MW00444426

The Collected Works of
Marie-Louise von Franz

MLvF

Volume 6

General Editors

Steven Buser

Leonard Cruz

Marie-Louise von Franz
1915-1998

Volume 6

Niklaus Von Flüe
and Saint Perpetua

A Psychological Interpretation
of Their Visions

Marie–Louise von Franz

CHIRON PUBLICATIONS • ASHEVILLE, NORTH CAROLINA

Logo of the Foundation of Jungian Psychology, Küsnacht Switzerland:
Fons mercurialis from Rosarium Philosophorum 1550 (Fountain of Life).

The Passion of Perpetua: A Psychological Interpretation of Her Visions
previously published by Inner City Books, © 2004, Toronto Ontario

www.ChironPublications.com

Interior and cover design by Danijela Mijailovic
Cover image by Martina Ott
Printed primarily in the United States of America.

ISBN 978-1-68503-029-2 paperback
ISBN 978-1-68503-030-8 hardcover

"The relationship Brother Klaus had to Nature, which was constellated though invasive archetypal contents, meant that he represented not only a typical Christian saint, but he simultaneously embodied the ancient image of the primitive medicine man, the Nordic shaman, and the prophet. It is as if an ancient 'pattern' of the individuation process had returned, but on a higher level, so that it might be reconciled with the spiritual development of Christianity, thereby broadening the latter to include this new dimension of nature. Accordingly, Brother Klaus's inner experiences and his lonely effort to realize them map out the individuation process of modern man. His visions, however, reveal with impressive clarity certain basic tendencies of the collective unconscious that strive to further develop the Christion religious symbols" (Marie-Louise von Franz, *Collected Works*, Volume 6, Paragraph 164).

"It was the record in the Gospels and the witness of St. Paul that built up the image of Christ as we know it. At the same time, it was above all the experience of single individuals in visions and dreams (like those of St. Perpetua) which confirmed the collective faith – that is to say, the conviction that God had really become man in Christ. These individual experiences gave real foundation to the doctrine. Dreams and visions are statements made by the human soul in a realm where consciousness and its conceptions are excluded. If we consider these spontaneous unconscious statements of the soul, we are able to perceive the Christian conception of the world originating in them as a phenomenon in itself" (Marie-Louise von Franz, *Collected Works*, Volume 6, Paragraph 169).

Foreword

The lives and visions of Niklaus von Flüe and Perpetua correspond to the pattern of Christian legends of saints and are therefore much closer to a historical context than fairytales. Marie-Louise von Franz explains the difference between legends and fairytales as follows: "Seen from a psychological viewpoint, local legends are to a large extent factual reports of magical incidents, which represent the experience of an individual by the world of archetypes into consciousness. ... Indeed, local legends offer psychological researchers the advantage of illuminating the total human situation, in which the numinous experience of the archetypes takes place. Legends illuminate more the suspenseful relation of this life to another world or to an awareness of the unconscious."[1]

Legends are answers or compensations to outer historical situations, which cannot be understood by rational consciousness alone. Legends explain or compensate a certain human or cultural development from the viewpoint of the collective unconscious and give historical reality a new meaning. Therefore, legends are closer to outer reality than fairytales.

On the other hand, fairytales describe unconscious developments as a compensation to the collective consciousness in general. For this reason, fairytales offer a more general or basic comment about constellated conscious situations, which means a more archetypal and less specific image. Marie-Louise von Franz writes in *Archetypal Symbols in Fairy Tales*: "Fairytales have an advantage over legends in that they more purely represent the archetypes and let them become more clearly comprehensible in their 'network of roots' and their dynamic function" and she continues "Fairytales

---

[1] Marie-Louise von Franz, *Archetypal Symbols in Fairy Tales*, Chiron Publications, Asheville, 2020, Vol. I of the *Collected Works*, § 27.

illuminate the unconscious forms and regularity of the natural laws of the soul in a more stripped down form."[2]

In which zeitgeist was Niklaus von Flüe born? His life was shaped by the events in the 15th century, that is, in the late Middle Ages or in the incubation phase of the modern era. This incubation phase began suddenly in the middle of the 14th century, more precisely in 1348 with the outbreak of the most devastating plague pandemic that Europe had ever experienced. The Black Death mowed down indiscriminately. It did not stop at clerics, knights and peasants, nobles and serfs, or men, women, and children. In the years that followed, minor epidemics flared up again and again. Extreme climatic fluctuations, as in the period between 1430 and 1440, which led to an extraordinary cooling, also resulted in bad harvests, famines, and a dramatic increase in mortality. This incubation phase in preparation for the modern age was also shaken by the constant armed conflicts between France and England, which went down in history as the Hundred Years War, which lasted from 1337 to 1453: the longest war in world history!

In these distant times from God, an image of the pure Mother of Jesus prevailed, which promised understanding, consolation, and relief especially to the countless women who lived in fear and need. The invocation of Mary helped them to better bear fear and pain, and released women from the hereditary guilt the Church accused them of. As a mother, Mary was understanding, as she knew the sufferings of women from her own experience. As a Jew in the Roman Empire, she also lived in dangerous times, was accused of an extramarital pregnancy and ultimately had to witness the painful death of her son on the cross.

In the middle of these uncertain times, in which the contrasts in all matters of daily life intensified and people needed new sparks of hope, Nikolaus von Kues, called Cusanus (1415 to 1478) was born in Germany. In 1438 he was papal envoy in Constantinople. On the return trip he realized the basic principle of his worldview: the coincidentia oppositorum. Everything lives and moves in the tension

---

[2] *Ibid.*

between the opposites. Such a coincidentia oppositorum is God himself. Every human being is also a coincidentia oppositorum because he or she unites all opposites in himself or herself: mortality and immortality, body, and soul, animality and deity.

The farmer and councilor of Obwalden, Niklaus von Flüe was born in 1417 as a farmer's son in Flueli-Ranft (Canton Obwalden CH) and died in 1487. He had many visions, one which had been anchored in popular belief for centuries, namely Mary as the beautiful stately wife of God. In another vision, the Swiss national saint also experienced the dark contrasts in the image of God himself. He saw a dark, terrifying face, which he interpreted as the face of God. This vision hardly astonishes us, for the idea of the devil was omnipresent during these difficult times. The experience shaped Niklaus so deeply that his visitors could read the mental change in his face.

Perpetua, on the other hand, lived in the 2nd century, 1300 years before Niklaus von Flüe. In those uncertain times, when Christians were alternately persecuted or tolerated, they met on Sundays for prayer, songs, and a common meal. From this, the church gradually emerged. With their emergence, a priestly hierarchy and a more streamlined organization of worship services developed, which corresponded to a departure from the original attitude of the Christian religion. Titles, functions, and guidelines were consequences necessary to organize a church, but which original Christianity lacked. Like any organization, the organized church ultimately led away from being spontaneously moved by individuals. This was suppressed by decrees, regulations, and creeds. The original religious feelings were replaced by an intellectual theology of the clergies.

Both the century of Perpetua and that of Niklaus were marked by a deep piety of individuals who wanted to find their way back to God, not to the God of the Church, but to the pure divine source from which all life flows.

The current pandemic has given the visions of Perpetua and Niklaus a new relevance. In the same century as Perpetua, another young woman, Saint Corona, was tortured to death for comforting her husband, as he had his eye gouged out prior to his beheading. That is why the Church later canonized her and consecrated her to *holy Corona*. Her name comes from the fact that God himself is said to have put a crown on her. She is still venerated in many places as the patron saint of epidemics, including in the Aachen Cathedral (D), which Emperor Charlemagne commissioned to build in the 8th century. Perhaps at the beginning of the 21st century we will experience a slow change or renewal of the image of God, which is revealed through the inner soul experiences of individual people. This would reconnect us to the archetypal current that works through the eons.

Alison Kappes (Hirzel) and Barbara Davies (Zürich) translated the original German manuscript into English in a most careful and respectful way. We are quite thankful to both ladies, as well as Chiron Publications, for making it possible to publish an English version for the first time as Volume 6 in *The Collected Works of Marie-Louise von Franz*.

On behalf of the Foundation for Jungian Psychology, Küsnacht, December 28, 2021

PD Dr. Hansueli F. Etter
President

❖❖❖   Table of Contents   ❖❖❖

Illustrations

Book 1

The Visions of
Niklaus von Flüe

◆

Introduction

1   Among the saints of the Catholic Church, Niklaus von Flüe is a very unique and highly original phenomenon, and his visions, too, bear the stamp of unconventional authenticity.[1] One has the impression that they have not been corrected and altered which, naturally, makes them of special psychological interest. These visions have been written about from very diverse points of view. M.-B. Lavaud's book *Vie profonde de Nicolas de Flüe*,[2] which contributes significantly in elucidating the visions, stands out amongst those written from the Catholic standpoint. Lavaud gathered together all the essential amplifications from the Bible and from the texts of the mystics that could be useful in interpreting the visions and has thus explained them in great depth. From the Protestant standpoint, F. Blanke's little book *Bruder Klaus von Flüe*,[3] which impressively throws light upon the originality of Niklaus von Flüe's personality in his lonely search for God, should be mentioned.

2   If, nevertheless, I venture to present a study of these visions, I do so because it seems to me that the application of Jung's psychological concepts to them reveals even greater depths and more meaningful spiritual connections than have previously been seen. Jung himself commented upon some of St. Niklaus's visions in his essay "Brother Klaus"[4] and in the first part of his book *The Archetypes and the*

---

[1] Cf. C.G. Jung, *Collected Works* (CW), Vol. 11, *Psychology and Religion: West and East*, London: Routledge & Kegan Paul Ltd 1958, §487: "It is nice to think that the only outstanding Swiss mystic received, by God's grace, unorthodox visions and was permitted to look with unerring eye into the depths of the divine soul, where all the creeds of humanity which dogma has divided are united in *one* symbolic archetype."

[2] M.-B. Lavaud, *Vie profonde de Nicolas de Flüe*, Fribourg: Librairie de l'université 1942. By contrast, Johannes Hemleben's interpretation in J. Hemleben, *Niklaus von Flüe*, Frauenfeld: Huber 1977, is very superficial.

[3] F. Blanke, *Bruder Klaus von Flüe*, Zürich: Zwingli, 1948.

[4] C.G. Jung, CW 11, *Psychology and Religion*, §§474–487.

Collective Unconscious.[5] My study is based upon his comments, and I shall refer to them in what follows in various ways.

3   If one applies Jung's method of amplification to interpreting these visions, one is struck by the connection between the motifs which appear in the images of the visions and those found in the pre-Christian, and particularly in the Germanic imagination. Despite their specific context within the visions, it would, however, *be inaccurate to see these motifs as surviving heathen elements*. Rather, they point to a problem which, it seems to me, is still relevant today and which I shall discuss in detail in the course of this study.

4   In recent times psychologists have often expressed the opinion that, once again, there is a need for priest-doctor personalities, that is, a combined psychotherapist-doctor role, which includes the role of a spiritual care-giver. This would reinvigorate the archetypal figure of the medicine man and the shaman[6] for it generates the idea of a personality whose healing influence comes about by means of his own connection with the "spirits," that is, with the powers of the unconscious psyche. There can be no doubt that Niklaus von Flüe had an enormous healing influence, for it would appear that he was just this kind of "mana personality"—a person who has a great invigorating effect upon the people around him and his environment.[7]

5   Upon closer inspection, the saints of the Catholic Church can be divided into two types: those who were of the common folk and whose sainthood came about through a "consensus" of the people amongst whom they lived, which, indeed, was the original form of a saint being "elected"; and those who were elevated to sainthood through official canonization by the Church, a practice which only came into existence after the 10th century. Among the latter, there

---

[5] C.G. Jung, CW 9/i, *The Archetypes and the Collective Unconscious,* London: Routledge & Kegan Paul Ltd 1959, §12ff. and §131.
[6] According to Eliade (in M. Eliade, *Shamanism: Archaic Techniques of Ecstasy,* Bollingen: Princeton University Press 1956, p. 14f.), the nordic shaman is a medicine man who, along with his normal skills and practices, also possesses the technique of ecstasy.
[7] In comparative religious history, "mana" is understood to mean "exceptionally effective." For more on mana personalities, see C.G. Jung, CW 7, *Two Essays on Analytical Psychology,* London: Routledge & Kegan Paul Ltd 1953, §§374–406.

are, of course, many personalities of the former type of saint, but this latter group also includes scholars and those who belonged to the educated class, who were less popular amongst the common folk. These were people whose great deeds furthered the existence of the Church rather than being of benefit to the general populace. Naturally, both types overlap in many respects. Nevertheless, Brother Klaus undoubtedly belonged exclusively to the first type of saint.

6   It is known that the Church's worship of the saints had its origins in the cultic worship of the early Christian martyrs and that worship of the latter naturally arose *after their death,* which led to the preservation and worship of their graves, of their relics, etc. Even today the canonization of a person is, in principle, subject to that person being able to accomplish posthumous miracles. The tendency of the populace in early Christian times to worship the remains and the graves of Christians who had been put to death because of their faith is derived from *the pre-Christian hero-cult,* which goes far back in time, supposedly even to the time before Classical antiquity. The pre-Christian Greeks believed that the "spirit of the grave" (*Grabgenius*) of a deceased significant personality was able to have a healing effect, or to exert a protective influence, on surrounding areas and that one could be guided by this "spirit of the grave" through dreams and visions. This is why attention was paid to this type of "hero's grave" at many Greek places of worship, and the Greeks of the Classical period pointed out that these graves constituted the foundation, or early stage, of a new cult. Epidaurus, for instance, the great place of worship devoted to Asclepius, the god of healing, is said to have originally been built upon the grave of a hero called Maleas, and it was here that the whole cultic healing enterprise of Asclepius developed, an enterprise comparable to that of Lourdes today. At Olympia, all the participants of the games had to make a sacrifice upon the grave of the hero Pelops. In addition, there was a "grave of an unknown hero," which had the following ground-plan.

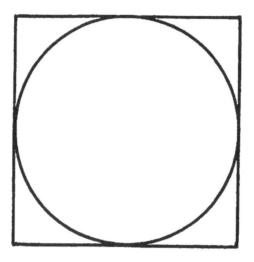

Grave of Unknown Hero, Ground Plan

7   This ground-plan is a mandala (a cultic circle) and, as such, it is a symbol of illuminating psychological significance.[8] It refers to a basic motif of how religious images are created that is to be found in all ages and in all corners of the globe, a motif that illustrates the idea of a centre of personality that transcends one's conscious personality. It clarifies a place within the soul that creates order and animates everything. "This centre," Jung[9] says, "is not felt or thought of as the ego but, if one may so express it, as the *self*." Although the centre is represented, on the one hand, by an innermost point, it is, on the other hand, surrounded by a periphery, or circumference, which includes everything that belongs to the self, namely, the paired opposites that constitute the totality of one's personality. Experiences of this inner wholeness are often accompanied by a feeling of becoming immortal for, indeed, this circle depicts something which is static and is therefore unshakeable, and eternal.[10] It is a foundation of existence (*Seinsgrund*) which is experienced as the divine within one's own soul and which periodically surfaces as a goal-image when a person strives to become conscious of their objective totality.[11]

---

[8] For further reading, see C.G. Jung, CW 9/i, *The Archetypes and the Collective Unconscious*, §§627–712 and the literature cited therein.
[9] *Ibid.*, §634.
[10] *Ibid.*, §637.
[11] See C.G. Jung, CW 12, *Psychology and Alchemy*, London: Routledge & Kegan Paul 1953, §328ff.

8   When the ground-plan of a hero's archaic gravesite has the form of a mandala, it would seem to indicate that the revered hero was a symbol for the people around him of a more complete and conscious personality, someone who was further along in his individuation process and could convey a sense of a larger and more complete human existence. Indeed, such a deceased person seemed almost to have incorporated the divine aspect of the human soul and, by becoming one with this divine inner-meaning, appeared to have attained eternity.

9   Thus, quite possibly, the psychological thought behind the cult of grave-worship was that an important personality represents an incarnation of the greater inner "divine" man. *After death, that is, after the living personal ego which covers up the greater figure, has been cast aside*, the "divine man," or self, becomes visible and has a positive effect. The Neoplatonist, Apuleius, of the second century A.D, said of this effect, "Everyone has a *Daimon* which is partially dependent upon our behaviour. If we take care of it, it will become a benevolent *Lar* (ancestral spirit) after our death. If not, it will become a *Larva* (haunting spirit). By religiously taking care of their inner lives, some men, for example Osiris, Asclepius, Amphiaraus and others, developed their Daimon to such a powerful extent that they became generally worshipped deities (*numina*)."[12]

10   Although these formulations belong to the late Greek and Roman period, they nevertheless mirror an ancient belief which possibly goes back to pre-Classical times, namely, the belief that there are certain powerful spirits of the deceased who live near graves and who have a blessed effect upon the living.[13] The posthumous power of the dead could be understood symbolically as being the effect of a spiritual force superior to the ego, a force called the self. Those who have endured the process of individuation to a greater extent, and who have realised it more consciously than those around them, are thereby elevated to the *imago* of the

---

[12] Apulei Platonici, *De deo Socratis*, Madaurensis de Philosophia libri rec., P. Thomas, ed. (Leipzig: Teubner, 1908), pp. 6–35. Citation translated from German by the translator, hereafter, shown as "trans."
[13] Siberian shamanic novices sleep upon the graves of deceased shamans to make themselves receptive to revelations and to the acquisition of power.

Anthropos; and the mandala form of their graves expresses precisely this idea of achieved spiritual wholeness.

11   It is likely that such traditions and viewpoints of late antiquity provided the fertile soil for the early Christian cult of the martyrs. One even finds that incubation was practised on some graves of the martyrs, just as it was on the graves of the Greek heroes. Only in the 10th century did the Church officially comment upon this local worship of powerful deceased individuals. At this time, the Church decided to introduce the practice of canonization along with certain preconditions pertaining to it. This was done in order to contain a practice which was spreading wildly and to steer it in the right direction. The conditions necessary for canonization include, amongst other things, an heroic attitude towards life, an above-average ethical and spiritual aptitude, and the posthumous performance of miracles.

12   In my introduction, I drew attention to the pre-Christian cult of heroes, on the one hand, and to northern shamanism, on the other, to emphasise certain universal human characteristics of the original priest-doctor idea which go beyond the specifically Christian concept. It seems that Niklaus von Flüe possessed these qualities to a very special degree. By saying this, I do not wish to undermine his importance as a Christian mystic, which, of course, he was above all else. Indeed, my intention is quite the opposite for, in my opinion, it was precisely because he was such a creative Christian mystic that he attained an archetypal dimension. C.G. Jung once remarked that Brother Klaus should be named the patron saint of psychotherapy.

◆

Chapter 1
The Times of Niklaus von Flüe

13 The fifteenth century, the century in which Niklaus von Flüe lived, was a time of great crises and change for the inner cantons of Switzerland, a time that Robert Duerrer has so impressively described.[1] I shall summarise his account:

14 With the end of the Battle of Sempach, the time of defensive freedom-fighting came to an end and a certain amount of independence towards the outside world was finally established.[2] Within the country, the principle of democracy had prevailed against the influence of the ruling nobility.[3] With the expropriation of large properties from foreign landowners and with the acquisition of agricultural areas by allied towns, the supply of grain became so reliable that the original cantons were able to become milk- and grain-producing economies for which they were better suited. They had, however, to ensure a market for their products, and thus, wherever possible, they took part in the expansion into the mountainous region of Ennet.[4] Unfortunately, this territorial expansion resulted in bands of youths raiding neighbouring areas at the slightest provocation, and, in 1461, the Swiss citizenry ended its fifteen-year peace with Austria in order to begin its conquest of Thurgau.[5] Mercenaries (*Reisläufer*) became increasingly disreputable and dangerous signs of disintegration arose. In rural communities,

---

[1] R. Duerrer, *Bruder Klaus. Die ältesten Quellen über den seligen Niklaus von Flüe, sein Leben und seinen Einfluss*, Sarnen: Ehrli, 1917–1921, Vol. 1, pp. xff. On the life of Niklaus von Flüe, see Leonard von Matt, *Der heilige Bruder Klaus. Offizielles Gedenkbuch der Heiligsprechung* (Zürich: NZN Verlag, 1947).

[2] Through the privileges granted by Emperor Sigmund.

[3] From 1404 onwards, the office of the highest official was rotated on a yearly basis in certain Swiss cantons. See R. Duerrer, *Bruder Klaus*, Vol. 1, p. xi.

[4] In 1403, the inhabitants of the Canton of Obwalden, together with those from the Canton of Uri, took part in the occupation of the Leventina Valley and, in 1496, when the Eschen Valley was being given back, they were able to secure special conditions for the safeguarding of the Gries Pass to Milan.

[5] For more details, see R. Duerrer, *Bruder Klaus*, Vol. 1, p. xiii.

for example, foreigners of ill-repute[6] were able to barter for Swiss citizenship. The fourteen-year war (1436-50) between the original cantons (Urkantone) and Zürich concerning the inheritance of the Count of Toggenburg[7] had an especially demoralizing effect. Brother Klaus took part in this war as a flag-bearer, and he got as far as Hirzel and Thalwil.[8] To his great sorrow, he witnessed the breaking of the agreements of the Sempach Letter that protected the civilian population and the Church. The practice of the time of electing two or three popes simultaneously undermined the people's trust in the authority of the Church,[9] especially as dignitaries of the Church repeatedly excommunicated entire regions after the people became involved in political or otherwise worldly affairs. Parishes were then often without both a priest and a divine service for years at a time. Brother Klaus's home parish of Sachseln had been without a priest since 1417,[10] which is why he had to be baptised in Kerns, a parish far from his home. Thus, it is easy to understand that in such decadent times, the so-called secularist movement gained ground[11] and people with a religious frame of mind felt increasingly on their own.

15   Brother Klaus was born in 1417 as the son of a respected citizen of Sachseln, Heinrich von Flüe,[12] and Klaus later stated that he had already had visions while still in the womb. He told this to the person he trusted most and who was his *directeur de conscience*. This was Heiny am Grund[13] from Lucerne, who was Klaus's father-confessor and the person who introduced him to the literature of the mystics of the time.[14] Indeed, it is primarily thanks to Heiny am Grund that Niklaus von Flüe was allowed to remain within the framework of the Church. Brother Klaus once told a monk[15] that he felt an

---

[6] The so-called "Mötteli-und-Koller-Handel," *ibid.*, Vol. 1, p. xiif.
[7] *Ibid.*, Vol. 1, p. xii.
[8] *Ibid.*, Vol. 1, p. 15.
[9] *Ibid.*, Vol. 1, pp. xviff.
[10] *Ibid.*, Vol. 1, p. xvif. according to the parish register of Sachseln of 1488.
[11] *Ibid.*, Vol. 1, pp. xviff.
[12] *Ibid.*, Vol. 1, p. 3. His mother was called Hemma Roberta.
[13] Sometimes written as *Haimo am Grund*.
[14] He was the local priest, firstly, of Kriens and later, of Stans. See more about him in Ch. Journet, *Saint Nicolas de Flüe*, Neuchâtel/Paris: Cahiers du Rhône 1947, p. 15.
[15] A remark made in confidence by Brother Klaus to a preaching monk, 8/9 June 1489; see R. Duerrer, *Bruder Klaus*, Vol. 1, p. 39.

extraordinarily great sense of awe towards the priesthood and that every time he saw a priest, it was as if he *saw an angel of God,* and it was primarily because of this that he felt great reverence for the most holy sacrament of the body and blood of Jesus Christ. He transferred this same reverence onto Heiny am Grund, who was suited to carry this inner image, but he chose to silently avoid other less agreeable clergymen. Evidently, Brother Klaus projected an image of his own future personality, that is to say, the archetypal idea of the Self, of all-encompassing wholeness onto the person of this priest, which explains his idea of a priest being an angel—a messenger of the Deity.

Chapter 2
The Prenatal Faces and
the Baptismal Vision

The aforementioned Heiny am Grund reports[1] that "Brother Klaus told him that both while still in his mother's womb and during his birth, Klaus saw a star in the sky which lit up the whole world and that since living in the Ranft, Klaus had, indeed, seen a star in the sky which so resembled the one he had seen while in the womb, he thought it was the same star. This means, Klaus went on to explain, that everybody would say that he shone in the world like this star. Brother Klaus also told Heiny am Grund that before his birth, while still in the womb, he had seen a large stone which he understood to be the stability and steadfastness of his own nature to which he must adhere and not allow himself to be distracted from. While still in the womb, Klaus also saw the holy oil and, when he was born into this world, he recognised his mother and the midwife and he saw himself being carried to his baptism from the Ranft to Kerns so clearly that he never forgot it. And he knew all of this at the time he was speaking as clearly as he'd known it when it happened. And at that time, Klaus also saw an old man at his baptism whom he did not recognize. But he did, indeed, recognize the priest who was baptising him."[2]

---

[1] R. Duerrer, *Bruder Klaus*, Vol. 1, p. 465f. and F. Blanke, *Bruder Klaus von Flüe*, p. 111. Parallel to this is the report by H. Woelflin (Lupulus), printed around 1501 (R. Duerrer, *Bruder Klaus*, Vol. 1, p. 531). See also A. Stoeckli, *Die Visionen des seligen Bruder Klaus* (Einsiedeln: Benziger, 1933), p. 10.

[2] Woelflin's report is based upon this, and he formulates it in the following manner: Klaus said that he saw a star in the sky "which shone more brightly than all the other stars, whose rays lit up the whole world. He later remarked that in his solitude, he often caught sight of a similar star so that he believed it was the same one which he had seen while in his mother's womb. At this time he also recognised *a mighty rock* and *the holy oil*, with which the Christians are anointed (...), and he emphasized, without boasting, that what he had seen was connected to his future life. He also added how, immediately after his birth, he clearly recognized his mother and the midwife, and how he had been carried over rocky terrain to his baptism in Kerns, the same terrain in which his life would come to an end, and how he

17   This statement of Brother Klaus's is extraordinarily puzzling and presents us with a difficult problem: Either we are dealing with an utterly unique and incredible miracle of an embryo and a newborn baby being able to consciously recall its perceptions or this statement is false, which would contradict the otherwise well-known integrity and sober straightforwardness of the saint. In Catholic literature, the veracity of this vision is, to some extent, both doubted and accepted[3] without the authors being able to give, in my opinion, conclusive reasons for their standpoint. Perhaps there is another explanation of how this strange statement came about, namely, that Brother Klaus had *a dream* about these prenatal occurrences and the events at his birth (examples of this do exist) and that he was so convinced as to the truth of his dream that he viewed its content as authentic information. This would correspond to the fact that in mythology and in the history of religion, there are parallels[4] of such prenatal psychic expressions of life of an embryo, an idea which seems to have an archetypal basis. For *biblical parallels,* Jeremiah I:4-5 could be considered[5]:"... Then the word of the Lord came unto me, saying: Before I formed thee in the belly I knew thee, and before thou camest forth out of the womb I sanctified thee, and I ordained thee a prophet unto the nations." Similarly, John the Baptist "recognised" Christ while still in the womb: He "leapt" inside the womb when his mother met the Virgin Mary.[6] The motif of children speaking while

---

was able to commit it all to memory as if it had all taken place in his old age. He recognized both the priest who baptised him and his godparents at that time. And, as he emphasized, *only an old man* who was amongst the people at his baptism, was an utter stranger to him."(Trans.) In R. Duerrer, *Bruder Klaus,* Vol. 1, p. 531f.; see also A. Stoeckli, *Die Visionen des seligen Bruder Klaus,* p. 10.

[3] An outline of the Catholic standpoint on this question can be found in Ch. Journet, *Saint Nicolas de Flüe,* pp. 158ff, and M.-B. Lavaud, *Vie profonde de Saint Nicolas de Flüe,* pp. 24ff. Lavaud tends to believe the report.

[4] Jung was the first to emphasize this, in contrast to F. Blanke, *Bruder Klaus von Flüe,* p. 112, who repudiates the existence of there being parallels. Jung said in a letter to Blanke (*ibid.,* p. 115f.): "Such statements seldom appear on their own." (Trans.) He supposes, therefore, that there must be parallels or that Brother Klaus got the idea from some earlier tradition. Joe Homer, for example, a medicine man of the Yuma tribe of Indians, saw God while still in the womb. See also Daryll Forde, *Ethnography of Yuma Indians: American Archaeology and Ethnology,* 1931, p. 28. I am indebted to Mr. Roy Freeman for courteously drawing my attention to the above point. As Blanke emphasizes, Katherina Emmerich, according to her own statements, had prenatal visions, but it is more than possible that she got the idea from Brother Klaus (see F. Blanke, *Bruder Klaus von Flüe,* p. 116).

[5] Given by F. Blanke, *ibid.,* p. 115, as a relative parallel.

[6] Holy Bible (King James Version: KJV), Luke 1:15: An angel of the Lord announced, "... And he shall be filled with the Holy Ghost, even from his mother's womb." See also, Luke 1:41.

still in the womb appears in various primitive myths. Such children always go on to become redeemers and heroic figures.[7]

18   Thus, like many other religious statements, Brother Klaus's comment is also not to be taken concretely, but rather as being "spiritually true."[8] It corresponds to an archetypal religious idea and symbolises, as the parallels show, his being chosen as a redeemer and religious leader.

19   These symbols, which, according to Niklaus, he perceived while still within his mother's womb and at his baptism are, in themselves, highly meaningful. There are *four*: the three symbols made of inanimate matter which he saw while he was within the womb—*the star, the stone and the holy oil*; then there is the fourth, which is the symbol of a human being—the figure of *an unknown old man* whom he saw shortly after his birth.

20   It has long been believed that the birth of an important person is announced by a star, for example the Star of Bethlehem.[9] In many places, it was believed that the human soul was a star, either prior to birth or after death.[10] In Egypt, for example, a star was used, among other things, to depict the *Ba,* the symbol of the self and of preconscious and postmortal individuality.[11] The postmortal "starification" of heroes is a widespread mythological motif.[12] In the allegorical tradition of the Church Fathers, stars were thought to represent ecclesiastical dignitaries "who by word and deed should

---

[7] See the examples in F. von der Leyen and P. Zaunert (eds), *Indianer Märchen aus Südamerika,* "Die Märchen der Weltliteratur," Jena: Eugen Diedrichs Verlag 1921, No. 3: "Die Sonne, der Frosch und die Feuerholzer." The child helps its mother, who has lost her way in the woods, to find her way again and talks to her. In No. 28, "Makunaima und Pia," there are twins talking in the womb. No. 79, "Die Zwillinge" has got the same motif. See also F. von der Leyen and P. Zaunert (eds), *Indianer Märchen aus Nordamerika,* No. 15, p. 104f., which is a North American myth of the Iroquois about a redeemer and in which good and evil twins converse with each other while in the womb, arguing about which way out each one wants to take at birth.

[8] C.G. Jung, CW 11, *Psychology and Religion,* §293; and, on the subject of the rational impossibility of religious statements, see C.G. Jung, CW 12, *Psychology and Alchemy,* §18.

[9] Holy Bible (KJV), Matthew 2:1–2.

[10] Upon the death of a Roman emperor, who was considered a deity, astrologers searched the heavens for a new star.

[11] See H. Jacobsohn, *Das Gespräch eines Lebensmüden mit seinem Ba. Zeitlose Dokumente der Seele,* Zürich: Rascher Verlag 1952, pp. 2ff., and A. Dieterich, *Eine Mithrasliturgie* (Leipzig and Berlin, 1903). In C.G. Jung, CW 5, *Symbols of Transformation,* London, Routledge & Kegan Paul 1956, §130, Jung writes, "The neophyte says, 'I am a star wandering together with you and shining up from the depths.'"

[12] E. Stucken, *Astralmythen* (Leipzig: Pfeiffer, 1907), pp. 48ff. I do not agree with Stucken's standpoint, and this reference is intended only as a source of information. *Perseus* and *Hercules* are represented as stars in constellations bearing their names. *Osiris* is a star in the *Orion* constellation.

shine on the world like stars." They are "afire with the heat of love and are rooted in heaven, in Christ, through their faith, love and hope" and "their influence upon the earth is through the comfort they give to the poor."[13] Or the stars are seen as the chosen Christians,[14] whereby Christ, too, is a star, the *stella matutina*, which brings both light to the world[15] and an end to the night of sin.[16] Finally, the Church also regarded stars as being the glorified bodies of the "resurrected,"[17] which calls to mind the ancient Egyptian concept of the transfigured soul of the dead, of the *Ba*, which appears as a star. The star is also a symbol of the *alchemical Mercurius* as the *principium individuationis.*[18] As such, it foretells of Brother Klaus's own archetypal destiny and of the possibility of individuation, which is why Brother Klaus's own interpretation of the star referring to himself is apt.

21   The second symbol, the "large stone" or rock, is a part of Brother Klaus's name, for "von Flüe" actually means "of the rock."[19] The von Flüe family's coat of arms includes a depiction of a chamois (later an ibex) standing on a mountain or three rocks.[20] Klaus interpreted the rock as being a sign of his steadfast and constant nature to which he should adhere and not allow himself to be distracted from.[21] The philosopher's stone of the alchemists was similarly reputed to be a symbol of the steadfast quality of the self. The symbolic meaning of a stone is such a broad topic that I would like to mention only a few of the main points made in C.G. Jung's chapter "The Stone Symbolism" in *The Visions of Zosimos.*[22] Jung points out that the central symbol of alchemy, the lapis, was, in fact, thought of by the alchemists as symbolizing the "inner spiritual man," that is the

---

[13] Cf. Albertus Magnus, *Apocalypsim*, B. Joannis Apostoli, *Opera Omnia*; A. Borgnet, ed., Paris, 1890–1899 Vol. 38: 494, (trans.).

[14] *Ibid.*, p. 504, (trans.).

[15] *Ibid.*, p. 524, (trans.).

[16] *Ibid.*, (trans.).

[17] *Ibid.*, p. 529, (trans.).

[18] Cf. C.G. Jung, CW 13, *Alchemical Studies*, London: Routledge & Kegan Paul 1967, §273. Mercurius is compared to a "crown of stars." As the light-bringer," he is compared to the morning star.

[19] F. Blanke, *Brüder Klaus von Flüe*, p. 113.

[20] R. Duerrer, *Bruder Klaus*, Vol. 1, p. 5. A diagonal beam of wood was added later.

[21] *Ibid.* Vol. 1, p. 465. This report from Heiny am Grund is also to be found in F. Blanke, *Brüder Klaus von Flüe*, p. 111.

[22] C.G. Jung, CW 13, *Alchemical Studies*, §§126–33.

Anthropos pneumaticos, which the alchemists tried to release from matter as the *natura abscondita.* Thus, the stone is, in fact, *a god of the macrocosmos hidden in matter. Every human being is the potential carrier, and even creator, of the stone.*[23] The alchemical lapis is actually an image of God, which, in its material state, compensates for the lofty spirituality of the Christ-image, which is too far removed from natural man. Jung says, "In the image of Mercurius and the lapis the 'flesh' glorified itself in its own way; it would not transform itself into spirit but, on the contrary, 'fixed' the spirit in stone. ..."[24] The lapis may therefore be understood as a *symbol of the inner Christ,*[25] of God in man. ... Though the lapis is a parallel of Christ, it is not meant to replace him. On the contrary, in the course of the centuries, the alchemists tended more and more to regard the lapis as the culmination of Christ's work of redemption ... [and] it came not from the conscious mind of the individual man, but from those border regions of the psyche that open out into the mystery of cosmic matter."[26]

22   The symbol of the stone, or the image of its divine effect, is, in itself, much older than alchemy and can already be found, for example, in a belief of the Australian Aborigines who thought that children's souls lived in a child-stone.[27] But the idea of magical stones also existed in Europe. Oreste's madness was cured by means of a stone, and Zeus found respite from his lovesickness by sitting on the

---

[23] Author's italics.

[24] *Ibid.,* Jung, Vol. 13, §127.

[25] Author's italics.

[26] *Ibid.*

[27] *Ibid.,* §128. Jung continues: "The stone as the birthplace of the gods (e.g., the birth of Mithras from a stone) is attested by primitive legends of stone-births which go back to ideas that are even more ancient—for instance, the view of the Australian aborigines that children's souls live in a special stone called the 'child-stone.' They can be made to migrate into a uterus by rubbing the 'child-stone' with a *churinga. Churingas* may be boulders, or oblong stones artificially shaped and decorated, or oblong, flattened pieces of wood ornamented in the same way. They are used as cult instruments. The Australians [Aborigines] and the Melanesians maintain that *churingas* come from the totem ancestor, that they are relics of his body or of his activity, and are full of *arunquiltha* or mana. They are united with the ancestor's soul and with the spirits of all those who afterwards possess them. They are taboo, are buried in caches or hidden in clefts in the rocks. In order to 'charge' them, they are buried among the graves so that they can soak up the mana of the dead. They promote the growth of field-produce, increase the fertility of men and animals, heal wounds, and cure sicknesses of the body and the soul. Thus, when a man's vitals are all knotted up with emotion, the Australian Aborigines give him a blow in the abdomen with a stone *churinga.* The *churingas* used for ceremonial purposes are daubed with red ochre, anointed with fat, bedded or wrapped in leaves, and copiously spat on (spittle, i.e. 'mana')."

stone of Leukadia.[28] In ancient Germanic culture, hollowed-out stones were placed upon graves, and sacrifices were made there, probably in the belief that the souls of the dead dwelt in the stones.[29] Similarly, it was believed that little children came out of such stones.[30] These are the so-called "Bautar stones."[31] According to the beliefs of other Germanic tribes, the ancestral spirits of the tribe lived either in, or by, the *hearth stone*, the oldest known burial place, and it was believed that such hearth stones had been cast down to earth by God.[32]

23   In India, a young man will tread upon a stone in order to obtain firmness of character.[33] Brother Klaus, too, interpreted the stone as referring to the "steadfast nature of his own being."[34]

24   The motif of being born from a stone is widespread and can also be found in an Iroquois myth: There are two healers who are twin

---

[28] *Ibid.*, §129.

[29] P. Herrmann, *Das altgermanische Priesterwesen,* Jena: Eugen Diederichs Verlag, 1929, p. 52f.: "Findings show that hollowed-out stones were put onto graves and offerings were poured into the stones to nourish the dead. In the north, so-called little bowl or dish stones are common, occasionally decorated with a cross in a circle, symbols of the sun." "From ancient times onwards, stones were placed in a circle around the graves. It is possible that they demarcated sacred ground from its surroundings and that temples developed from this custom. This explanation of worshipping and offering up sacrifices at stones which were thought to accommodate the dead is compatible with the idea of the souls of ancestors living within the stones, as the Penates did in the *Seida* (sacred stones) of the Lapps. In Germany, the Church strove to prevent 'offerings at stones' well into the eleventh century." (Trans.)

[30] *Ibid.*, Hermann, p. 54: "In Denmark, little children come out of stones. An Icelander prayed to several stones and the Icelandic Canon Law of 1123 states, 'People should not have anything to do with stones.' King Knud forbade the Danes to worship stones, as was done in England. In Gilja, in Iceland, there stood a stone which was worshipped by the whole clan and in which it was said their protective spirit lived. Kodran explained that he did not want to be baptised until he knew who was the stronger: the protective spirit of his family who had brought only good luck, or the bishop. Thereupon he went to this stone and 'sang' over it until the stone burst. Thus Kodran thought that his protective spirit had been vanquished, and he allowed himself to be baptised." (Trans.)

[31] *Ibid:* "In olden times, it was the custom to put some kind of monument, for example memorial stones and cairns, on graves. Some stones without an inscription date from as far back as the Bronze Age right up to the eleventh century. Without doubt, the *Bautar stones* of the north originally marked places where the soul dwelled, for they were mostly found on graves. They are uncarved gravestones, or memorial stones without inscriptions. ... They are occasionally found in larger groups in hilly fields of graves, together with all kinds of stone arrangements, mostly standing between one to six metres high." (Trans.)

[32] *Ibid.*, p. 64: "A pole was erected in the house as an outer sign of the living ancestral spirit of the hearth, *the ancestral pole*, from which the raised hide evolved. In later times, the hearth stone was thought to be a stone that God had cast down from heaven onto earth." (Trans.)

[33] C.G. Jung, CW 13, *Alchemical Studies*, §129.

[34] R. Duerrer, *Bruder Klaus*, Vol. 1, p. 465, (trans.). See also C. G. Jung, CW 13, §129f.: "According to Saxo Grammaticus, the electors of the king stood on stones in order to give their vote permanence. The green stone of Arran was used both for healing and for taking oaths on. A cache of 'soul stones,' similar to *churingas*, was found in a cave on the river Birs near Basel, and during recent excavations of the pole-dwellings on the little lake at Burgaeschi, in Canton Solothurn, a group of boulders was discovered wrapped in the bark of birch trees." Jung emphasises that the idea of the magical stone then lived on in the importance given to gem stones and he relates a Navajo myth of a turquoise goddess whose immortality is represented by her stone-like nature.

brothers: the one, "Maple-Shoot," is good and the other, "Flint," is evil. In the Wichita tribe, the healer is called the "Great Southern Star," who, however, performs his healing work on earth as the "Flint Man." He has a son who is called "Young Flint." Once their work is completed, they both return to the sky. As Jung points out, in this Indian myth, as in medieval alchemy, the Saviour coincides with the motif of the stone, the star and the "son," who is *super omnia lumina* (i.e., the light of all lights).[35] Precisely, this same combination of archetypal motifs is found again in the prenatal visions of Brother Klaus, a beautiful example of the relationship of archetypal motifs without any influence from consciousness.

25   In myths, a stone often means immortality, which is why heroes are often transformed into a stone in order to prevent the decay of their bodies.[36] In its most comprehensive sense, the lapis is a symbol of *the saviour, of the Anthropos and of immortality*. Psychologically speaking, it represents the greater "inner man," or the self. Thus, we can also interpret the stone in Brother Klaus's vision as being *the star that has come down to earth.*

26   According to the alchemists, the alchemical lapis is not an ordinary stone, but is a "stone which has a spirit." It is identical to the all-healing substance (the *medicina catholica* or panacea) and thus to the various tinctures of alchemy, such as water, oil, and the elixir of life. If seen in the light of alchemical amplification, the holy oil, which was the third symbol Brother Klaus saw while still in the womb, is, in fact, a variation of the same basic motif, or rather, a further development of the same archetypal content. Alchemical mercury was also seen as being an "oil" (*oleum*), i.e., an *aqua unctuosa,* and the Christian alchemists themselves often compared

---

[35] C.G. Jung, CW 13, §132.

[36] *Ibid.*, §132f.: "The culture hero of the Natchez Indians came down to earth from the sun, and shone with unendurable brightness. His glance was death-dealing. In order to mitigate this, and to prevent his body from corrupting in the earth, he changed himself into a stone statue ..." ... "The civilization of the Nile Valley ... turned its divine kings into stone statues for the express purpose of making the king's *ka* everlasting." "Thus the Apocalypse of Elijah says of those who escape persecution by the Anti-Messiah: 'The Lord shall take unto him their spirit and their souls, their flesh shall be made stone, no wild beast shall devour them ...'" and: "In a Basuto legend reported by Frobenius, the hero is left stranded by his pursuers on the bank of a river. He changes himself into a stone, and his pursuers throw him across to the other side. This is the motif of the *transitus*: the 'other side' is the same as eternity."

it to the Church's chrism.[37] The Church uses the holy oil in confirmations, ordinations, and in the sacrament of extreme unction.[38] Among other things, it was believed to be the "energized form" of the state of grace of the Holy Ghost (*charisma*).[39] It means "mana"[40] and is a substance which bestows immortality—the fluid star, or stone, so to speak; or, in alchemical terms, it is "the soul of the stone"; and in this third new aspect, it comes, so to speak, even one step closer to the realm of the human soul. Indeed, it is possible to see a certain development in the sequence of symbols: The star represents that which is "outermost"—the projected image of the self and "inner light" into the far-reaches of the cosmos; the stone is the star which has come down to earth—the tangible star; and the oil is, so to speak, its "hidden soul", or, to put it in religious terms, it is a substance in which the Holy Ghost has become manifest. Thus, the oil symbolizes a *meaning* which points towards the numinous presence of the divine, a presence which is sensed, for example, in the experience of synchronistic phenomena.[41] A meaning such as this would seem to suggest the existence of a spiritual, or inner, order, even in inorganic material objects. All three symbols which the saint saw in his prenatal vision point towards his vocation to achieve individuation. They also indicate what kind of divinity wants to be realized in the life of Brother Klaus—namely, it is *the alchemical lapis*, an analogia christi, that wants to become manifest in him.

---

[37] Marie-Louise von Franz, *Aurora Consurgens*, Toronto: Inner City Books 2000, pp. 261–276, and J.D. Mylius, *Philosophia reformata*, Frankfurt am Main: Jennis 1622, p. 260, in C.G. Jung, CW 13, *Alchemical Studies*, §422: "'The *prima materia* is an oily water and is the philosophic stone, from which branches multiply into infinity'... Here the stone is itself the tree and is understood as the 'fiery or as the 'oily water'. ('... water and oil do not mix'!)."

[38] F. Blanke, *Bruder Klaus von Flüe*, p. 113.

[39] Marie-Louise von Franz, *The Passio Perpetua*, (trans. E. Welsh) Irving: Spring Publications, 1980, p. 61.

[40] According to religious history, "mana" refers to the primitive idea of "a magical potency which is regarded both as an objective force and as a subjective state of intensity." The word is Melanesian. There are, however, amongst other peoples many parallel expressions for this divine numinous "power." C.G. Jung, *The Structure and Dynamics of the Psyche*, London: Routledge & Kegan Paul Ltd. 1960, Vol. 8, §114.

[41] C.G. Jung, CW 9/ii, *Aion*, London: Routledge & Kegan Paul Ltd. 1959, §§252–265.

27 But, in addition to these three things that depict distinctly alchemical images, i.e., symbols of inanimate matter, there is a fourth that, as such, characteristically represents a marked contrast to the other images, namely, the appearance of the *unknown old man* at Klaus's baptism. The fourth image leads us into a new area,[42] into life on this side, into the here and now, into the human realm. Nevertheless, it is again unmistakably a symbol of the self. Jung wrote to Blanke[43] that this old man represents the archetype of the wise old man, i.e., of the spirit. In the Christian tradition, he would correspond to the *antiquus dierum*; in the Cabala, to the *senex sanctissimus* or *caput album* as well as to the *antiquus dierum*. Here, however, he would be the personification of the *granum salis*, which the one who is being baptized receives from the *Sapientia Dei* within whom God Himself is present.

28 Thus, the unknown old man, the star, the stone, and the oil are, in fact, the child's silent godparents. The same old man reappears quite often in Brother Klaus's visions and reveals further aspects of Brother Klaus's own divine nature.

29 The unknown old man who appears at the baptism of a child is a fairytale motif. In the Grimm's fairytale "Ferdinand the Faithful and Ferdinand the Unfaithful," it is said that there was once a father who was so poor that he couldn't find a godfather for his little son, so he asked an *unknown poor old man* to be godfather. The old man appears in the church and baptizes the boy "Ferdinand the Faithful." He gives him a key and tells him that when he is fourteen years old, the boy will find a castle on a heath to which the key fits and, once inside, he will find his godfather's gift. This is, in fact, a white horse. Later, this white horse turns out to be a talking horse that accompanies and advises the boy throughout all his heroic deeds. Finally, he chases the horse three times round in a circle, after which the horse turns into a handsome prince. In some variations,[44] however, it is said *that this horse is really God Himself;*[45] while in

---

[42] *Ibid.*
[43] In a letter to Blanke on 18 March 1946, quoted in F. Blanke, *Bruder Klaus von Flüe*, p. 118.
[44] Cf J. Bolte and G. Polivka (eds), *Anmerkungen zu den Kinder- und Hausmärchen der Brüder Grimm*, Leipzig: de Gruyter 1918, Vol. 3, p. 22.
[45] *Ibid.*

others, the horse is identical to the old man who appeared at the baptism.[46] I mention this fairytale here because this motif of the horse is again important in a later vision of Brother Klaus's and because, during puberty, Brother Klaus did not find a castle, but a "magical tower."

---

[46] *Ibid.*

♦

Chapter 3
The Vision of the Tower

30 As a boy, Klaus was very pious and, from a psychological standpoint, extremely introverted. He often stole away from his friends and looked for a secluded place where he could pray. "As he got older," says Woelflin,[1] "he performed more and more good deeds and, while still a minor, he hardened his body by fasting every Friday and soon increased this to four days of fasting a week. He fasted secretly for forty days each Lent by eating only a little bread and some dried pears each day." When reproached for being too hard on himself, Klaus answered, "It is according to God's will."[2]

31 This deep introversion seems to be in accordance with the tendencies of Klaus's own unconscious for, as is reported in another vision which he had at the age of sixteen, a friend, Erni an der Halden,[3] says that Brother Klaus confided in him that when he was sixteen, he saw *a beautiful, high tower* standing where his little hermitage and chapel now stand, which is why he decided at a very young age to lead "a solitary life, which is what he did."[4]

32 As M.-B. Lavaud[5] points out, the tower is a symbol of God.[6] Perhaps it is also an image for the role Klaus was to have for his people, namely, as a tower which defends and unifies them.[7]

---

[1] R. Duerrer, *Bruder Klaus*, 1:532f., (trans.). On Niklaus's life, see also Werner Duerrer, *Augenzeugen berichten über Bruder Klaus*, Lucerne: Rex Verlag, 1941.
[2] (Trans.)
[3] The parish register of Sachseln of 1488; R. Duerrer, *Bruder Klaus*, Vol. 1, p. 464.
[4] A. Stoeckli, *Die Visionen des seligen Bruder Klaus*, p. 13. Stoeckli translates '*ein einig wesen*' (a solitary life) (trans.) with '*ein einsames Leben*' (a lonely life) (trans.).
[5] M.-B. Lavaud, *Vie profonde de Nicolas de Flüe*, pp. 27ff.
[6] Holy Bible (KJV), Psalm 61:3 "For thou hast been a shelter for me, and a strong tower from the enemy"; and Proverbs 18:10 "The name of the Lord is a strong tower: the righteous runneth into it, and is safe."
[7] F. Blanke, *Bruder Klaus von Flüe*, p. 69; see also M.-B. Lavaud, *Vie profonde de Nicolas de Flüe*, p. 27: "The first mention of a tower in Genesis refers to a nonsensical undertaking of men who settled on the plain in the land of Shinar (Gen. 11:4). Niklaus, on the other hand, brought the people together despite their various languages and cultures and the split between the Reformed Church and the Catholics ..." (Trans.)

33   Lavaud goes on to remind us of the parable from St. Luke:[8] "If any man come to me, and hate not his father, and mother, and wife, and children, and brethren, and sisters, yea, and his own life also; he cannot be my disciple." And later, "Whosoever does not bear his cross, and come after me, cannot be my disciple. For which of you intending to build a tower, sitteth not down first, and counteth the cost, whether he have sufficient to finish it?" Here, the tower has to do with forsaking "all that he hath"[9] and with the necessity of ending the unconscious *participation mystique* of family relationships. This is not only the precondition of living a Christian life but is also a precondition of the individuation process. The tower, moreover, is generally an allegory for the Church[10] or the Virgin Mary[11] and is, therefore, a feminine, maternal symbol. Perhaps it is pertinent to mention here that a brother of Klaus's mother, Matthias Hattinger von Wolfenschiessen, was a so-called *Waldsbruder*[12] (hermit) who lived in a tower similar to the one Klaus later built for himself. (The mother's brother is often a personification of the mother's animus, her inner attitude, making it possible to imagine that his mother's side of the family had an influence on Brother Klaus.)[13]

34   Psychologically speaking, the negative aspect of a tower often means being trapped in introverted defence mechanisms that make one feel cut off and isolated. A tower, as is a dungeon, is also an image of the self, especially when *one's fear of the self predominates*.[14] Seen positively, the tower is the motherly *temenos*, the holy realm, under whose protection the process of individuation can unfold. Precisely in those fateful years of puberty when a drive towards the outer world awakens, the unconscious keeps Brother Klaus focused on this image of extreme limitation of the self which, however, is simultaneously an image of the goal of the "towering" personality he was to become.

---

[8] Holy Bible (KJV), Luke 14:26ff.
[9] Luke 14:33.
[10] C.G. Jung, CW 6, *Psychological Types*, London: Routledge & Kegan Paul Ltd. 1971, §381.
[11] *Ibid.*, §379 and §390.
[12] F. Blanke, *Bruder Klaus von Flüe*, Vol. 1, p. 7.
[13] H. Federer, *Wander- und Wundergeschichten aus dem Süden*, Berlin: G. Grote'sche Verlagsbuchhandlung, 1924. Federer, too, had already suspected that Klaus's mother's influence underlay Klaus's piety.
[14] C.G. Jung, CW 12, *Psychology and Alchemy*, §325.

35   Relatively late in life, when he was around thirty years old, Brother Klaus married Dorothea Wiss[15] who came from a respectable family. They had ten children[16] and lived together for a good twenty years. He also held several positions within his community[17] but he turned down the offer to become mayor.[18] He took part in various expeditions of war, as a standard-bearer and later as a captain, though without deriving any pleasure from them.[19] Towards the middle of his life, or shortly thereafter, he began to suffer from states of depression and inner restlessness,[20] and it was during this time that he had most of the visions we know of.

---

[15] R. Duerrer, *Bruder Klaus*, Vol. 1, p. 27.
[16] *Ibid.*, and see Ch. Journet, *Saint Nicolas de Flüe*, p. 16.
[17] F. Blanke, *Bruder Klaus von Flüe*, Vol. 1, p. 8; R. Duerrer, *Bruder Klaus*, Vol. 1, p. 39.
[18] *Ibid.*, Vol. 1, p. 463.
[19] For more, see Ch. Journet, *Saint Nicolas de Flüe*, p. 18f. His name was found among a list of 699 Swiss who tried to free Nuremberg from being besieged by the troops of the margrave (military governor) of Brandenburg. See G. Méautis, *Nicolas de Flüe,* Neuchatel: Secrétariat de l'Université, 1940, p. 30.
[20] F. Blanke, *Bruder Klaus von Flüe*, p. 12.

◆

Chapter 4
The Time of Depression and Temptation

³⁶ Unfortunately, the information which has been handed down about events in the development of Brother Klaus's inner life cannot be put into chronological order, which is why I have had to order them according to the likelihood of their inner occurrence. The period of his married life until the moment of his "cutting off," as he called it, i.e., until he made his decision to live the life of a hermit, is distinguished by two types of visions: The first type mirrors a heavy conflict which finds its resolution in his decision to "cut off"; the second type is the big visions which seem to be an answer to Klaus's own questions on faith and to those of his time. The experiences he had which reflect more his personal conflicts shall be considered first. Around 1460, Brother Klaus said of his depressive states: "God submitted me to a terrible temptation which tormented me day and night, which made my heart so terribly heavy that even the company of my dear wife and children was tiresome to me."[1]

³⁷ During this period of his life, Klaus was tempted by the devil on various occasions. In the parish register of Sachseln, Erni Rorer reports[2] that Brother Klaus told him how the devil made him suffer greatly every day, but how the Virgin Mary always comforted him.

---

[1] R. Duerrer, *Bruder Klaus*, Vol. 1, p. 39: Klaus tells a preaching monk: When it suited him (i.e., God) "to win me back by showing me his mercy, he used his cleansing file and his driving spur, i.e., severe temptation, for he could not bear me to be still, neither during the day nor at night. I was so dejected that I could not bear the company of either my dear wife or my children. While I remained in this state, my above-mentioned trusted and dear friend, to whom I told every secret, came to visit me to have a talk and gave me certain things which he hoped would relieve me of my temptation. But I told him that I had tried this and similar things as well, and had found no comfort." (Trans.) Heiny am Grund suggests at this point that Brother Klaus contemplate the Passion of Christ.

[2] *Ibid.*, Vol. 1, p. 463.

In Klaus's search for his "true self,"[3] "the devil caused him great misfortune, especially on one occasion when he wanted to go to Melchtal to cut down thorn bushes in the meadow and the devil cast him down a slope with such force that he was badly hurt and fainted when he was picked up."[4]

³⁸ Klaus told Reverend Oswald Yssner[5] that "it seemed that the devil appeared to him as a richly dressed nobleman mounted on a beautiful horse and, after a long discourse, advised Klaus to give up his pious attitude which would not help him to win eternal life, but rather he (Klaus) should live as other people do."[6]

³⁹ In one of Brother Klaus's major visions, three noblemen appear to him in whom he later recognized the Holy Trinity. And, on another occasion, a noble traveller appears to him wearing a bearskin of shining gold, a figure that Brother Klaus believes to represent Christianity. Thus, it is only the *content* of what the nobleman says which makes Brother Klaus think, in this instance, it is the devil. But if, for a moment, one disregards this classification within the confines of dogma and views it instead from a psychological standpoint, a nobleman means nothing other than, indeed, a noble man, and, as such, he symbolizes, presumably, the noble aspect of Brother Klaus's own being, his own inner, noble, and distinguished personality. It is interesting to see the great extent to which this inner figure was realized in Niklaus von Flüe's life for,

---

[3] *Ibid.*, Vol. 1., p. 464.

[4] *Ibid.*, (trans.). See also the detailed description of Hans von Flüe's in R. Duerrer, *Bruder Klaus*, Vol. 1, p. 469: "[Brother Klaus] never desired anything other than to worship God, though the devil brought him suffering and discontentment. At some point, he [Hans von Flüe] went to Melchtal in Bergmatten with his father to check the cattle. His father wanted to rip out the thorn bushes to clean the mats with them. When the devil appeared and threw his father into a large thornbush some thirty paces away so roughly that he [Klaus] lost consciousness, and he no longer knew anything at all. When Hans reached Klaus, Hans sat him up and carried his still unconscious father to the fire in the barn and when, after a long time, his father returned to consciousness, even though he was hurt all over, he spoke patiently, as if there was nothing else he could say, and said, 'In God's name, how horribly the devil has treated me, but it must be God's will.'" (Trans.) See also Woelflin's report in R. Duerrer, *Bruder Klaus*, Vol. 1, p. 534.

[5] R. Duerrer, *Bruder Klaus*, Vol. 1, pp. 466ff.

[6] (Trans.) According to Woelflin (R. Duerrer, *Bruder Klaus*, 1: 546) this encounter, however, took place in the time *after* Klaus's 'withdrawal.' In contrast to reports from other witnesses, Woelflin says that the devil tormented Brother Klaus 'terribly,' also after his withdrawal from the world, and as he didn't achieve anything by pulling Klaus out of his hermitage by his hair, he appeared as a richly dressed nobleman and said to him that it was completely senseless to live such a lonely and strict life beyond the reaches of human society for, in doing so, he could not reach the glory of heaven. If Klaus truly wanted to achieve this with all of his heart, it would be more useful to adapt to the normal customs of society. (Trans.)

aside from his inner development, he was, in fact, elevated to the level of the nobility in his outer life and was later often visited by aristocrats, princes and bishops who asked his advice as if he were one of them. And Ulrich, a nobleman from Memmingen in Swabia, even settled in the Ranft and built his hut beside Brother Klaus's own place of refuge, in the place known as "Mösli."

40   Paradoxically, precisely this nobleman advises Brother Klaus "to live as other people do, for he will not win eternal life if he continues on in *this* way." Perhaps Niklaus von Flüe consciously strove both too hard and too one-sidedly to achieve the pious goals he had set for himself, i.e., he was too intent upon the realization of his own ideas, and precisely because of this, he lost contact with the natural nobility of his own being. The somewhat cramped piousness that typified this period of his life was probably not in tune with the unconscious. By contrast, the rider and his horse mirror those who are in contact with the animal side of their nature in the right way.[7] In the canton of Uri, it is still considered to be a "sacrilege" to "not do as others do."[8] The desire to be something special challenges the divine powers of both good and evil, which then most often stomp on any such plans. It is precisely this nobleman who stands out from the mass who unexpectedly advises Klaus to adapt. So apparently, precisely in this area of trusting in his special destiny, Klaus should not strive to be special according to the dictates of his ego. Rather, he should remain humble so that the Self can unfold according to its own natural law.

41   While in other circumstances, Klaus correctly interpreted his visions with a rare instinctual certainty, in this depressed period of his life, it would seem he felt confused. This explains his negative interpretation of the nobleman, that is, of being the devil himself.

42   Another vision from this period shows the same conflict even more clearly. Welti von Flüe reports[9] that, among other things, Klaus

---

[7] C.G. Jung, CW 5, *Symbols of Transformation*, §421: "... the hero and his horse seem to symbolize the idea of man and the subordinate sphere of animal instinct."
[8] Eduard Renner, *Goldener Ring über Uri: ein Buch vom Erleben und Denken unserer Bergler, von Magie und Geistern und von den ersten und letzten Dingen*, Zürich: Helvetische Bücherei, 1941, pp. 310ff.
[9] Parish register of Sachseln, in R. Duerrer, *Bruder Klaus*, Vol. 1, p. 469, (trans.); F. Blanke, *Bruder Klaus von Flüe*, p. 24f. and p. 88.

had once told him that "Shortly after he had begun his life in retreat, he went to the meadow in Melche to cut the grass and, on the way, he prayed to God, asking for the grace to live a pious life. At that moment, a cloud in the sky spoke to him and told him to submit to the will of God. It said he was a foolish man and should be willing to submit to what God wanted of him."

43   At first, this vision seems to be contradictory, for Klaus asks God for the grace to live a pious life and God scolds him and calls him a foolish man who should finally submit himself to doing God's will! Perhaps Klaus's conscious idea of what a pious life was not what God wanted of him.[10]

44   In mythology, clouds can appear to encompass archetypal contents coming from the unconscious. Zeus and Hera unite in a cloud, and, in Revelations, the Son of Man arrives on a cloud. The Virgin Mary was thought of as being "a cloud, a provider of shade and coolness," and, at the same time, clouds and fog are said to be the products of the devil, who sends out "the fog of the unconscious" from the north.[11] Clouds, so to speak, represent potential[12]—they symbolise an archetype in its relatively undefined state upon which consciousness cannot yet find its bearings. It was only much later that God revealed His "terrifying" face to St. Niklaus—in his current state, he would not have been able to have borne it. But in this vision of the cloud, God indicates that what Klaus imagines to be God does not altogether correspond to the reality of God[13] in his unconscious soul. This is the same tragic situation we find ourselves in when we channel all our conscious efforts into doing the right thing, only to

---

[10] See also F. Blanke, *Bruder Klaus von Flüe*, p. 25: "The voice coming out of the cloud is also an admonishing, punitive voice. ... Klaus's sin is his absolute indecisiveness. He is not reproached for being overly involved in the happenings of the world and of having forgotten the task which has been set—such reproaches would have been unjust. Rather he was reproached for lacking the will to make the most difficult and final decision. Klaus himself was not aware of this." (Trans.) I do not completely agree with Blanke, for I do not perceive in Klaus's hesitation an "imperceptible secret attachment to the world" (trans.), but rather a pure lack of understanding, as Blanke also intimates above. I rather think that he would have been willing to do anything but did not know *what* was intended.
[11] C.G. Jung, CW 9/ii, *Aion*, §158.
[12] *Ibid.*, §240.
[13] C.G. Jung, CW 11, *Psychology and Religion*, §479: "This is what always happens when things are interpreted, explained, and dogmatized until they become so encrusted with man-made images and words that they can no longer be seen. Something similar seems to have happened to Brother Klaus, which is why the immediate experience burst upon him with appalling terror."

be constantly reprimanded by the unconscious for being on the wrong track. Although we mean well, we are unable to get the message and cannot understand the intention of the unconscious. It is only after Klaus has a further vision that he is shown how his inner developmental process can take a step forward in the direction of a dramatic *dénouement*, to understand more clearly what his unconscious destiny is aiming at.

Chapter 5

The Vision of the Lily That Was Eaten by a Horse

45 Woelflin alone reports the following vision of the saint:

"When, on another occasion, Brother Klaus went to a meadow to look at his livestock, he sat down on the ground and, as was his custom, he started to pray with all his heart and to give himself up to divine contemplation. Suddenly, he saw a wonderfully perfumed white lily growing out of his mouth and extending upwards until it touched the sky. When, however, a little later his livestock (which were his means of supporting his family) passed by him and he had lowered his gaze for a moment, his eyes came to rest upon a horse that was more beautiful than the others. And he saw how the lily in his mouth bent itself down to this horse and was eaten by it as it passed by."

46 Brother Klaus interpreted the vision by saying that "the treasures of heaven cannot be found by those who lust for worldly pleasures, and that if heaven's offerings are mixed up with the concerns and interests of earthly existence, they will be stifled like the seed of God's word is stifled when it is sown amongst thorns."[1]

47 As Blanke[2] emphasises, it is possible that Brother Klaus had seen an image of Christ with a lily sprouting out of His mouth, for, at this time, such an illustration in which a lily replaces the sword in the

---

[1] R. Duerrer, *Bruder Klaus*, Vol. 1, p. 535, (trans.) See F. Blanke, *Bruder Klaus von Flüe*, p. 20f. and pp. 84f.
[2] *Ibid.*, p. 85.

mouth of the Son of Man in Revelations existed in various paintings throughout Switzerland. In this form, the lily is an image of the *anima Christi*. The bride in the Song of Solomon is described as "the lily of the valleys,"[3] and the Church Fathers interpreted this passage as referring to Mary, the mother, bride and sister of Christ.[4] But the connection between the lily and the horse in Brother Klaus's vision probably also points towards a completely different meaning, one which has closer connections to folklore. Indeed, according to Germanic pagan mythology, the lily represents *the* royal flower, par excellence.[5] It symbolises the power and force of a kingdom's law, which is why it also appears in very many royal and noble coats-of-arms. The lily is associated with mermaids, white women, and valkyries,[6] as well as with the "white woman" and the goddess Ostara, Donar's sister, whose name lives on in the word "Easter."[7] Blooming or budding plant stalks, especially the switch of an apple tree, are, along with the lily, also emblematic images for royalty, which is why, for example, Alfred the Great's crown jewels depict the king with two lily stalks in his hand.[8]

48   Viewed within the context of such amplifications, the lily, then, is an image for Brother Klaus's "royal" and purely contemplative

---

[3] *Cant. Cant. Vulgata*, 2: 1: *Ego flos campi et lilium convallium*; Holy Bible (KJV), Song of Solomon 2:1, "I am the rose of Sharon and the lily of the valleys." In this connection, see C.G. Jung, CW 6, *Psychological Types*, London: Routledge & Kegan Paul, 1971, §392.

[4] *Ibid.*

[5] M. Ninck, *Wodan und germanischer Schicksalsglaube*, Jena: Eugen Diedrichs Verlag, 1953, p. 196. The lily is the symbol of the Merovingians and, from the eleventh century onwards, it appears in the hand of the French king and the German emperor. [It is the sword lily (or Iris) spoken of below (ed.).]

[6] Thus, the picking of unknown lily-like flowers brings in its wake the appearance of the "white lady" or other "virgins" (*valkyries*).

[7] M. Ninck, *Wodan und germanischer Schicksalsglaube*, p. 223.

[8] *Ibid.*, p. 195: "The governing power of the king and judge is emphasized in a series of additional characteristics such as blooming and growing. In Old High German, the staff or sceptre, the sign of royal authority, is called *chunincgerta*, in the Germanic language *cyneguard* or "royal crop," also hazel rod. Accordingly, we find the crop [or switch] represented in medieval statues ... almost always in bud and in bloom. Footnote: examples include: the king with the two *lily stalks* in the crown jewels of Alfred the Great (depicted in E. Winckelmann, *Geschichte der Angelsachsen*, Stuttgart: Hoffmannsche Verlagsbuchhandlung, 1847, p. 149) is King Rachis in *Leges Langobardorum*, Göttingen: Franz Beyerle, 1962, pp. 183–192). Also there is the enthroned Mathilde of Toscana with the flower in her hand, in Cod. Vat. Lat. 4922, and the plant motifs. Buds and creepers are often attached to the crown ..." (Trans.) And M. Ninck, *Wodan und germanischer Schicksalsglaube*, p.196: "Based on an ancient symbol ... the lily (the white lily, the lily of the sword [*fleur de lys*: Iris] and the water lily) became the truly royal flower. For the Merovingians, whereas the lily [*fleur de lys*] at first crowned their sceptre, it later became a sign of royalty in itself, and this was not limited to the Franks alone. From the eleventh century onwards, the lily was used as an image for their seals by both the French king and German emperor, and it was to be found in innumerable coats of arms of the nobility ..." (Trans.)

anima[9] that is focused on the Beyond. It is, so to speak, a symbol of his unwavering inner search for God that was growing within him like a plant striving towards the light. At the time Brother Klaus lived, there were still strange stories circulating. For example, in Hiltisrieden in 1430 when the foundation stone of a curate's house was being laid, a lily was discovered to be growing right through the heart of a corpse that was found there. Later, circa 1444, the story moved to a place between Sempach and Hiltisrieden, where Duke Leopold had apparently been killed in battle, and it was said that a lily grew out of his heart. Indeed, there are legends about a lily growing out of the mouth or heart of the dead in several other regions.[10]

49   Therefore, perhaps we could say that, while still alive, Brother Klaus had already 'deadened' himself to life to such an extent that this "soul-flower," which endures beyond physical death, was, in some miraculous way, able to be seen during his lifetime. Perhaps the appearance of this vegetative form of his anima is connected to his fasting, and Jung writes[11] that perhaps one explanation of Brother Klaus's fasting is that he was somehow able to draw his nourishment from his surroundings, which would mean he was able to live in a kind of plantlike way. This explanation is not intended to diminish in any way the miraculous aspect of Klaus's ability to fast.

50   Now in his vision, the lily bends itself over Brother Klaus's favourite horse, and the horse devours it. Far more than in the Bible,

---

[9] In Jungian psychology, "anima" means the feminine spiritual disposition in men which appears in dreams and other products of the unconscious, often personified as a woman. See C.G. Jung, CW 9/i, *The Archetypes and the Collective Unconscious*, §§111–147 and E. Jung, 'Die Anima als Naturwesen', in *Studien zur analytischen Psychologie C.G. Jungs*, Zürich: Rascher Verlag, 1955, Vol. 2, pp. 78–120.

[10] Alois Lütolf, *Sagen, Bräuche, Legenden aus den fünf Orten*, Lucerne, 1862, p. 374f., and F. Pfeiffer, *Marienlegenden*, Stuttgart, 1846, pp. 77–82 and pp. 105–109.

[11] C.G. Jung, CW 18, *The Symbolic Life*, London: Routledge & Kegan Paul Ltd., 1977, §1498: "Naturally I have no explanation to offer concerning such phenomena as the fast of Brother Klaus but I am inclined to think that it should be sought in the realm of parapsychology. I myself was present at the investigation of a medium who manifested physical phenomena. An electrical engineer measured the degree of ionization in the atmosphere in the immediate vicinity of the medium. The figures were everywhere normal except at one point on the right side of the thorax, where the ionization was about sixty times the normal. At this point, when the (parapsychological) phenomena were in progress, there was an emission of ectoplasm capable of acting at a distance. If such things can occur, then it is also conceivable that persons in the vicinity of the medium might act as a source of ions—in other words, nourishment might be effected by the passage of living molecules of albumen from one body to the other. In this connection it should be mentioned that in parapsychological experiments decreases of weight up to several kilograms have been observed during the (physical) phenomena, in the case both of the medium and of some of the participants, who were all sitting on scales."

the horse in Germanic mythology is an immensely important symbol, even more so than the lily. Indeed, it is the actual form in which the God, Wotan,[12] appears who, by the way, used to storm about in the olden days as a wild hunter or as a group of dark horses near the mountain of Pilatus, that is, very close to Brother Klaus's dwelling.[13] *Not only does Wotan almost always appear on a horse, but also as a horse.*[14] His sons were called *Hengist* and *Horsa* ("Stallion" and "Horse"), and Ninck emphasises that "the god's essence and his totem animal flow together to make an indivisible whole."[15] This is why, as Tacitus says, in Germanic mythology, the horse has a closer relationship to the gods than even the priests do.[16] Wotan himself is even called *Jak* (Gelding) or *Hrossharsgrani* (Horsehair Beard),[17] and, conversely, his names are given to horses. From a psychological standpoint, the horse generally embodies animallike instinctive psychic energy in its pure essence. It is a form of libido[18] which, with its mythological associations, circles around the maternal and the physical, and around things that come from the underworld as well as ghostly things.[19] Horses tend to get excited and panic. Perhaps we should pay special attention to this characteristic because, not long after this vision, Brother Klaus tried to run away to "*ellend*" (a foreign land) which means there might be a psychological connection between the vision and his impulse to leave. Brother Klaus considered the horse devouring the lily to be a mishap and thus interpreted the horse negatively. But, from our modern standpoint of looking at dreams, we would have to say that he

---

[12] M. Ninck, *Wodan und germanischer Schicksalsglaube*, p. 75ff.

[13] *Ibid.*, p. 78 (for R. Cysat, see following): "Thus there were other ghosts in these high, wild alps. Many can be heard and seen at night, sometimes riding, and sometimes appearing in the form of those people who one knows during the day. Some ride up the mountain and through the woods towards the lake of Pilatus and canter as if there were many hundreds of them, so loud is their thunder and power ..." (Trans.) In the dialect of Lucerne, when a storm was approaching, people would say, "It is the *Türst*" [huge Wotan-like figure] (trans.) or "It is the *Wüetisheer*" [Wotan's army] (trans.), and when the big black dog with eyes of fire could be seen racing down the ravine, it was characteristically compared to a "*Wätterleich*" [bolt of lightning] (trans.). See also, *ibid.*, pp. 79–81.

[14] *Ibid.*, p. 92.

[15] *Ibid.*, p. 93, (trans.).

[16] Tacitus, *Germania,* Munich: Verlag der Bremer Presse, 1922, p. 9. See M. Ninck, *Wodan und germanischer Schicksalsglaube*, p. 93.

[17] *Ibid.*, p. 73.

[18] C.G. Jung, CW 5, *Symbols of Transformation*, §422.

[19] *Ibid.*, §421 for the meaning of "mother." Concerning Odin as a black death horse, see A. Lütolf, *Sagen und Bräuche, Legenden aus den fünf Orten*, p. 44.

overlooked one thing, namely, that *the lily itself bends down to the horse (incurvari!).* One could say that the lily "took a liking" to the horse. The vision depicts an objective event,[20] namely, the uniting of the plant with the animal, the former bending down towards the latter and being incorporated by it.[21] The vision is an image of an *enantiodromia,* an inner psychic process, the moment in which the upward striving spiritual form of the psyche turns back towards animal life. The lily comes out of his [Klaus's] body and then goes back down into a body, the body of an animal that Brother Klaus especially likes. This movement of the lily reminds one of what is said in the *Tabula Smaragdina* about the philosopher's stone: *Vis eius integra est, si versa fuerit in terram"* (Its strength is perfect when it has turned towards the earth (!)). And, *"Ascendit a terra in coelum, iterumque descendit in terram et recipit vim superiorum et inferiorum."* (It rises from the earth to the sky and descends again onto the earth, and receives the power of the above and below unto itself).[22]

51   If we take the lily to be a symbol of the *anima candida* who is detached from the world, then here is a hint that the latter bends towards the matrix[23] of the animallike unconscious psyche (that is, the horse) *of its own accord* in order to unite with it.[24] The beautiful horse, which the lily bends down to, reminds us of the Grimm's fairytale "Ferdinand the Faithful and Ferdinand the Unfaithful," mentioned above. On a heath where a castle stands, the youthful hero finds a beautiful white horse that is able to speak (which corresponds to Brother Klaus's vision of the tower). In some versions, this white horse is identical to the unknown old godfather

---

[20] C.G. Jung, CW 8, *The Structure and Dynamics of the Psyche*, §532: according to Jung's standpoint on dreams, a dream or a vision is a self-portrayal of an unconscious psychic event; it contains no judgemental objective even if consciousness can, on occasion, experience it in this way.
[21] Wotan's horse is an especially greedy creature: in the old Faustian legend, for example, Mephisto appears as a horse which, while its master is carousing with his friends, eats up all the hay in the haystack. As Ninck emphasizes, the horse is actually Wotan and represents the greed of wanting instant and perpetual satisfaction in the face of the all-devouring abyss of time. The animal's gaping jaws, too, are an image of the magical power which emerges as the yawning gulf opens. The word "*Ginschlund*" is related to the word "*ginna*" which means to do magic, to attract, to beguile. See M. Ninck, *Wodan und germanischer Schicksalsglaube*, p. 138.
[22] J. Ruska, ed., *Tabula Smaragdina*, Heidelberg: Winter, 1926, p. 184f.
[23] See C.G. Jung, CW 5, *Symbols of Transformation*, §421 on the meaning of the horse as a mother.
[24] I am grateful to Dr. R. Kluger-Schärf for this interpretation.

or to God Himself. This fairytale from northern Germany most probably contains old Germanic ideas, i.e., the white horse brings to mind Wotan's horse, Sleipnir, which, indeed, was often considered to be identical to God. Seen against the background of such amplifications, the meaning of the lily disappearing into the horse hints at a *unio mystica* of the soul with the divine, represented by the anima.

For the moment, then, the soul-flower of the saint *is* in the horse, and, accordingly, we could expect Brother Klaus to be gripped by some urge which would correspond to the symbolic nature of the horse, namely by the urge to go on a "ghost ride." Indeed, it is not only in Germanic mythology that the horse acts as a companion into the other world, into the spiritual realm. In the initiation rites of other races, too, the horse often appears as a psychopomp and as the carrying animal on an ecstatic journey into the Beyond.[25] The medicine man, who is the medium and shaman of primitive races, flies upon a horse's back into the sky or into the realm of the dead. The horse helps him to reach another world, which is why many shamans carry a staff with a horse's head upon it. "The symbolic ride," Eliade[26] says, "expresses the shaman's leaving his body and his mystical death." This is why I believe that Brother Klaus's horse vision was an announcement telling him that his soul-flower, which longs for heaven and ecstatically reaches up towards it and which represents his emotional longing for an experience of God, wants to become emotionally active and to take him on a ghost ride into the Beyond. Indeed, we know that, like a horse, Brother Klaus was once gripped by a desire to roam about the country and leave everything behind him, namely when he took leave of his wife and children with the intention of going away and living in a foreign land.

---

[25] For evidence of this, see M. Eliade, *Shamanism*, pp. 323, 408, 467ff.
[26] *Ibid.*, p. 470.

◆

Chapter 6
The Liestal Vision

₃ Erny Rorer reports[1] that Brother Klaus once recounted the following episode in this way:

₄ "One day, he [Brother Klaus] decided to leave his country, to leave his wife, his children, and all he had behind him, to live in a foreign land. So he set off and when he was close to Liechtstall (Liestal), it seemed to him that this place, and everything in it, had turned red. He was so frightened that he immediately went up to a solitary farmhouse to talk to the farmer there. He told him of his intention to leave, but the farmer did not approve and told Brother Klaus to return home and to serve God amongst his own people for God would prefer that; and he told Klaus he should find his peace in this way for he was a Swiss citizen who would not necessarily be liked by foreigners. So Brother Klaus left the farmer's house the same evening and went into a field. He lay down near a fence and, while asleep, he had a vision of a shining light coming from Heaven which opened up his abdomen, which he felt so painfully as if he had been cut open with a knife. He understood that he should return to the Ranft, which he immediately did."[2] But he did not return

---

[1] R. Duerrer, *Bruder Klaus*, Vol. 1, p. 463, (trans.) and almost the same report by Heiny am Grund (in Duerrer, op. cit, Vol. 1, p. 466), and in summarised form by O. Yssner (in Duerrer, Vol. 1, p. 468). See F. Blanke, *Brüder Klaus von Flüe*, p. 89.

[2] See R. Duerrer, *Bruder Klaus*, Vol. 1, p. 466, where Heiny am Grund says, "He [Brother Klaus] also said to him: 'Once when he said he wanted to go abroad and came to Liechtstall, the town and everything in it seemed red to him. So he left and came to a solitary farm and to a farmer to whom he told his plans, and this farmer told him he should go home to his own people and serve God there for this would be better than staying amongst strangers for it would be more peaceful for him at home because not everybody likes the Confederates. So he left the farmer's house the same evening, and spent the night in a field by a fence, and after he fell asleep he saw a shining light coming from the sky that opened

to his family home; instead, he went to an alp, the Klisterli, in upper Melchtal. Erny Rorer reports,[3] "and when he reached home, he stayed in Melchtal for eight days, living in thick thorn bushes and wild undergrowth, and when people realized this, many went to him and caused him great distress."

55   Woelflin reports[4] that Klaus's brother went to Klaus and tried to convince him to stop starving himself. Klaus then decided to return to the Ranft and, with the help of some friends, to build himself a small retreat—on 16 October 1467, in the year he was to turn fifty.

56   It is often asserted that Brother Klaus had intended to go to the 'Friends of God' (*Gottesfreunden*) in Alsace but, as Blanke correctly emphasizes, this is not clearly stated in any of the original source books.[5] In my view, it seems more probable that he was gripped by a desire to leave without any destination in mind. In any case, this is what Wotan sometimes incites in those whom he meets. R. Cysat, from Lucerne,[6] tells of a story from the sixteenth century, for example, in which a farmer's son from Entlebuch quarrels with his father over money and, suddenly, on the so-called Branegk, meets up with a funny "elegant" warrior (who is Wotan). The warrior asks him what the trouble is and offers him money and the opportunity to team up with him. The youth is then gripped by a sudden urge to strike out on his own. He has "nothing in his mind except to leave and be gone." He did not stop until he reached Einsiedeln, where some people from Unterwald recognized him on the street and talked him into returning home. But he had to spend a few days in Einsiedeln to come to his senses again and—as it is said—"to find himself." I believe that Brother Klaus had a similar experience: He

---

up his stomach which was so painful, it was as if he were being cut open by a knife and this convinced him that he should return to the Ranft and go on serving God there as he had before." (Trans.)

[3] R. Duerrer, op cit, Vol. 1, p. 463, (trans.); F. Blanke, op cit, p. 91f.

[4] R. Duerrer, *Bruder Klaus*, Vol. 1, p. 540, (trans.); F. Blanke, *Brüder Klaus von Flüe*, p. 92.

[5] F. Blanke, op cit, p. 91. On Brother Klaus's relationship to the "Friends of God," see Otto Karrer, "Eine unbekannte Nachricht über Niklaus von Flüe" in *Schweiz. Rundschau*, Einsiedeln: Benziger, 1927/28, 27, pp. 258–62.

[6] R. Brandstetter, *Die Wuotansage im alten Luzern. Der Geschichtsfreund*, Stans, 1907, Vol. 62, I, p. 139. The same as "*Luftreise*," *ibid.*, p. 131; see also M. Ninck, *Wodan und germanischer Schicksalsglaube*, pp. 78ff.

simply felt he had to go, to leave everything behind without any definite idea about where he was going—an outer projection of the longing to be free and the wish to experience the classical "ghost ride" of the medicine man. When he then suddenly sees the whole town of Liestal and its environs bathed in red, he is deeply afraid. Thus, we must first look at the negative implications of the colour red to interpret this motif correctly. Red is most often associated with fire and blood[7] and thus refers to emotionality and passionate feeling.[8] In ancient Egypt, red was thought to be the colour of "evil passion," of the god Seth. A world bathed in red suggests war and bloodshed. The Germanic Valkyries prophesy a battle in the following verse:[9]

57
> *Blood rains from the cloudy web*
> *On the broad loom of slaughter.*
> *The web of man grey as armor*
> *Is now being woven; the Valkyries*
> *Will cross it with a crimson weft.*[10]

58 Red paint and red threads are used in many places for black magic.[11] In this context, red is also the colour of death. Artemidor says[12] that crimson colours are "sympathetic" towards death. And in ancient Greece, the dead were wrapped in crimson cloth before being buried, and the sarcophagi were painted vermilion.[13] In many primitive tribes, even corpses were coloured red.[14] The war dress of many peoples was also red to clearly indicate their warlike nature.[15] But in its positive aspects, red stands for the colour of life. It reflects the "mana" of a being and it also means immortality and the power

---

[7] It has almost become a stock sentence in the traditional texts on Brother Klaus to say that in Liestal he saw a "blaze of fire" (e.g., see Journet, Lavaud, Mojonnier and others), but this, however, is a rational creation of these commentators. In the source material, there is *no* mention of fire.

[8] C.G. Jung, CW 8, *The Structure and Dynamics of the Psyche*, §384.

[9] M. Ninck, *Wodan und germanischer Schicksalsglaube*, p. 182.

[10] Ian Cassells, *The Raven Banner: A guide to Viking Caithness*, Thurso, 1995.

[11] Cf Eva Wunderlich, "Die Bedeutung der roten Farbe im Kultus der Griechen und Römer" in *Religionsgeschichtliche Versuche uned Vorarbeiten*, Giessen, 1925, pp. 14ff.

[12] *Ibid.*, p. 46.

[13] *Ibid.*, pp. 49ff.

[14] *Ibid.*, p. 51.

[15] *Ibid.*, pp. 73ff.

to heal.[16] In Brother Klaus's experience in Liestal, red appears on the outside in his projection of this colour onto the world. This means that the theme "world" (that is, crowds of people ["town"] and foreign lands) is, so to speak, *loaded with destructive emotion.* Accordingly, we could guess that Brother Klaus must have had a deeply passionate nature which could burst out negatively when it came into contact with the outer world and that this was one of the reasons why his unconscious forced him into complete seclusion. There is possibly another clue that would support my guess: Hans Salat (1535/37) reports in his biography that once, when Klaus was participating in an assembly of the court and council of his parish, a man spoke out harshly against the law, and Klaus saw "flames in terrifying shapes" coming out of the man's mouth.[17] As a result, he decided to avoid all worldly prestige and power, "for both are so difficult to deal with in a serious and irreproachable manner."[18]

59   Although this vision is certainly true on an objective level,[19] Brother Klaus's highly sensitive reaction to "world"-oriented emotionality permits us to assume that the latter would have been dangerous for him if he had been allowed his too intense a temperament to flow out into the world. This could have resulted in Klaus feeling, for example, constant indignation about the wrongdoings of those around him, which would have made him feel restless and would have "eaten him up" inwardly. People who have such a passionate nature seem to be especially threatened by dissociation, which can be triggered by inner or outer events. The ability to have control over one's passion is also expected of the shamans of the north. For example, the Yakuts require their shamans to be serious and tactful but, above all, they may not show arrogance or hot-headedness. "One must feel an inner strength in him that

---

[16] *Ibid.*

[17] R. Duerrer, *Bruder Klaus*, Vol. 2, p. 677.

[18] Cf A. Stoeckli, *Die Visionen des seligen Bruder Klaus*, p.14.

[19] Psychologically speaking, "objective level" means that the dream or vision depicts something outside of oneself, something relatively psychologically independent of the dreamer, which, in this instance, would refer to this man being consumed by the fires of hell; on the "subjective level," it would represent an inner dynamic process which, in this instance, could be, for example, that a part of Brother Klaus (his shadow) succumbs to the fire of passion.

does not frighten, yet is conscious of its power."[20] Simultaneously, almost everywhere in the world, shamans are thought to be connected to blacksmiths and to *have mastery over fire*.[21] Their "mana" is often described as "burning," and they have a creative inner fire[22] along with a lack of sensitivity to outer heat or cold. The blaze which Brother Klaus saw with such shock in the wrongdoer could, therefore, have made such a great impression upon him because it symbolised his own negative opposite, along with a destructive developmental potentiality within himself (his shadow), which could only be avoided by his renunciation of all worldly power. By withdrawing from the world, he instinctively found the healing countermeasure, namely, locking himself up to be alone with himself, or rather, with his inner confrontation with all that was "red," which, at that time, threatened him in the outer world. Indeed, if applied to the outer world, red corresponds to fire that destroys. But if applied to the inner world, red corresponds to the *ignis noster* of the alchemists, about which a text, the famous *Turba Philosophorum*, says,[23] "Out of those composites which have been transformed into red spirit the *principium mundi* is derived" (the earliest beginning, or the basic principle, this is the ark of the world).[24] After internalising "red," a new way of life begins for Brother Klaus, too, namely, his life as a recluse in the woods. But in the Liestal episode, red is still visible externally and makes him too fearful to go any further afield into the world.

In his desperate situation, he goes to the owner of a solitary farm and asks his advice, and this man tells him he would do better to serve God at home, for Swiss Confederates are not too popular abroad. As a child would, Brother Klaus willingly obeys this advice. This is one of his most curious and perhaps most admirable

---

[20] M. Eliade, *Shamanism*, p. 29.
[21] *Ibid.*, pp. 470ff.
[22] *Ibid.*, p. 475.
[23] J. Ruska, *Turba Philosophorum*, Berlin, 1931, p. 201; Cf C.G. Jung, *Alchemical Studies*, Vol. 13, §103, fn. 52: "Contrary to Ruska (*Turba*, p. 201: fn. 3), I adhere to the reading in the MSS because it is simply a synonym for the moist soul of the prima materia, the radical moisture. Another synonym for the water is "spiritual blood" (*ibid.*, p. 129), which Ruska rightly collates with (fire-coloured blood) in the Greek sources ... Mercurius ... is called (fiery medicine)." (These explanations also show a meaningful connection between the colour "red" and the "holy oil" in Brother Klaus's visions.)
[24] Or (according to J. Ruska, *Turba Philosophorum*, p. 201) "*des Wissens*" (i.e., of knowledge) (trans.).

qualities, namely, that in critical moments of danger, he could submit to reality with great simplicity. Much later, when he has his terrifying vision of God, he saves himself by simply throwing himself on the ground, and in this Liestal vision, he submits to the advice of an unknown, simple farmer. Aware of his own confusion and that he was too far from his instincts to be able to judge the situation he found himself in, Klaus correctly consults the farmer as if he were an oracle and accepts his advice without any argument. In such moments, Klaus appears to have a divine quality which the alchemists called *res simplex*[25] and *homo simplicissimus*,[26] that is, *the capacity for complete simplicity and spontaneity of action out of one's inner wholeness*. A similar *homo simplex* shines through in certain koans of Zen Buddhism.[27] It appears to be a manifestation of the divine in man, as it were, or as Jung says,[28] "an answer of Nature, who has succeeded in conveying her reaction direct to the conscious mind."

61   In a parallel report about this episode, H. Woelflin and H. Salat[29] say that Klaus was drawn back to the Ranft as if he were being pulled by a rope. This motif is significant, as rope often plays a role in the initiation rites and practices of the shamans of the circumpolar peoples,[30] but also in many other cultural areas. Thus, on the graves of the kings of Tibet a rope is depicted to signify that the king did not die but has ascended to heaven.[31] Certain priests were able to assist the dead in climbing up to heaven on ropes[32] and were thus called "the owners of heavenly ropes." On the other hand, certain gods were thought to be "binding"[33] so that a rope can also be a

---

[25] Cf C.G. Jung, CW 12, *Psychology and Alchemy*, §371.

[26] Cf Bernhardus Trevisanus, *"Parabel von der Fontina"* in: Jean-Jacques Manget, *Biblioteca Chemica Curiosa*, Geneva: Chouet, 1702, Vol. 2, p. 388f. Here, it is a *homo simplicissimus*, who is the only one allowed to serve and see the renewal of the king at the fountainhead. The *res simplex* refers to the divine.

[27] The "koan" is understood to be a paradoxical question, statement, or action of a Zen master as a means to instruct the student in "Sartori" (enlightenment), and for this reason, it is then related to others. It seems to be the wish of the Zen master to help the student to have an "insight into his own nature," into the nature of "original man" and into the depths of his own being. Cf C.G. Jung's foreword to D.T. Suzuki's *Introduction to Zen Buddhism* in C.G. Jung, CW 11, *Psychology and Religion*, §894f.

[28] *Ibid.*, §895.

[29] R. Duerrer, *Bruder Klaus*, Vol. 1, p. 540, and Vol. 2, p. 678.

[30] Cf M. Eliade, *Shamanism*, pp. 430ff.

[31] *Ibid.*, p. 431.

[32] *Ibid.*, p. 433.

[33] *Ibid.*, p. 430.

symbol of a *definitive spiritual commitment to a godhead.* Generally speaking, the cord seems to represent a suprapersonal, objective, meaningful connection to "the Beyond" (the collective unconscious).[34] In its instinctive aspect, it symbolises, so to speak, the "feeling of being at home," but in its spiritual aspect,[35] it symbolises a binding and indissoluble connection to the elements of the unconscious.[36]

62 The dream of the following night seems to confirm that the farmer's and Brother Klaus's decision was right, for, in the dream, a light appears in the sky and, like a knife, it opens Brother Klaus's belly. This "light" or "glow" in the sky is most likely connected to the star which the saint saw while still in the womb and which now comes down, as it were, to him personally. The *principium individuationis* which touches each individual ego, touches, in this instance, the belly, the seat of desire and of deeper spiritual emotions.[37] It is a sudden enlightenment which strikes Klaus, not as a thought, but rather within the depths of his animal personality. As Jung says,[38] "Light means an 'illumination'; it is an illuminating idea that 'irrupts.'" Within Brother Klaus, it is a substantial psychic energetic tension which apparently corresponds to a very important unconscious content. Later, this content becomes manifest in his profound primal experience of God, which he has before he dies. But in this phase of Klaus's life, the light cannot be defined more exactly. It "touches" him only emotionally and brings about his definitive withdrawal from the world. The process of individuation,

---

[34] The rope is like a ladder or a bridge over which the soul goes into the Beyond, the latter often being seen as a "lost paradise." The same idea is found also in Tibet; cf *ibid.*, p. 431.

[35] Cf C.G. Jung, CW 8, *Structure and Dynamics of the Psyche*, §398 on the archetypes as a "meaningful" aspect of instinct.

[36] In most of the ceremonies of the Hopi Indians, a cotton rope is tied to the "prayer-sticks" which symbolize the connection of the Hopi to the world of the spirits. Cf Ruth DeEtte Simpson, *The Hopi Indians*, Southwest Museum Leaflets, Southwest Museum: 1953, pp. 25ff.: "Attached to the prayer-stick is a breath-feather and a long cotton string which always symbolizes communication between the Hopi and the Spirit-world."

[37] On the meaning of the "belly" in archaic thinking, see, for example, R.B. Onians, *The Origins of European Thought about the Body, the Mind, the Soul, the World, Time and Fate*, Cambridge: Cambridge University Press, 1951, pp. 84ff.

[38] C.G. Jung, CW 11, *Psychology and Religion*, §479: "Light means illumination; it is an illuminating idea that 'irrupts.'" Using a very cautious approach, we could say that we are dealing with a considerable amount of psychic tension which apparently corresponds to a very important unconscious content. "This content has an overpowering effect and holds the conscious mind spellbound." This tremendous power of the "objective psychic" content has in all epochs been called "daimon" or "god."

that is to say, the Self, which up until now has seemed to be projected entirely onto the outer world,[39] grips Klaus and results in his realisation that he should go home to the Ranft. Here, too, it reminds us of the experiences of enlightenment of certain Zen Buddhists about which a master (Shih-shuang) once said,[40] "Transform your body and your spirit into a bit of inanimate nature, like a stone, or a piece of wood. When you are completely turned inwards so that all signs of life disappear, then suddenly a plenitude of light will enter you, like a light out of the deepest darkness. Then the Self, free of all sophistry, will be revealed, *the original face of your own being*, then *the marvellous landscape of your original home* will be unveiled. There is only one direct way which is open and without hindrance and you can enter upon it as soon as you have given everything away." I find the return of Brother Klaus to his home to be *symbolically* important in the sense of a turning towards the "landscape of your original home," a turning inwards to his own true self.

63   The "illumination" in his vision has, at the same time, the character of an extremely painful wound. The closest parallels to this are again to be found in northern shamanism, as well as in the initiation rites of medicine men of many primitive peoples. As Mircea Eliade[41] points out, most often the choosing of a shaman is preceded by an inner crisis in the chosen one, and often the gods indicate their choice by striking a shaman-to-be by lightning, or by having a meteorite (!) land near a novice.[42] Almost always, however, the rites of initiation consist of a dismemberment or the cutting of some part of the novice's body[43] whereby, in the majority of cases, individual inner organs are "renewed." With some Australian Aborigines, too, the initiation of a medicine man consists of, amongst other things, a medicine man opening up the stomach of

---

[39] For example, as a star in the cosmos.

[40] Citation taken from T. Suzuki, *An Introduction to Zen Buddhism*, Kyoto: Eastern Buddhist Society, 1934, p. 64. The italics are the author's.

[41] M. Eliade, *Shamanism*, p. 19.

[42] *Ibid.*, p. 22: A Siberian woman became a shaman when a fireball entered her body. Injuries, too, were often thought to be a sign of being chosen.

[43] *Ibid.*, p. 34 and pp. 36ff.

the initiate and placing small stones which have magical powers inside it,[44] or the medicine man throws an invisible spear at the novice which splits open his neck.[45]

During his initiation, the Siberian shaman receives his "tutelary spirit," which, among other things, is called his "lightning," or his "enlightenment," for, as they say,[46] the *angakok* (tutelary spirit) consists of "a mysterious light which the shaman suddenly feels in his body, inside his head, within the brain ... a luminous fire which enables him to see in the dark, both literally and metaphorically speaking, for he can now, even with closed eyes, see through darkness and perceive things and coming events which are hidden from others; thus they look into the future and into the secrets of others." That the motif of dismemberment or wounding repeatedly appears in so many initiation rites means, psychologically speaking, that there is a lesion or wounding of the natural unconscious ego which the Self bears down upon like a heavy weight (the motif of St. Christopher). The dream of Gilgamesh[47] from the epic of the same name is a nice parallel to this, for in the dream, Gilgamesh, the sun hero, predicts his fateful meeting with Enkidu, the mortal "real" human being. Gilgamesh dreams that the stars in the sky are like a host of warriors and one of them falls down on him.[48] Later, he dreams that a mountain falls down on him.[49] As Dr. R. Kluger-Schärf said in her interpretation of this,[50] the dream shows the moment in which Gilgamesh begins to get caught up in the individuation process. As in Brother Klaus's prenatal visions, here, too, the motif of the star and the rock or stone are connected to each other. The visions of the Egyptian alchemist Zosimos of Panopolis (third century A.D.) also

---

[44] *Ibid.*, p. 52 and pp. 46ff.

[45] *Ibid.*, p. 47.

[46] *Ibid.*, p. 90.

[47] Cf A. Heidel, *The Gilgamesh Epic and Old Testament Parallels*, Chicago: Chicago University Press, 1949, p. 35.

[48] Cf *ibid.*, p. 26: "Gilgamesh arose to reveal the dream ... 'Last night I felt happy and walked about among the heroes. There appeared stars in the heavens. The host of heaven fell down towards me. I tried to lift it, but it was too heavy for me. I tried to move it, but I could not move it.'" His mother interprets the dream to mean the coming of Enkidu.

[49] *Ibid.*, p. 46f.: "I have seen a second dream. ... In my dream, my friend, a mountain toppled. It struck me, caught my feet. ... The light became glaringly strong, a unique man appeared. ... He pulled me out."

[50] In an unpublished work.

provide us with an example of such a wounding of the ego.[51] In the most important part of his vision,[52] Zosimos sees a priest standing at an altar in the form of a shallow bowl who says, "I am Ion,[53] priest of the innermost hidden sanctuaries, and I am undergoing terrible punishment. For early in the morning, someone came running in great haste, and overpowered me and cut me into pieces with the sword ..." Whereupon Zosimos sees with his own eyes how the priest transforms into a spirit through great suffering. This motif symbolises the alchemical *separatio* and resembles many parallels in primitive rites. As C.G. Jung has stated, such primitive, cruel rites of dismemberment serve the purpose of transforming the initiate into a new and more efficacious person. Indeed, seen in this light, the initiation takes on the aspect of a healing—it is not a torment, as Zosimos maintains in his interpretation of his vision, but rather it is "the 'hylical man.' Such a one is dark, and sunk in materiality. He is essentially unconscious and therefore in need of transformation and enlightenment. For this purpose his body must be taken apart and dissolved into its constituents, a process known in alchemy as *divisio*, *separatio* and *solutio*, and in later treatises as *discrimination* and *self-knowledge* [in which] every step forward along the path of individuation is achieved only at the cost of suffering."[54] This is why, when we come into conscious contact with the individuation process, we experience it as being painful, even deadly.

65   More precisely, however, it is not the ego but the Self which seems at first to be wounded (Christ, Wotan, Ion, the mercurial dragon, etc.), and it is only when the Self is realised in a human being that the latter begins to share in the suffering.[55] Individuation is, as

---

[51] Cf C.G. Jung, CW 13, *Alchemical Studies*, §§439ff. and C.G. Jung, CW 11, *Psychology and Religion*, §345.

[52] C.G. Jung, CW 13, *Alchemical Studies*, §86, and C.G. Jung, CW 11, *Psychology and Religion*, §345.

[53] Jung points out that this "Ion" already appears in the Sabean tradition as *Junan ben Merqulius* (Son of Mercury). In my opinion, this Ion of *Zosimos* and the "Ion" of the Sabeans are identical with the *Ioun-mutef* the highest priest of initiation in the Egyptian death rituals. He is the son of Thot (Hermes-Mercurius). Cf A. Moret, *Mystères égyptiens* (Paris: Librairie Armand Colin, 1927), pp. 75ff.

[54] Cf C.G. Jung, CW 11, *Psychology and Religion*, §411.

[55] Cf C.G. Jung, CW 11, *Psychology and Religion*, §427: "Only subjective consciousness is isolated; when it relates to its centre it is integrated into wholeness. Whoever joins in the dance sees himself in the reflecting centre, and his suffering is the suffering which the One who stands in the centre 'wills to suffer.' The paradoxical identity and difference of ego and self could hardly be formulated more trenchantly."

Jung says,[56] "an heroic and often tragic task, the most difficult of all, it involves suffering, *a passion of the ego*:[57] the ordinary, empirical man we once were is burdened with the fate of losing himself in a greater dimension and being robbed of his fancied freedom of will. He suffers, so to speak, from the violence done to him by the Self.[58] The analogous passion of Christ signifies God's suffering on account of the injustice of the world and the darkness of man. The human and the divine suffering set up a relationship of complementarity with compensating effects. Through the Christ-symbol, man can get to know the real meaning of his suffering: He is on the way towards realizing his wholeness. As a result of the integration of conscious and unconscious, his ego enters the "divine" realm, where it participates in "God's suffering." The cause of the suffering is in both cases the same, namely "incarnation," which on the human level appears as 'individuation.'" This is why, in the Acts of John, Christ says, 'As you dance, ponder what I do, for yours is this human suffering which I will to suffer.' "[59]

66   Thus, behind the image of God lies a process of transformation in which man begins to participate—in so far as he approaches God. Brother Klaus was, as we know, a deeply religious person with an instinctive relatedness to God, and such a person must have, as Jung says, "an intensive relationship to God which lays him open to an invasion far transcending anything personal." But at the same time, he must have been born with "an unusual extension of consciousness."[60]

---

[56] *Ibid.*, §233.
[57] Author's italics.
[58] *Ibid.*, §233, fn. 8: "Cf. Jacob's struggle with the angel at the ford."
[59] *Ibid.*, §415.
[60] *Ibid.*, §731.

Chapter 7
Retreat to the Ranft

67 After his experience of the light, Brother Klaus returns home and crawls under a bush until his brother convinces him to give up his fasting and his life in the woods. Then, Klaus somehow makes the decision to build a hermitage for himself in the Ranft with the help of his friends. Erny Rorer reports[1] that the place was described to Klaus in the following manner: He saw four bright lights coming from heaven showing him the place where a hut and a chapel should be built, and it was carried out in accordance with Klaus's wish and his vision.[2] His wife and his children gave their consent for him to withdraw in this way[3] and they were at peace with the situation and often visited him at his hermitage, mostly on Sundays.[4] Klaus never felt tempted to move back in with them.[5] With his experience of the light, his total fasting began, which he persisted in until his death. Of course, there is no shortage of voices accusing this saint of being peculiar.[6] But, as Jung emphasises,[7] we should not liken Klaus to an eccentric who has misanthropically crept away and gone into hiding. Rather, we must search for the reason for Klaus's retreat into his

---

[1] R. Duerrer, *Bruder Klaus*, Vol. 1, p. 463.
[2] According to Woelflin (R. Duerrer, *Bruder Klaus*, Vol. 1, p. 540) there are four lights *like candles*. Cf also, R. Duerrer, *Bruder Klaus*, Vol. 1. p. 429, fn. 48: "*Vidit enim caelos apertos et quatuor fulgurantia descendere lumina in vallem istam, ubi sua in adolescentia egregiam . . . vidisset turrim. . ., Consulto itaque suo patre spirituali mansit in illo loco silvestri. . .*". Cf also A. Stoeckli, *Die Visionen des seligen Bruder Klaus*, p. 13.
[3] R. Duerrer, *Bruder Klaus*, Vol. 1, pp. 27ff., on 16 October 1467, twenty years prior to his death. Probably his father, Heinrich von Flüe, also still lived at his house and one brother, Peter von Flüe; the oldest son, Hans, was twenty years old, his wife was around forty, and his youngest son, Nikolaus, was only sixteen weeks old.
[4] *Ibid.*, p. 547.
[5] *Ibid.*, cf Ch. Journet, *Saint Nicolas de Flüe*, p. 17, fn. 3.
[6] See also the report of P. Numagens, in R. Duerrer, *Bruder Klaus*, Vol. 1, pp. 232ff.
[7] C.G. Jung, CW 11, *Psychology and Religion*, §474.

singular inner life, a reason which is hinted at in his visions. These events and experiences were of more value to him than ordinary human existence. They were probably the focus of his daily interest and "the source of his spiritual vitality."[8] Discussions similar to this one concerning Brother Klaus's spiritual health occur not only in connection with other saints but also in connection with medicine men and shamans of ethnic cultures. Drawing upon numerous examples, M. Eliade[9] describes how the vocational calling of the medicine men and shamans comes about, namely, sometimes through one's birthright (especially from the mother's side, and we might recall here that the brother of Klaus's mother was a forest hermit!), sometimes through dreams and trance experiences, and almost always after experiencing a phase of heavy spiritual crisis, which is often understood as being in a state of possession, either by ancestral spirits or some other kind of spirits or gods.[10] The knowledge of the medicine-man-to-be is often transmitted to him via dreams. A love of being alone, of withdrawing into the forest, of immersing oneself in water, and of confused circumstances are the classic symptoms of experiencing a vocation.[11] A retreat into the mountains and animallike behaviour, both of which Brother Klaus exhibited after his return home from Liestal, are also characteristic of a vocation coming to light.

68

In shamanism, animallike existence indicates the integration of ancestral spirits in animal form. The question as to whether or not we are dealing with a pathological situation here seems to me to be answered best by the native people themselves who say that the main difference between someone who is possessed and a shaman is that the latter is someone who *has healed himself,* whereas a possessed person lacks this ability.[12] Thus, the illness of a shaman is a

---

[8] *Ibid.,* §476.
[9] Eliade, *Shamanism,* pp. 22ff.
[10] *Ibid.,* p. 24.
[11] *Ibid.,* p. 26. This brings to mind how Brother Klaus was said to have often bathed in the icy waters of the Melchaa.
[12] For more, see *ibid.,* p. 27; concerning the extraordinary abilities of shamans, see *ibid.,* pp. 28ff.

transitional sign of his being "chosen,"[13] and this is how we should understand Brother Klaus's confusion, which came to an end when he decided to face the inner spiritual demands that were being asked of him. Evidently, once he had withdrawn into his hermitage, everything settled down.

69 According to H. Woelflin[14], from this time onwards Klaus spent the first part of his day in prayer and contemplation. In the afternoon, he would step outside, sit in the sunshine and, if he felt like it, he would pay a visit to his fellow hermit, Ulrich at Mösli. Ulrich was a Swabian nobleman from Memmingen who had followed Brother Klaus's example and built a hermit's cell near to Brother Klaus's cell. Ulrich had many books, and Brother Klaus often discussed religious matters with him. According to other witnesses, Klaus also went to Einsiedeln now and again. When he wanted to be contemplative and to avoid his all-too-many visitors, he would spend a day or two in the forest.[15] Some who visited Brother Klaus have described his outer appearance in the following manner: Hans von Waldheim says of him,[16] "he looks like a man in the prime of his life at the age of fifty, with brown hair without any grey in it. He has a well-formed, thin face with good colour, his stature is tall and thin and he speaks German well and in a charming manner." People had told Waldheim beforehand that Brother Klaus always had ice-cold hands, was as pale as a corpse,[17] and was always of a sad disposition, but this was not true. When Waldheim visited him, Klaus had warm hands, and his complexion had the same colour as any other natural, healthy person in good physical condition. Furthermore, he was not at all sad. Rather, he was affable, happy, and friendly.[18] Brother Klaus most often had *his mouth half open*, a detail

---

[13] *Ibid.*, p. 28.

[14] R. Duerrer, *Bruder Klaus*, Vol. 1, p. 546.

[15] R. Duerrer, *Bruder Klaus*, Vol. 1, p. 61.

[16] *Ibid.*, (trans.).

[17] In fact, Bovillus (R. Duerrer, *Bruder Klaus*, Vol. 1, p. 567) reports that because of his fasting, Brother Klaus began to suffer from "a cold stomach," so that instead of his spiritual nourishment, he was forced "to warm up his stomach and chest daily by the fire of a wood stove." (Trans.) One can still see a stove in his cell today.

[18] *Ibid.*, Vol. 1. p. 62; cf also, 1: 62f.: "Brother Klaus received us there with a happy and smiling face and he gave each one of us his hand, which was not cold but of a natural warmth." (Trans.) When Waldheim

which is depicted in the portrait on his gravestone.[19] Perhaps this reflects an attitude of awe-inspired inner contemplation.[20] On the other hand, another visitor, the deacon Albrecht von Bonstetten, who, it must be said, visited Klaus after he had had his fearful vision of God on the 31 December 1478, writes:[21] "Klaus was of a good height, was very thin, with a brown and wrinkled face. He had tangled, uncombed black hair with streaks of grey and his beard was a thumb's length. His eyes were average-sized and the whites of his eyes were clear. He had a well-shaped nose. He was not talkative and was rather dismissive of those whom he did not know. If one touched him, his hands were cold. He was always barefoot and wore a grey robe. He stood tall and he had a manly voice."[22]

70

The four lights[23] which Brother Klaus saw descending, shining like candles, at the place in the Ranft[24] where he then built his hermitage are probably connected to the star and to the light which struck Klaus in Liestal. But now the *one* light in the visions of that earlier time has become *four* lights. This may be the result of his earlier psychic wounding through which the Self reached him. Of course, the number four as a symbol of inner wholeness reflects, as Jung has demonstrated, the quaternion structure of consciousness. While *one* light represents the unity of the Self, *four* lights represent the fact that a conscious realization of this unity starts with, or is made possible by, the four functions of consciousness.[25] Thus, both his return home and the internalisation of his problems have

---

told him the legend of the sinner, Maria Magdalena of Marseille, his eyes overflowed with tears. (R. Duerrer, *Bruder Klaus*, Vol. 1, p. 63f.).

[19] Strangely enough, exactly this expression can be found on the so-called "stele of Wildburg," an Old-Germanic stone column which was found in Württemberg and which probably depicts a Germanic priest. Cf P. Herrmann, *Das alt-germanische Priesterwesen*, p. 17.

[20] Myconius describes Brother Klaus in the following manner (R. Duerrer, *Bruder Klaus*, Vol. 1, p. 611f.): "He was extraordinarily tall and of a handsome build, but so thin that his skin appeared to rest directly on his bones. His complexion was dark, his hair was black sprinkled with grey. His beard was not long, but sparse and divided in the middle. His eyes were deep black and, because of their heavenly lustre, could make one tremble with fear. When he spoke, the veins of his neck and throat seemed to be filled with air, not blood. He wore a single, simple piece of clothing which reached down to his ankles. His head and his feet were bare at all times. He had a manly voice and spoke slowly. When he spoke of God, he seemed to know all the secrets of the Scriptures even though he was not able to read at all." (Trans.)

[21] *Ibid.*, p. 87, (trans.).

[22] Cf Ch. Journet, *Saint Nicolas de Flüe*, pp. 62ff.

[23] Cf R. Duerrer, *Bruder Klaus*, Vol. 1, p. 540.

[24] R. Duerrer, *Bruder Klaus*, Vol. 1, p. 463.

[25] See C.G. Jung, CW 9/ii, *Aion*, §410.

constellated the problem of becoming conscious of the Self for Brother Klaus, for his decision indicates his willingness to subjugate both his ego and his plans to this unknown inner force, i.e., to the Self, which, in this instance, asks Klaus to *commit himself to one place.* Here, as in very archaic cults, the Self manifests as a numen of a place, or as a *genius loci.* But perhaps the dark and closed-in wooded valley of the Ranft is to be understood symbolically as the most deep withdrawal into oneself and as a turning towards the flow of inner life within one's own soul.

71   Considering what Brother Klaus did from the perspective of several hundred years later, it would seem that he established a pattern, or set an example, which all of Switzerland gradually followed and which he himself urged his fellow citizens to adopt, namely, to confine themselves to a *réduit* (redoubt) as a defence against the outside world and thereby prevent shadow problems from exploding on the outside. The people then had to deal with these shadow problems on an inner level. Nevertheless, it still took the defeat at the Battle of Marignano for the confederates to be convinced by this insight. Thus, the "red spirit" of one's own aggression is transformed into a starting point for the dawning of consciousness. As Jung once said, in Switzerland, we have managed to reach the point of keeping our shadow problems within our own border. The next step would be for each individual to take on the conflict within himself.[26] This is the very step which Brother Klaus made by confining himself and his problems to the *réduit* of the Ranft. A wonderfully clear instinct led him to this solution. This turning inwards is so meaningful because it was not forced upon him by a clash with the outside world or by a defeat from the outside, and it does not suggest a rift or flight from the world or from the shadow. It really seems to be more like an act of insight into the meaningfulness of the inner life.

72   This concludes our discussion of the visions and experiences which shed light upon this period of inner conflict in Brother Klaus's life and also indicate the personal suffering he went through until

---

[26] C.G. Jung, CW 10, *Civilisation in Transition*, London: Routledge & Kegan Paul, 1964, §455.

the time of his "breaking away." However, within this same period of time, Klaus had four more great visions which go more deeply into a problem that extends beyond the personal realm.

◆

Chapter 8
The Vision of the Three Visitors

73   Woelflin gives the following report of this important vision which, I believe, is a variation on the appearance of the nobleman on horseback, despite the fact Klaus at first thought him to be the devil and, now in this vision, believes him to be God:[1]

74   "Three distinguished-looking men who, by their dress and bearing, seemed to be of noble rank, appeared to him [Klaus] while he was occupied with his household duties. The first one to speak said: 'Niklaus, will you surrender to our power with your body and soul?', to which Klaus immediately replied, 'I submit to no one but almighty God whose servant I long to be with body and soul.' Upon hearing his reply, the three men turned away from Klaus and burst out laughing (*in hilarem proruperunt risum*). And, again, the first one turned to Klaus and said, 'If you have dedicated yourself exclusively to God's eternal service, then I promise you that in your seventieth year, God, in His mercy, will look upon your deeds with compassion and will relieve you of all your burdens. Therefore, in the meantime, I admonish you to endure steadfastly and, in eternal life, I will give you the bear's claw (*ursinam ungulam*) and the flag of the victorious army (*validi exercitus vexillum*). *But the cross that is to remind you of us* I shall leave behind for you to carry.' Whereupon the noblemen left. Thus, Brother Klaus realised that if he were able to bravely overcome the torment of many temptations, a mighty army would accompany him into eternal glory."

---

[1] R. Duerrer, *Bruder Klaus*, Vol. 1, p. 537f. (Trans.); cf F. Blanke, *Bruder Klaus von Flüe*, p. 88, and A. Stoeckli, *Die Visionen des seligen Bruder Klaus*, p. 12.

75 At first, this vision appears to be self-explanatory, and it seems that the three men represent the Holy Trinity. But when we take a closer look, we notice some curious points: firstly, the fact that when they first appear, Klaus himself is not sure whether the three men are not demonic tempters; secondly, the absurd laughter of the visitors; thirdly, the fact that the first of the three men refers to God in the third person, as if he were not God himself, and yet he then speaks in the first person, as if he were God; and finally, the peculiar symbol of the bear's claw and the flag of the mighty army in the Beyond, which the three men offer him. According to the rules of dream interpretation, motifs must first be taken for what they are. This would mean accepting that while these three noblemen *remind* us of the Christian Trinity, nevertheless they do not exactly correspond to the Trinitarian dogma. Rather, they are the spontaneous appearance of a triadic image of God, an archetype which, as C.G. Jung has shown, was generally widespread long before the idea of the Christian Trinity took hold.[2] The unchristian elements of these three figures once again seem to point towards older Germanic ideas, as in the vision of the lily and the horse we spoke of earlier, but here they point more towards Wotan, especially the reference to the bear's claw which Niklaus will receive in the Beyond as a sign, or "totem"—his own individual symbol.

76 The great Germanic god Donar is often referred to as *Björn* (Bear), and Wotan sometimes called himself *Björn* or *Bjarki* (Little Bear), but also especially *Hrammi* (Bear's Paw).[3] Even today, in the central part of Switzerland, you can find a bear's paw nailed to house doors as a talisman.[4] Indeed, the paws symbolise *pars pro toto* the power a bear has, so that the motif actually expresses the fact that Brother Klaus will find he has the strength and the power of a bear in the Beyond. But perhaps it also means that this aspect of his being can only be truly realised after his death. In Revelations,[5] it is written:

---

[2] C. G. Jung, *CW*, Vol. 11, *Psychology and Religion*, §§172–176; see also P. Sarasin, *Helios und Keraunos* (Innsbruck: 1924) and D. Nielsen, *Der dreieinige Gott* (Copenhagen: 1922), and W. Kirfel, *Die dreiköpfige Gottheit* (Bonn: Dümmler, 1948).
[3] M. Ninck, *Wodan und germanischer Schicksalsglaube*, p. 19 and p. 49.
[4] Cf R. Duerrer, *Bruder Klaus*, Vol. 1, p. 538, fn. 41.
[5] Holy Bible, Revelation 2:17.

"To him that overcometh will I give to eat of the hidden manna, and will give him a white stone, and in the stone a new name written, which no man knoweth saving he that receiveth it." Thus, Brother Klaus's new and secret name in the Beyond would be "Hrammi" (Bear's Paw)—one of Wotan's names.[6]

77   Benoit Lavaud, who has compiled all the biblical amplifications of the symbol of the bear,[7] came to the paradoxical conclusion that sometimes the bear represents the wicked ruler[8] (e.g., the "beast" of the Revelation has the feet of a bear),[9] but that it is also an image of Yahweh, though in his "dark" manifestations. Thus, in Lamentations,[10] it says about God, "He was unto me as a bear lying in wait, and as a lion in secret places. He has turned aside my ways ..." Here, the bear represents the *dark side of God* whose 'terrifying countenance, will later be revealed to Brother Klaus more clearly. But apparently, in the Beyond, Brother Klaus will be the herald of this dark side of God's image which, although it can be destructive for anyone who is possessed by it, within his soul it will be transformed into a healing power. Incidentally, it should be noted that, right up to the present time, the bear is one of the most widespread protective spirits of the Nordic shamans.[11] In earlier times, for many peoples of eastern and northern Europe, the bear was so sacred that its name was not to be spoken out loud. Instead, one referred to him indirectly as "He," "the House-father," "Little Grandfather," "Father," "Mother," "Clever Father," "The Old One," "The Holy Man," "The Holy Woman," "The Honey-eater," or "Gold-foot." In Greece, the bear was sacred to Artemis and the Mother-Goddess. In addition, the female spirit who follows a hero,

---

[6] M.-B. Lavaud, *Vie profonde de saint Nicolas de Flüe*, p. 46; Lavaud also cites this place in the Revelation and interprets the banner of the paw as being a *bravium* in the sense of the Gospel according to II Timothy 4:8. Lavaud interprets the bear, on the one hand, as being the devil (M.-B. Lavaud, *Vie profonde de saint Nicolas de Flüe*, p. 46) and, on the other hand, as being a symbol of God. (*Ibid.*, p. 61).

[7] *Ibid.*, p. 46 and p. 61.

[8] Holy Bible, Proverbs 28:15.

[9] *Ibid.*, Revelation 13:2.

[10] *Ibid.*, Lamentations 3:10–11; cf also, Proverbs 28:15 and Hosea 13:7–8.

[11] M. Eliade, *Shamanism*, pp. 72, 105, 458f. and the literature quoted there: C. Hentze, *Le culte de l'ours ou du tigre et le t'aotie*, Zalmoxis I, 1938, pp. 50–68; A.F. Hallowell, "Bear-ceremonialism in the Northern Hemisphere," *American Anthropologist* (28, 1926), pp. 1–175; N.P. Dyrenkova, "Bear-worship among Turkish tribes in Siberia," *Proceedings of the 23rd International Congress of Americanists*, New York: September 1928, p. 411ff.; H. Findeisen, "Zur Geschichte der Bärenzeremonie," *Archiv für Religionswissenschaften,* Berlin: 1941,Vol. 37, pp. 196ff.

the Fylgia of the Germanic people, is often a bear. Bear claws were thought to be a talisman against the evil eye, and in Prussia, a bear's paw was put into the tombs of the dead so that they could climb the "Mountain of the Beyond." In Christian times, the bear was sometimes seen as being one form in which the devil chose to appear, and at other times as being the animal of the Mother of God.[12]

78   Because Brother Klaus does not understand all of this and *cannot* understand it, the three divine visitors tell him that they will leave him the cross—the Christian symbol of wholeness—to bear during his lifetime that, however, feels like a dead weight to the person who has to carry it and makes the suffering and torture that Christ underwent in bearing His own cross an inner reality for the bearer. This is an indication of the next developmental step that is required, namely, to follow the path of *inner alignment with Christ* and to become one with that god who has the "bear's paw" as his distinctive sign, and in whom the power and effectiveness of animal nature will be redeemed and integrated. Seen from a psychological standpoint, the cross means the "torment of becoming conscious, of moral conflict and the uncertainty of one's own thoughts."[13] Accordingly, it would mean that Klaus can only obtain the "prize" of the bear's paw by suffering what the cross means.

79   Responding to Klaus's answer that he would submit himself to God alone, the three men turn away and burst out laughing.[14] There seems to me to be a similarity here to Klaus's cloud vision in which Klaus asked God for a "life of devotion," and God scolded him and told him he should submit himself to His will. Indeed, the laughter of the visitors points to a similar incongruence, namely, to the fact that once again Brother Klaus's idea of God differs from the reality of God that is staring him in the face. The most striking difference here is the Wotanlike characteristics which God, as he now appears,

---

[12] *Handwörterbuch des deutschen Aberglaubens*, H. Bächtold-Stäubli, (ed.) (Berlin: 1927–1942) p. 890 and p. 899. In Lappland the bear is called *siavo*; "holy," or "the holy beast." As "Corn Bear" (*ibid.*, p. 893), it was a symbol for vegetation and fertility and thus played a role in Germanic marriage rites.
[13] Cf, amongst others, C.G. Jung, CW 16, *The Practice of Psychotherapy*, London: Routledge & Kegan Paul, 1954, §223.
[14] Again, it is precisely Wotan who often has the characteristics of a divine trickster that could explain such absurd laughter especially well.

unexpectedly has. In fact, Wotan often walked about on earth in the company of two companions, for example, with Hönir and Lodur at the time when he gave life to the first people, Askr and Embla.[15] And on other occasions, he often travelled incognito around the country with Hönir and Loki, and together, they paid an unexpected visit to someone.[16] In Saxony, *Odin* joins with *Saxnot* (Tyr) and *Thuner* (Thor) to form a supreme divine trinity, which finds an echo in the sequence of "Tuesday, Wednesday, Thursday."[17] The same triad latently still exists in many local legends: Three men sleep in Zobtenberg, as well as in a mountain crevice near the Lake of Lucerne. Similarly, three men who live in the Dominiloch on the mountain of Pilatus will, at some point, free the country in a time of need.[18] The three summits of the hill of God (*Gotteshügel*) in Alt-Upsala are to this day associated with *Odin, Thor* and *Frey*.[19] Otherwise, Wotan often appears with his brothers Wili and We, or with the two ravens Hugin and Munin, or with the wolves Geri and Freki, or with the dogs Wil and Wal. In the sixteenth century, he was still said to be eerily moving around the region of Lucerne as the three-legged *Türsthund* (*Thurse*: giant),[20] and his horse is often similarly depicted as being three-legged.[21] Especially in Sachseln, where Brother Klaus lived, Wotan was believed to haunt the place

---

[15] M. Ninck, *Wodan und germanischer Schicksalsglaube*, p. 69.

[16] *Ibid.*

[17] *Ibid.*, p. 117 and p. 142; cf also, p. 337: "A little example … may show the extent to which the names of the highest Germanic gods were officially destroyed by means of a truly astonishing act of censorship by the Church. As an authentic attestation from the eighth century that *Wotan* besides *Thunar* and *Saxnot* was one of the foremost gods of the Saxons, the so-called baptismal vow of the Saxons had up until then been quoted. "*Forsachistu. diabolae? ec forsacho diabolae. end allum diabolgeldae? end ec forsacho allum diabolgeldae. end allum diaboles uuercum? end ec forsacho allum diaboles uuercum and uuordum, Thunaer ende Uuoden ende allum them hina genotas sind*" etc. Cf also P. Herrmann, *Das altgermanische Priesterwesen*, p. 76ff. According to him, in Upsala the Third God, which is depicted as a phallus is *Frey* (instead of *Ziu* or *Tyr* or *Saxnot*).

[18] *Ibid.*, Ninck, p. 142. He thus compares them to the three mountain summits of Pilatus. The Swiss word for Wotan, *Türst*, from *Thurse* (*Riese*, giant (trans.)), may be an amalgamation of *Thor* and Wotan.

[19] Cf A. Lütolf, *Sagen, Bräuche, Legenden aus den fünf Orten*, pp. 56–57. Equally, three such "tells" [ancient mounds] sleep in the alps of Niederbauen in Emmeten in Canton Unterwalden in the so-called hell holes. Sleeping all around them is an army of mercenaries from Unterwalden. When a man comes, one of the "tells" asks him, "Which time counts now?" The sleeping warriors are waiting for a time of war in order to attack. (Cf also, *ibid.*, p. 92f. the same legend about the Giswilerstock near Brünig and near Flüelen.) Also in the areas of Uri and Schwyz, ghost battles have been seen in the sky; (*ibid.*, p. 129).

[20] Cf R. Brandstetter, *Der Geschichtsfreund*, Vol. 62, p. 122.

[21] M. Ninck, *Wodan und germanischer Schicksalsglaube*, p. 142. Cf also, C.G. Jung, CW 9/i, *The Archetypes and the Collective Unconscious*, §437ff.

as the so-called "Dancing Dog of the Arbour" (*Tanzlaubenhund*) with only *one* eye, the size of a plate, on his forehead, and he was once seen by Niklaus's own daughter.[22] On rune stones, a triadic figure is *the* sign for Wotan.[23]

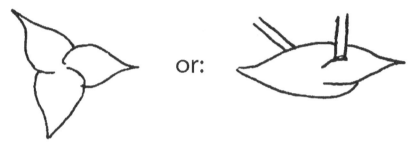

or:

Triadic Figure

80

The powerful, that is, victorious (*validus*), army with which Brother Klaus will enter into the Beyond calls to mind the army of the slain (*Einherjer*) who serve Wotan.[24] The servitude which the three visitors ask of Brother Klaus seems to be something like a demand for allegiance.[25] Wotan's retinue bore, among other things, the honorary title of "Victorious Bears" (*Sige-beorni*).[26] In the folklore of circa 1600 in the area around Lucerne, Wotan's army of

---

[22] Cf R. Duerrer, *Bruder Klaus*, Vol. 2, p. 926: "At a time when Brother Klaus was still participating in everyday life, he held his little daughter in his arms while working at a place where one enters the Melchtal and she cried out to her father that there was a big black dog with one eye in the middle of its forehead. Brother Klaus, who recognized the evil spirit, said to her that she should not be afraid for nothing would happen to her. At that moment, the dog disappeared." (Trans.) According to Duerrer, this was the "Dancing Dog of the Arbour" (*Tanzlaubenhund*) of the people of Sachseln; he was lying in the arbour below the church. A later offspring of Brother Klaus met the dog once again nearby. Cf also A. Lütolf, *Sagen, Bräuche, Legenden aus den fünf Orten*, p. 342f. The arbour, a place for dancing and for taking exercise, was below the parish church in Sachseln. Here lived the Dancing Dog of the Arbour who walked daily to the little chapel of light (*Lichttägelkappeli*) which is by the footpath on the way to Flüeli (on the spot where the Lourdes chapel is today). Holding playing cards in its front paws, the Dancing Dog of the Arbour once met a man and asked him to play a game of cards with him. In another place, he is called the "Eternal Dog" or the "World Dog."

[23] M. Ninck, *Wodan und germanischer Schicksalsglaube,* Plate VIII of the illustrations: Rune stones from Sanda, around 1050 AD; cf also. *ibid.,* Plate III: Rune stones from Tjängvide (Gothland), eighth to ninth century.

[24] *Ibid.*, p. 121–22: According to Ninck, Odin is the God of Victory and as the "Father of the Slain" (*Walvater*) he is the god and comrade of all who have fallen in battle.

[25] In the Beyond, in Valhalla, the army do battle daily, but each evening they drink mead together. "All the 'slain' (*Einherjer*) of the court of Odin fight every day. They select those to be slain, ride home from battle, and sit together reconciled with each other." (Trans.), (*ibid.*, p. 122). For this reason "to die" is the same as "to go to Odin," (*ibid.*, p. 132). And "to kill" means to consecrate one's life (to Odin) (*wihan*), (*ibid.*, p. 125).

[26] *Ibid.*, p. 159.

the dead was still thought of in a positive way, whereas almost everywhere else it was thought of as being an evil, wild ghost-hunt.[27] Their leader, God himself, appears as a "great and powerful lord," and to belong to His army was considered a privilege rather than a curse. The army was called "the raging army" (*Wuott ins Heer*),[28] "God's army" (*Guottisheer*)[29] or, more commonly, "the blessed ones" (*die säligen Lütt*), and the latter, it was said, were "even friendly and charming" to the living. It was also believed that some people lived in close companionship with "the blessed ones" and that, now and then, they strolled around with them, which was considered to be a great honour, and people who did this were thought of as being more pious, more reverent and more fortunate than others, even "almost saintly."[30] Thus, it becomes clearer what the posthumous union of Brother Klaus with this "powerful army," which the three noble wanderers augured, could mean.

81   As a motif, the flag with the bear's paw fits in this connection for, as Ninck emphasises, the flag always represents being under Wotan's protection.[31] If it flutters, it promises victory; if it droops, it is a bad

---

[27] Cf *ibid.*, p. 81 and especially R. Brandstetter, *Der Geschichtsfreund*, pp. 106ff. Seen negatively, these dead are the "fiery ones" (*die feurigen Leute* or *die Züssler*), and whoever sees them will always meet with a bad end. Cf also, A. Lütolf, *Sagen, Bräuche, Legenden aus den fünf Orten*, p. 135. Recently, the connection between the wild hunt and Wotan has been called into question and has been put down to a popular etymological connection of the "raging army" (*wütendes Heer*) and "Wotan." Cf J. Vandryes and E. Tonnelat, *Les religions des Celtes, des Germains et des anciens Slaves* (Mana: Presses Universitaires de France, 1948), p. 363 and fn. 354, but it seems to me that these doubts are taken too far. I believe the opposite to be true: the "raging army" (*wütendes Heer*) is a later interpretation of "Wotan's army" (*Wotan's Heer*), a shift in meaning that came about when Wotan was no longer so well known. It has been authentically handed down that Wotan is the leader of the dead.

[28] R. Brandstetter, *Der Geschichtsfreund*, p. 134.

[29] In accordance with "the good souls" (i.e., the souls in purgatory); Cf R. Brandstetter, *Der Geschichts-freund*, p. 134; also A. Lütolf, *Sagen, Bräuche, Legenden aus den fünf Orten*, p. 444 and p. 450ff.

[30] R. Brandstetter, *Der Geschichtsfreund*, p. 135, also cited in M. Ninck, *Wodan und germanischer Schicksalsglaube*, p. 82. R. Brandstetter, *Der Geschichtsfreund*, p. 134: The chronicler Cysat from Lucerne reports, "Now these ghosts are highly thought of by the elders and they are a part of society, and the living who stroll around with them were considered holy and blessed! These ghosts were the souls of those whose life had come to an end before their allotted time, who did not die a proper and natural death ... and each of those who had died by means of some weapon bore a sign, as did the rest who also bore a sign of how they had lost their lives. There was always one who went ahead, crying out, 'Make way! Make way, for the blessed ones are coming.' There were also melodious string players who could be faintly heard ... and some of the living were especially devoted to them as companions and friends; they sometimes strolled around with them and sometimes they were visited by them in their homes." Because of this, these people who joined them were more highly thought of and were regarded as being "blessed." (*Ibid.*, p. 136, (trans.)). It was a great honour, and such people were thought of as being "more pious, reverent and almost saintly," and only because of this are they "more fortunate." (*Ibid.*, p. 137, (trans.)).

[31] M. Ninck, *Wodan und germanischer Schicksalsglaube*, p. 90: "The flag is, above all, a symbol of fate. ... For Odin, who oversees the fighting, is closely connected with fate and because he receives the power

omen.[32] Priests carried such animal symbols not only among the troops on the battlefields, but also through fields as a magical means of making the soil fertile.[33] Apparently, Brother Klaus is elected to be such a priest. It is altogether quite striking how Brother Klaus's later role in the Ranft brings to mind the role of priests in old Germanic times, as well as the role of the shamans of the north. In old Germanic times, priests were simply noblemen, heads of families or men and women with natural authority.[34] The priests were called *êwart* or *êsago*, and they were the guardians and spokesmen of "rights" (*ê*, that is, *religio*).[35] Apparently, they had long hair and wore a long robe with a stolelike belt.[36] The famous seeress Weleda of the Westphalian Bructere lived in a tower[37] from where she announced her prophecies. If one reads about the many political consultations and other dealings for which Brother Klaus's opinion was asked, which are recorded in Duerrer's source book, it would seem Klaus really was such an *êwart*, a guardian of the *ê* (the divine order).

---

to be effectual from the Norn's hand which creates and determines fate … thus the flag comes under his special protection. 'The flag of battle fluttered on high,' say the songs of the *Edda* (Gnaefar gunnfani). … The Bayeux Tapestry, the important Norman pictorial monument which William the Conqueror brought to England, has a dragon made out of cloth on a pole as its standard …" (Trans.).

[32] *Ibid.*, p. 91: "Terror is amongst your ranks, death's decay is your lord. Your battle flag does not flutter, Odin is hostile towards you." (Trans.)

[33] P. Herrmann, *Das altgermanische Priesterwesen*, p. 72: "Tacitus himself differentiates between *signa* (attributes of the gods), such as the sword of Tius, or the spear of Wotan, or the hammer of Donar … and *effigies* (symbols). Or the symbols were animal images which were carried at festive processions by the priests through the hallways as well as through the rows of soldiers ready for battle: such as the eagle of Tius; the wild pig and bear, Donar's animals; the dog and wolf. … The Langobardians of Italy bowed before the image of a snake. They worshipped the snake as a symbol of their highest god, Wotan." (Trans.)

[34] *Ibid.*, p. 9.

[35] *Ibid.*, p. 15: "The names for a priest are numerous. … According to how he made and protected laws, he was referred to as 'keeper of *ê*' (*êwart*, '*êwarto*', *wart des ê*); this *ê* is our sadly forgotten word for *religio* (i.e., the conventional, unforeseeable divine order or the law …), or he was called *êsago*. … The other side of his activity as the one who performs sacrificial rites is emphasized by the east Germanic word *got*, '*gudja*,' and the Scandinavian *Gode* (*gudi*, 'god'), which is related to the word '*gut*'(i.e., 'god-head') … If, however, 'god' meant 'magic' or even 'fetish,' then, the word '*goden*,' brings sorcerers and shamans to mind. Originally, he was only the 'vocation caller,' 'the counsellor,' 'the magician.' What the 'magician' of Iceland managed to achieve and how the farming aristocrat became the political leader of the regional area belonging to the temple and thus laid claim to his universal power to rule as the sovereign lord of the region is an extremely instructive chapter in the historical development of religion. The 'high-priest' of Burgundy bore the name *sinistus* ('the oldest one'; cf *Siniskalk*, the old servant; Latin: *senex*); perhaps this goes back to a time when the eldest in the family chose to become a priest, as in the original communities of Jerusalem. Later, like the Arabian sheik, he was not the eldest in years, but the most honourable—an offspring from an old noble family. (Trans.)

[36] Cf *ibid.*, p. 14.

[37] *Ibid.*, p. 17.

82   There is one strange motif, however, that unexpectedly connects this vision that seems to be so transparently pagan to Christianity, namely, the cross which is left behind and which Brother Klaus should bear for the rest of his life as a reminder of the three visitors. This makes it impossible to view the vision as *a simple regression into paganism.* Rather, this motif points towards the "Christification of the individual through the Holy Ghost," which Jung describes in his paper "Answer to Job."[38]

83   The *Imitatio Christi*, which is clearly expressed in the motif of the carrying of the cross, shows that the three visitors wanted Brother Klaus to realise *a spiritual development which does not reject, or run counter to, what is Christian, but rather reveals new aspects of it and demands the integration of further archetypal contents.*

84   As Jung states in *Psychology and Religion*,[39] the Christian cross, psychologically speaking, symbolises a step in becoming conscious in which man becomes aware of his ethical conflict and of his responsibility. Within the Trinity, the cross is essentially a part of the hypostasis of God the Son. But in relation to the Holy Ghost, it symbolises a step in spiritual development in which the ego voluntarily submits itself to a more comprehensive inner wholeness: the Self. The effect that the Self has upon the psyche is known in Christian terms as the "Holy Ghost," that is, as the breath that heals and makes whole and establishes the integrity of the personality, which, in these circumstances, is highly appropriate. For the last two thousand years, history has known of the *figure of the primeval Cosmic Man, the Anthropos,* "whose image has merged with that of Yahweh and also of Christ. *Similarly, the saints who received the stigmata became Christ-figures in a visible and concrete sense, and thus carriers of the Anthropos-image. They symbolize the working of the Holy Ghost among men."*[40] We need hardly emphasise how true

---

[38] C.G. Jung, CW 11, "Answer to Job," *Psychology and Religion*, §758: "But the indwelling of the Holy Ghost, the third Divine Person, in man, brings about a Christification of many, and the question then arises whether these many are all complete God-man. ... That is to say, even the enlightened person remains what he is, and is never more than his own limited ego before the One who dwells within him ..."

[39] C.G. Jung, CW 11, "A Psychological Approach to the Trinity," *Psychology and Religion*, §180 and especially §272ff.

[40] *Ibid.*, §276. Author's italics.

this is of Brother Klaus. Jung goes on to say[41] that there are many symbols of the Self which take a nonhuman form, for example, the sphere, circle, square, and octagon; or chemical-physical forms, such as the stone, ruby, diamond, quicksilver, gold, water, fire, spirit, etc. Thus, these symbols express the nonhuman character of the Self—of wholeness. Seen within the context of what Jung has said, we could understand Brother Klaus's vision to mean that it was presaged for him to become a Christlike person and "carrier of the Anthropos-image," thus making him a living harbinger of a spirit that manifests theriomorphically as a bear. But we may not overlook the fact that in his vision Brother Klaus is not given a bear. Rather, he is given only a flag with the image, that is, the *symbol*, of a bear's paw. This hints that the dark side of God's spirit is not to be experienced in the form of an archaic state of possession as it was, for example, in old Germanic times when there was a custom of people going berserk. Rather, it should be integrated on a symbolic level. The path to achieve this will lead him to his alignment with Christ.

85 Because this last motif is presented more clearly in a later vision, I want to postpone any further interpretation of this point. Instead, I would like to pursue the strange motif of the wandering divine visitor for this motif is of central importance in the first of several visions recently found in Lucerne.

---

[41] *Ibid.*

Chapter 9

The Vision of the Singing Berserker

86 The text begins:[1]

"... and which he knew. And it seemed to him that he saw a man dressed as a pilgrim. He carried a staff in his hand and wore a hat tied on and its brim was turned up in the manner of someone who wants to set out on a walk, and he wore a cloak. And Klaus knew within himself that he [the pilgrim] came from the sunrise or from far away. Though he did not say so, *he came from the place where the sun rises in the summer.*[2] And upon reaching Klaus, he stood before him and sang the word '*Alleluia*' three times. And when he began to sing, his voice echoed and (the earth and) everything between heaven and earth supported his voice, as the small pipes of a pipe organ support the large ones. And Klaus heard three perfect words coming from some single source, emerge and then snap back into place, like a spring closing under pressure. And after he had heard these three perfect words, each word separate from the other, Klaus did not wish to say anything other than that one word. And when he [the pilgrim] had completed the song, he asked Klaus for a donation. And he [Klaus] had a penny in his hand and did not know where he had got it from. And he [the pilgrim] took off his hat and accepted the penny being placed in it. And the man [Klaus] had never realised what a great honour it was to receive a donation in a hat. And the man [Klaus]

---

[1] A. Stoeckli, *Die Visionen des seligen Bruder Klaus*, p. 15f., (trans.).
[2] The italics are the author's.

wondered very much who he [the stranger] was and where he came from, and the pilgrim said, 'I come from there', and he would say no more. And he [Klaus] stood in front of him and looked at him. And the wanderer was transformed and appeared bare-headed, wearing a robe of blue or grey, but Klaus no longer saw the cloak, and he [the stranger] was such a noble, well-built man that he [Klaus] could only look at him with yearning and desire. His face was tanned, which gave him a noble appearance. His eyes were as black as magnets, his limbs were so well formed that they were of particular beauty. Although he was clothed, his garments did not prevent his limbs from being visible. And while Klaus continued to look at him with fixed attention, the pilgrim returned his gaze. Many great wonders then came to pass: the mountain of Pilatus collapsed to the ground (that is, it flattened itself to the ground) and he [the pilgrim] revealed a view of the whole world so that it seemed to him that all the sins of the world were revealed, and a great crowd of people appeared, and behind the people Truth appeared and truth revealed itself in all their faces.[3] And on the hearts of all, there appeared a large growth the size of two fists joined together. And this growth was egoism, which led the people astray [seduced them] to such an extent that they could not bear to look the pilgrim in the face, just as people cannot bear flames of fire, and they ran terrified back and forth, cursing and swearing, and he watched them run into the distance. And the Truth that had stood behind them remained."

[87] As the vision continues, the pilgrim's face changes to look like a "Veronica cloth," and the pilgrim reveals further new aspects of himself to Klaus. But because of the length of the text of the vision, it seems better to begin our interpretation at this stage. The biographer, Woelflin, deals with the beginning of this vision only

---

[3] A. Stoeckli, *Die Visionen des seligen Bruder Klaus*, (i.e., they stood opposite it). But it rather means that they turned their back on the truth.

briefly by saying that Brother Klaus, while lost in spiritual rapture, once wandered through lonely areas, far away from human habitation,[4] where he saw an old man approaching from afar who was "of noble appearance and well-dressed, and he sang a song for one voice which he developed into three-part harmony."[5] Brother Klaus experienced this as being a lesson in the "indivisible nature of the divine, which is differentiated into three people and yet is in wonderful harmony."[6] Later in the vision, he comes to the palace with the fountain, which, in the original text that has since been found, is described in a similar way. Here we can clearly see how Woelflin already alters the text to fit the conventional Christian standpoint by leaving out many details.[7]

88   This wanderer, who comes singing from where the sun rises, once again has characteristics similar to Wotan, both in his clothing and in the manner in which he mysteriously wanders around. Saxo calls Wotan the "Inexhaustible Wanderer."[8] Wotan's other names include "Vegtamr" (he who has left), "Gangleri" (he who is tired of the being on the move), "Gangrapr" (he who gives advice while moving from one place to the next).[9] Ninck says,[10] "There are many stories of how Wotan moves around as a *beggar*, as a *singer*, as a *stranger who pays visits to kings* under the assumed name of 'Gest', who tells them stories in their halls or at their bedside, who sings them songs and who competes with them in solving riddles … " His appearance corresponds exactly to the image of the wanderer. He wears a coat and a wide-brimmed hat which covers his forehead.[11] His cloak is coarse and is blue, with blue-stripes, grey or spotted. … He is tall with a long beard. He has only *one* eye which blazes like fire. His hair and his beard are grey with age, but nevertheless "he was so handsome and noble as he sat amongst his friends that it

---

[4] The typical "magical flight" of the shaman and medicine man.
[5] A. Stoeckli, *Die Visionen des seligen Bruder Klaus*, p. 11.
[6] *Ibid.*, p. 11.
[7] E.g., the motif of the bearskin.
[8] Hav. 103, cited in M. Ninck, *Wodan und germanischer Schicksalsglaube*, p. 69.
[9] Cf, *ibid.*, p. 73, (trans.).
[10] *Ibid.*, p. 69. The italics are the author's.
[11] He was called, for example, *Sidhoettr* (i.e., *der breithutige*: the One with the Wide-brimmed Hat) (trans.); cf W. Menzel, *Odin*, Stuttgart, 1855, p. 166f.

made everyone light-hearted" (Snorri).[12] In Klaus's vision, too, the wanderer is a beggar and a singer and *his clothing matches even down to the colour of his coat.* In medieval times, it was Ahasuerus, the eternal Jew, who assumed this role of Wotan.[13] In the inner cantons of Switzerland, Wotan's army is accompanied by delightful music, especially when Wotan makes a friendly appearance. It is said that "he and his followers approach in a friendly manner surrounded by melodious sounds, as if there were all kinds of stringed instruments playing."[14] In many places, Odin was thought of as being a minstrel with magical powers who wanders around and attracts the living into the land of the dead with his magical sounds.[15]

89   It is interesting that this vision is presented as an experience of a "spiritual journey." This, too, fits for the nordic shamans who, along with many primitive medicine men, know of this "great journey" of the spirit during which their bodies most often remain at home, as if they were dead. This is especially true of those who are possessed by Wotan.[16] In the very area from which Brother Klaus comes, stories from the sixteenth century were told of how Wotan removes individuals from one place to another and sometimes carries them off even as far as Milan.[17] Apparently, Klaus, too, went on such "spiritual journeys," which is strongly reminiscent of the Jungian method of active imagination.[18] The biographer J.J. Eichhorn[19] reports a legend in which Brother Klaus was once found by his own people "enraptured, standing upright with his back against the wall of his cell, looking upwards with his eyes rolled back, his mouth open and a 'terrifying' look upon his face. And when he was himself

---

[12] M. Ninck, *Wodan und germanischer Schicksalsglaube*, p. 70.

[13] Cf C.G. Jung, *Civilisation in Transition*, CW 10, §374: "Wotan is a restless wanderer who creates unrest and stirs up strife, now here, now there, and works magic. He was soon changed by Christianity into the devil, and only lived on in fading local traditions as a ghostly hunter. ... In the Middle Ages the role of the restless wanderer was taken over by Ahasuerus, the Wandering Jew, which is not a Jewish but a Christian legend. The motif of the wanderer who has not accepted Christ was projected on the Jews."

[14] R. Brandstetter, *Der Geschichtsfreund*, p. 137; cf also, *ibid.*, p. 138f.: "*es tönt mit allerley Seittenspiel, Harpfen, Luten, Gygen, Zittern, Violen, Triangel und derglychen*" (all kinds of stringed instruments ring out: harps, lutes, violins, zithers, violas, triangles and similar). (Trans.)

[15] Cf A. Lütolf, *Sagen, Bräuche, Legenden aus den fünf Orten*, p. 47.

[16] Cf M. Ninck, *Wodan und germanischer Schicksalsglaube*, pp. 100ff.

[17] R. Brandstetter, *Der Geschichtsfreund*, 131ff; cf also *ibid.*, p. 111f, pp. 127ff.

[18] For this see C.G. Jung's Introduction to R. Wilhelm's *The Secret of the Golden Flower*, in *Alchemical Studies*, Vol. 13, §20.

[19] R. Duerrer, *Bruder Klaus*, Vol. 2, p. 979.

again, he told those who were present, 'My children, I was in the village.' This meant, 'I visited my friends in spirit.'"[20] Duerrer interprets this as being an expression of the joy Klaus experienced in contemplation, and he compares it to Brother Klaus's statement that "contemplation can be savoured like a dance."[21] These ecstatic journeys, however, are also a special effect which the *Türst* (Wotan) engenders, and furthermore, they belong to the classical practices of shamans and medicine men the world over.[22]

90   When, in the inner cantons of Switzerland, the *Türst* (Wotan) makes a friendly appearance, his army of "blessed ones" play beautiful music, as mentioned above, and he appears as a "mighty lord." In Brother Klaus's vision, however, it is the noble wanderer himself who makes the music[23]—and the whole cosmos responds to him. This brings to mind the Hippocratic idea of the *Ulomelie*, a holistic concord of all things in nature,[24] and in this cosmic "harmony," the wanderer appears to play a key role. This may indeed point towards the basis of every synchronistic phenomena for we often express the experience we have of things suddenly falling into place with the symbolism of a lock or key; for example, in English "it clicks," and in Bavarian, *"Jetz hot's gschnakelt"* ("now it's clicked").[25] The philosopher's stone, too, was often compared by the alchemists to the "Key of David which closes and no one opens, and which opens, and no one closes."[26]

---

[20] Cf also, the portrait (*ibid.*, p. 776) where he is portrayed "as having been absent or in a state of ecstasy." (Trans.)

[21] *Ibid.*, Vol. 2., p. 980.

[22] Cf M. Eliade, *Shamanism*, p. 143, p. 297 and p. 363f., as well as P. Herrmann, *Das altgermanische Priesterwesen*, pp. 43ff.

[23] According to W. Menzel, *Odin*, pp. 183ff., Wotan was thought of as being the creator of song (*Ynglinsaga*, 6). He is also the lord of the "wish-violin" (*Wunschgeige*) or of a violin which can kill and bring back to life again.

[24] Cf C.G. Jung, "Synchronicity: An Acausal Connecting Principle," CW 8, *Structure and Dynamics of the Psyche*, Routledge & Kegan Paul: London, 1960, §924. See also §930. Jung refers to the preconditions of synchronistic phenomena as an "acausal orderedness" (§965), and this wanderer appears here as his "lord" (*Herr*).

[25] (Trans.) In American English from the language of automated machinery, it's "the penny dropped."

[26] Cf Holy Bible, Revelation 3:7, and *Rosarium philosophorum, Artis Auriferae quam Chemikam vocant* (Basel, 1610), Vol. 2, p. 181: "The philosophers speak of salt and the soap of wisdom and the little key which closes and no one opens and closes again, and no one can open it; without this little key, they say, no one in the world can reach the completion of this science." (Trans.) And *ibid.*, p. 162: "This stone is, in fact, a key, for it is made out of *the strongest spirit (fortissimi spiritus)*."

91   In a report from Greenland,[27] at a so-called *Seid* (a kind of shamanic meeting) which is conducted by a Völva (a female seer or shaman), there is a connection between the idea of locking and that of singing. Before the Völva begins with her magic, she firstly asks for women to be brought to her who can sing the *vardlok(k)ur* ("the lock of the ghosts"). This is a wonderful song, which attracts the protective spirits with whose help the seeress, or female shaman, will be able to answer all questions, do her magic, and reveal what is hidden. In Brother Klaus's vision, too, it is *after the song of the wanderer that the Truth and the spiritual inner world of man is revealed*, and the spiritual inner world of man. As is told in the *Edda*, the magical songs which Odin extracted from the giant were previously "locked up"; and a Skalde, Egil, thus sings:[28]

92   *Forth it flows but hardly;*
For within my breast
Heaving sobbing stifles
Hindered stream of song
Blessed boon to mortals
Brought from Odin's kin,
Goodly treasure, stolen
From Giant-land of yore.

93   We still speak of "*loosening* one's tongue" and of being "closed." But it is the atmosphere that by Wotan creates which unlocks feelings, poetic ecstasy, and clairvoyant trances, which is why the wanderer, too, appears as the lord of this secret.[29]

94   The mechanism that snaps closed brings to mind a snap-lock. Perhaps this is why the idea of a locked-up treasure has a part to play. It indicates that a strong, autonomous psychic dynamic is involved—a sudden impulse, and at the same time, a "locked" secret.

---

[27] Cf P. Herrmann, *Das altgermanische Priesterwesen*, p. 47f, and also M. Eliade, *Shamanism*, p. 367f.
[28] See M. Ninck, *Wodan und germanischer Schicksalsglaube*, p. 321. "*Sona-torrek*" ("Sons' Loss"), English, trans., W.C. Green (1893), from the original *Egils saga Skallagrímssonar* (*Egil's Saga*).
[29] Cf C.G. Jung, CW 10, *Civilisation in Transition*, §375: "He is the god of storm and frenzy, the unleasher of passions and the lust of battle; moreover he is a superlative magician and artist in illusion who is versed in all secrets of an occult nature."

Indeed, the wanderer does not want to say anything about himself, neither who he is nor where he comes from. Odin also once said of himself:[30] "I have been known by many names since I have been amongst people."

95 Nevertheless, we are once again dealing with a Christian motif, for the wanderer sings "Alleluia," the word of Christian worship.[31] He praises the Christian God just as an angel or worshipper does, and he is not in any way antagonistic towards Him. The three complete words which he sings and which, naturally, have always been thought of as being connected to the Trinity,[32] also bring to mind the *tria verba pretiosa*, an Arabic alchemical text of the same title by Calid, in which these three precious words are meant to indicate a progressive process of the four qualities of the lapis becoming one.[33] The medieval author of *Aurora Consurgens* had already made the connection between the triadic division of this motif into the body, soul, and spirit, and the Trinity.[34]

96 The alchemist Zosimos,[35] who was familiar with Christian teachings, said of the lapis:[36]

97 "Our stone hath its name in common with the Creator, for it is triune and one" (*triunus et unus*). And the *Carmina Heliodori*[37] refer to the stone a "thrice-blessed source" (or "one sprout with three faces"). Despite these parallels, one cannot, of course, ignore these associations to the Trinity as being the most important ones. As in the vision prior to this one, we are once again dealing with a strange combination of Christian *and* pagan motifs which would seem to reveal a special tendency of the unconscious, namely, to reconcile the opposites of our chthonic-pagan past and its instinctual basis

---

[30] Cf M. Ninck, *Wodan und germanischer Schicksalsglaube*, p. 71, (trans.).
[31] "Praise be to Yahweh."
[32] Cf M.-B. Lavaud, *Vie profonde de Nicolas de Flüe*, p. 53.
[33] *Rosarium philosophorum*, Basel, 1610, Vol. 1, p. 227f.
[34] Cf M-.L. von Franz, *Aurora Consurgens*, Toronto: Inner City Books, 2000, p. 397.
[35] (Rosinus); *ibid.*, p. 278.
[36] *Rosarium philosophorum*, *Artis Auriferae quam Chemikam vocant*, 2: 192.
[37] Günther Goldschmidt and Richard Reitzenstein, eds., *Heliodori Carmina quattuor ad fidem codicis Casselani. – Alchemistische Lehrschriften und Märchen bei den Arabern*, Giessen: Töpelmann, 1913, p. 29.

with the standpoint of our spiritual Christian conscious standpoint.

98   Although the wanderer does not wish to reveal from where he comes, or where he is going, or his name, nevertheless he does, in a manner of speaking, reveal himself indirectly for suddenly he is no longer wearing a cloak and hat but instead has on a blue or grey robe,[38] and he is "so noble and handsome to behold," that Brother Klaus "could only look at him with yearning and desire." His skin is tanned, his eyes are "as black as magnets," and his beautiful limbs are visible through his clothing. There is a very similar description of the Türst (Wotan) in the reports of Renward Cysats, where the Türst is described as being a black, slender man with a long nose[39] who appears as a "great and powerful lord" or a "well-groomed" nobleman and warrior. In the reports of the Icelandic chronicler Snorri Sturluson, it is said of Wotan that he was more distinguished than all the other gods and that it was he who had taught them all their arts and skills.[40] In addition, he knew how to change "his skills, his appearance and his form, at will."[41]

99   Even though in some old Germanic texts Odin is described as being weak-sighted, blind or one-eyed,[42] compared to our text in which it is said his eyes are "as black as magnets," nevertheless, in some old texts he is called "*Baleygr*" ("Eyes like Flames").[43] Incidentally, Brother Klaus also had fiery dark eyes.[44]

100   In Brother Klaus's vision, the wanderer comes from where the sun rises in summer—which also has to do with the motif of music. According to Jacob Grimm, the Gothic word *swigla* (flute) and the old Germanic word *swegel* (heaven) and *swegle* (radiant) are

---

[38] This is a classical form of dress of Wotan; cf M. Ninck, *Wodan und germanischer Schicksalsglaube*, p. 70.
[39] R. Brandstetter, *Der Geschichtsfreund*, p. 139.
[40] Ninck, *Wodan und germanischer Schicksalsglaube*, p. 6.
[41] *Ibid.*, p. 73. (Trans.). As is known, the Romans identified him with Mercury.
[42] *Ibid.*
[43] *Ibid.*, (trans.).
[44] According to M .Ninck (*ibid.*, p. 82), Wotan's colour is sometimes black, sometimes fair.

etymologically related. Similarly, our German word *hell* (bright) is probably related to *hallen* (resound/echo) and *tönen* (sound/resound).[45] From a Christian standpoint, the east is an allegory for the Blessed Virgin Mary or for Christ. During Advent, the following is sung in church: "*O oriens splendor lucis aeternae et sol iustitiae, veni et illumina sedentes in tenebris et umbra mortis.*"[46] Psychologically speaking, the wanderer comes out of an area of the unconscious where a new "enlightenment" for mankind is being prepared.

101   In the scene which follows in Brother Klaus's vision, the pilgrim becomes the one truth that reveals all. Along with other names, Wotan, too, bears the title *Sannr* (*wahr*: true)[47] for he had once received the original truth from Mimir[48] and he both possesses and bestows clear-sightedness upon all that is hidden.[49] Thus, Snorri Sturluson refers to Wotan as the "songsmith, who, with his songs, can open up earth, mountain and rock and can take what is within."[50]

102   In Brother Klaus's vision, too, the next thing to happen is the decisive peripeteia, that is, the flattening of Mount Pilatus by means of which the pilgrim "opens up the whole world." Viewed from Sachseln, Mount Pilatus does, indeed, oppressively block the entire view to the north-west, which is the direction Klaus apparently projected his idea of "the world" onto, for this was the direction he chose when he wanted to leave. Pilatus, with its three peaks, is not only *the* numinous and dominating mountain of this area, but, according to a local legend, it is also *the* place, par excellence, where "*Wuott ins Heer*" (Wotan and his army) haunt most often,[51]

---

[45] Cf also J.W. Goethe: '*Die Sonne* tönt *nach alter Weise*' ("The sun-orb sings, in emulation"—Bayard Taylor (trans.) M. Ninck, *Wodan und germanischer Schicksalsglaube*, p. 166, mentions a Low German expression *de krik vam dage* (*das Schrillen des Tages*: the shrillness of the day (trans.)).

[46] M.-B. Lavaud, *Vie profonde de Nicolas de Flüe*, p. 55, (trans.); see Lavaud's footnotes for further information.

[47] M. Ninck, *Wodan und germanischer Schicksalsglaube*, p. 73, (trans.).

[48] *Ibid.*, p. 308: The Valkyrie teaches *Sigurd* about the runes: "She thought up *Hropt* (Odin), she carved Hropt and instructed the people in its meaning, intoxicated with drink. ... On the mountain, he stood with Brimir's sword/ On his head he wore his helmet/ *Then Mim's head murmured wisely first, and spoke words of truth ...*" (Trans.)

[49] *Ibid.*, p. 313.

[50] *Ibid.*, p. 7. He spoke only in rhyme.

[51] Cf R. Brandstetter, *Der Geschichtsfreund*, p. 122, (trans.).

especially on a bare quadrangular rocky place on its summit.[52] This is why Ninck describes Pilatus as being the real Odinsberg (Odin's Mountain).[53] In old chronicles, the name is interpreted as meaning *mons pileatus*, the mountain with the magical hood.[54] Thus, the disappearance of Pilatus is easy to explain for it becomes invisible, so to speak. Another name for Pilatus was "Fracmont" (*Freck-münd*—Cheeky Mouth), which comes from *fractus mons*,[55] (*Brochen Birg*—Fractured Mountain).[56] The material mass which blocks the view disappears and thus the world opens up, i.e., the nature of the world is revealed, and, as is shown, the inner workings of the human heart also become visible, and the human failing of egoism becomes apparent. Just as people run from fire, in this vision, they scatter in all directions when confronted with the "Truth." Like Wotan, this pilgrim also knows how to magically open mountains and rocks,[57] but, more than this, he also reveals the inner world and the egoism in the hearts of people. For the god Wotan, too, selfishness is indeed the most repulsive of faults, for he is *the* god of emotions, of love and of unconditional surrender.[58]

103   As Jung has shown,[59] Wotan is "a god of rage and frenzy, who embodies the instinctual and emotional aspect of the unconscious. Its intuitive and inspiring side also manifests itself in him, for he

---

[52] *Ibid.*, p. 110. According to A. Lütolf, *Sagen, Bräuche, Legenden aus den fünf Orten*, pp. 20ff. there is a so-called *Gnappstein* on Pilatus, which would seem to come from a Celtic place of worship. For more on Pilatus, see also *ibid.*, p. 26.

[53] Cf M. Ninck, *Wodan und germanischer Schicksalsglaube*, p. 85: "We will see that Wotan–Odin is lord of the mountain and was often thought of as sleeping in the mountains. Pilatus was such a mountain of the gods. Still in Cysat's time, one climbed it in terror for there were surely many evil spirits on it. In the small lake below the summit, which was thought to be bottomless, Pilate's spirit was once evoked and, according to court records, with the help of an exorcist or conjuror, the people were able to see its tracks in the 'four-sided' place, which was there at the summit, about the size of a large parlour or room divided into four, all of it infertile and without grass'. As the legend of the raging army and the wild hunt is particularly lively alive in the area around this mountain, it is reasonable to suppose that the three-peaked mountain of Pilatus which towers over the countryside was Wotan's mountain, the storm god, the father of all gods and human beings, the god of all counsel (thus, the *Thingbezirk*) and the god of wizards (thus, exorcism). For just as the raging army is clearly related to storms and weather, so, too, is Pilatus the weather mountain. Old chronicles state that the mountain's name goes back to *mons pileatus*, 'mountain with a helmet', or 'capped mountain'. Odin's hat is the cap of fog of the weather mountain ..." (Trans.) Cf also *ibid.*, p. 134f. and A. Lütolf, *Sagen, Bräuche, Legenden aus den fünf Orten*, p. 26.

[54] Cf *ibid.*, p. 26.

[55] *Ibid.*, p. 21.

[56] Cf *ibid.*, pp. 20ff., (trans.).

[57] M. Ninck, *Wodan und germanischer Schicksalsglaube*, p. 7 and p. 137.

[58] According to Snorri, Wotan also knows of all the hidden treasures; cf *ibid.*, p. 137.

[59] C.G. Jung, CW 10, *Civilization in Transition*, §393f.

understands the runes and can interpret fate. The Romans identified Wotan with Mercury, but his character does not really correspond to any Roman or Greek god, although there are certain resemblances. He is a wanderer like Mercury, for instance, rules all the dead like Pluto and Kronos, and is connected with Dionysus by his emotional frenzy." According to Jung, a further parallel would be the Greek god of revelation, Hermes, who, as *Pneuma* and *Nous*, means wind. He would be the bridge to the Christian *pneuma* and to the descent of the Holy Ghost at the miracle of Pentecost. As "Poimandres," Hermes, too, is capable of "seizing" men.[60] One could interpret the wanderer in Brother Klaus's vision as being a "spirit of Truth," who, however, has retained the original emotional components of *Ergriffenheit* (of being deeply moved)[61] more strongly than is usually associated with the Holy Ghost. Thus, he would be a "spirit of Truth" who does not descend upon mankind "from above," but rather rises up out of the depths of his instincts. The wanderer asks Klaus for a donation, and in the vision, he finally reveals himself as being the one who arouses love and is, indeed, the secret of love itself. Thus, the wanderer speaks to an ecstatic feeling that any narrow-hearted selfishness stands in the way of. Then the face of the pilgrim is transformed into a face "like a Veronica," and, once again, he takes on a new form—Wotan is also known as "Wotan Svipall" ("Wotan, the Changing One") or "Wotan Grimmir" ("Wotan, the Masked One") and "Wotan Tveggi" ("Wotan, the Twofold One"),[62] and all these names relate to his ability to change form.

104   The vision continues:

"And the pilgrim's face changed 'like a Veronica' and he [Brother Klaus] had a great longing to look at him further. And Klaus saw him again as he had seen him earlier, but his clothes were different and he stood before him wearing pants and a coat over which there was a bearskin that was sprinkled

---

[60] *Ibid.*, §394.
[61] (Trans.)
[62] M. Ninck, *Wodan und germanischer Schicksalsglaube*, p. 73.

with gold. But Klaus readily recognised it as being a bearskin. The bearskin suited the wanderer particularly well, and Klaus saw that the pilgrim looked particularly handsome in it. And as he stood in front of Klaus and allowed himself to be looked at in his noble bearskin, Klaus realised that the man wanted to leave. Klaus said, 'Where do you want to go?' The pilgrim answered, 'I want to go up country'. More he would not say. As the pilgrim left, Klaus stood gazing after him. Then Klaus saw that his bearskin shone as though one had passed a shining weapon over it, the glitter of which one could see upon a wall. And he [Klaus] thought there might be something that was being hidden from him. And when the pilgrim was about four steps away, he turned round and he had his hat on again and he lifted his hat and bowed to Klaus and took his leave of him. Then he [Klaus] knew such love for him [the pilgrim] that he felt quite at one with him and he realised that he did not deserve this love but that it was within him. And Klaus saw in his spirit that his face, his eyes and his whole body were filled with loving humility, like a vessel filled with honey which could hold not a single drop more. Then he could no longer see the pilgrim but was so sated with him that he desired nothing further of him. It seemed to Klaus that he [the pilgrim] had made known to him [Klaus] everything that was in heaven and on the earth."

105 Exactly what is meant by the phrase "like a Veronica" is rather uncertain. Stöckli believes[63] that the wanderer has adopted a facial expression "like the one on Christ's sudarium [sweat cloth]." This, in my view, fits, and is even likely as, in this area, there was a legend which connected the shape of Mount Pilatus with the sudarium of St. Veronica. A handwritten document from the fifteenth century tells[64] "how Veronica came to Rome and how Pilate came to Rome

---

[63] A. Stoeckli, *Die Visionen des seligen Bruder Klaus*, 26.
[64] Cf A. Lütolf, *Sagen, Bräuche, Legenden aus den fünf Orten*, pp. 7ff. This is a fifteenth-century Codex (1478), which is now in the cloister in Engelberg. The legend, however, must have been widespread by at least the fourteenth century in the area around Pilatus. (*Ibid.*, p. 20).

via the Tiber and to Rotte (Rhone) and to Freckmund (Pilatus)."[65] The story tells us that after the death of Christ, the emperor Tiberius fell ill with leprosy, so he sent his servant, Albanus, to Jerusalem to find a good doctor (possibly Jesus). Albanus sought out Pontius Pilate, who, however, kept him waiting, for he feared the discovery of Christ's killing. But the people sent Albanus to a pious woman called Veronica who told him what had happened to Jesus. She also told him that she had wanted to have the face of Jesus painted onto a cloth so that she would have a memento of him. But then Jesus himself suddenly approached her "and then Jesus Christ our Lord took the cloth out of my hand and pressed it to His holy and divine face and gave it back to me. And there on the cloth was His holy face in all its original colour and detail. Thus the cloth with the imprint of His holy face and its characteristics was called a Veronica, after my own name."[66] Thereafter, the cloth became a "sacred relic" with which one could heal the sick. Albanus then takes Veronica with him to Rome, and she heals Tiberius. Pontius Pilate, however, whose offence became known in this way, was summoned to Rome, had to stand trial, and then committed suicide. But wherever his corpse was thrown, terrible storms arose so that his corpse had to be retrieved out of the River Tiber and later out of the River Rhone, near Vienne, where it had been brought. Finally, his corpse was put into the lake on Mount Pilatus. Ever since, he has often appeared in the company of a horse-shaped demon. He sits upon a throne, and his hair and beard are ice-grey. Brother Klaus probably knew of this legend, and it is therefore likely that when he said the face of the pilgrim was transformed into "a face like a Veronica," he meant that it looked like the face of Jesus on the cloth of St. Veronica. In art, it is portrayed as the face of one who is being tortured—a face that is in pain. This would fit with what happens next in the vision for, in his newly transformed state, the divine visitor now appears in a splendid bearskin sprinkled with gold. Thus, he is a *Beri-serkr* (a Berserker), a *Bärenhäuter* (one who wears a bearskin). This type of

---

[65] *Fractus mons*, i.e. Pilatus.
[66] A. Lütolf, *Sagen, Bräuche, Legenden aus den fünf Orten*, p. 9.

transformation, this so-called "going berserk," is a quality that belongs to Wotan whereby, in moments like this, his body was as still as death while he moved around in the form of an animal. Thus, he could "visit" distant countries and perform great deeds.[67] Not only could Wotan do this, but his followers. This Berserker-nature was often hereditary in respectable families. The "seizure," or "fit" would begin with a feeling of restlessness or drowsiness.[68] Then the hero would leave as a bear, a wild boar, or as a wolf's soul and would kill its enemies,[69] though sometimes, in a blind rage, he would kill his own family by mistake. After such a fit, the one who had "gone berserk" would be weak and easy to overpower.[70] But while having the fit, he could bite the edges of shields, swallow burning coals, and even walk through fire.[71] Behind this state is a mood called "*gramr*" or "*grimr*," a word which means the same as "anger" and, simultaneously, "sovereign lord" or "prince."[72] (In the case of Brother Klaus's vision, this establishes a connection between the one who goes berserk and the motif of the nobleman!) It is this "holy rage" of Wotan that ensures victory. The old Norse expression for "going berserk with rage" means literally "to change form" or "to change one's coverings." This refers to a psychic predisposition to leave one's body in a transformed shape which is called "*hamfong*."[73] The root of the word "*hamr*" also means skin, shadow, form, protective spirit, and it also appears in the word "*hamingja*" (tutelary spirit, or good fortune),[74] which is how the Germanic people referred to the anima. As the state of "going berserk" does, in fact, begin with suffering, to say that the pilgrim's face looks "like a Veronica" fits very well, for it

---

[67] M. Ninck, *Wodan und germanischer Schicksalsglaube*, p. 34.
[68] *Ibid.*, p. 35 and p. 40.
[69] *Ibid.*
[70] *Ibid.*, p. 37.
[71] *Ibid.*, p. 37 and p. 41.
[72] *Ibid.*, p. 42.
[73] *Ibid.*, p. 43. Only those that are clairvoyant can see the soul as a bear or wolf. Others cannot see it; cf *ibid.*, p. 44.
[74] *Ibid.*, p. 43: "The corresponding word '*hamo*' in Old High German denotes 'skin,' 'covering,' 'clothing,' and lives on in the word '*Hemd*' (shirt) and '*Leichnahm*' (corpse) (OHG *Lthhamo* ('Gestalt', i.e., form), '*Fleischhülle*' (covering of flesh), '*lebend*' (lively), '*Leib*' (body). In Middle New German: '*ham*' and '*hamel*'; and English: '*heam*' is 'afterbirth'; in Walloon '*Hamelette*': '*Glückshaube*' (caul), '*Haut*' (skin), '*der Gebärmutter*' (of the womb) in which '*Glückskinder*' (children of good fortune) are born, and the caul must be carefully preserved or buried for it was thought to be a protective spirit of the child." (Cf Icelandic '*fylgja*': afterbirth; originally 'protective spirit')."

is precisely after this that he appears as the Berserker. That mention is made here of a covering which, according to a local legend, was said to be a sacred relic, is not out of place but rather points to the fact that the pilgrim represents something like a *Hülle* (a covering), a *Hamr* (the soul), i.e., the protective spirit of Brother Klaus.

The rage of the Berserker is always also a condition of ecstasy and of *being in a frenzied state*, a state in which the one who is possessed can, amongst other things, have an uncanny spiritual effect on people and things from afar.[75]

As Jung wrote in a letter to Fritz Blanke,[76] the bear represents the theriomorphic characteristics of the greater personality. "On his spiritual pilgrimage and in his instinctual (bear-like, i.e., hermit-like) subhumanness, Brother Klaus recognises himself as Christ. ... The brutal coldness of feeling that the saint needed in order to abandon his wife and children and friends is encountered in the subhuman animal realm. Hence the saint casts an animal shadow. ... Whoever can suffer within himself the highest united with the lowest is healed, holy, whole. The vision is trying to show Klaus that the spiritual pilgrim and the Berserker are both Christ, and this opens the way to forgiveness of the great sin which holiness is. (*Sine peccato nulla gratia.*) He is frightened to death by God's wrath because this wrath is aimed at him, who has betrayed his nearest and dearest and the ordinary man for God's sake."

Brother Klaus's vision continues: "The bearskin shone as though one had passed a shining weapon over it, the glitter of which one could see upon a wall." And Brother Klaus thinks that there might be "something that was being hidden from him." This mysterious shining is not mentioned by chance for it indicates that the one who wears the bearskin is a *divine being*. The words "*Ziu*" (a Germanic name for god), the Latin word "*deus*" (god) and the ancient Indian word "*deva*" (god) share an etymological root which refers to the brightness of the daytime sky.[77] The divine is a brightness, a shining, and its shine shows its "mana." The association to a polished weapon

---

[75] Cf *Ibid.*, p. 44.
[76] C.G. Jung, *Letters*, Vol. 1, London: Routledge and Kegan Paul, Ltd., 1973, pp. 363ff.
[77] M. Ninck, *Wodan und germanischer Schicksalsglaube*, p. 68.

is also not irrelevant. Old Germanic names for swords were, for example,[78] "the Glowing One," "the Shine of Victory," "the Flickering Shine." And when Wotan was entertaining guests one evening in Asgard, he asked for swords to be brought into the hall "which were so highly polished that they shone and no other lighting was needed throughout the entire banquet."[79] Furthermore, expressions for "honour" and "one's standing in the world" in Old High German are nearly all related to a root word which means brightness, light, clarity: Swedish: "*tir*" (to light up); Old High German: "*toerr*" (pure, clear); Old Norse: "*teitr*" (happy, beaming) which is related to "*tîr*" (adornment), which is used by Brother Klaus to describe the shining of the bearskin.

109   Psychologically speaking, the shining of the bearskin has to do with divine "mana," and thus it is understandable that Brother Klaus experiences this as something being "hidden" from him, that is, as a fascinating secret.[80]

110   After the wanderer has left, a strange feeling of love (*Minne*) for him suddenly wells up within Brother Klaus, and he feels sated with love, like a honey-pot filled to the brim. This love (*Minne*) which suddenly lights up in the man with the bearskin (*Bärenhäuter*) is *the* form of love, or Eros, which belongs to Odin in whose honour the so-called "*Minnebecher*" (cup of love) was drained at banquets.[81] And, as Ninck emphasises, "*Minne*" is a word which means much more than the word "love": It means an intensely loving way of thinking[82] that establishes a spiritual connection from afar with those who are travelling and with the dead. It is a deep fervour and, simultaneously, a devoted way of caring while in a state of rapt contemplation. It was out of this *Minne* amongst men that the Germanic practice of

---

[78] *Ibid.*, p. 248.
[79] *Ibid.*, p. 248f. (Trans.)
[80] The wanderer's shining hints at something which he does not wish to, and cannot, say openly: His shining is, so to speak, a "rune" which hints at his divine nature.
[81] Cf M. Ninck, *Wodan und germanischer Schicksalsglaube*, p. 245, and P. Herrmann, *Das altgermanische Priesterwesen*, p. 70: "The first full cup belonged to the love of God, most often to Odin, who was approached with this sacrifice with the request for victory and power. Similarly one drank to Njörd and Frey, to a good harvest and to peace, and then came the *Bragebecher*, the cup of the great god, of Thor, and finally they drank to the memory of their own blood relatives." (Trans.)
[82] Cf M. Ninck, *Wodan und germanischer Schicksalsglaube*, pp. 140ff.

swearing allegiance arose.[83] Such feelings of love for another man is indirectly hinted at here when Brother Klaus experiences "desire and yearning" when he is permitted to see the noble form of the pilgrim. Thus, it almost looks as if the Berserker wants to seduce him into swearing his allegiance in the Germanic sense.[84]

In addition, Brother Klaus's simile of the vessel filled with honey is pertinent if one thinks of the *Minnebecher* (cup of love) of the ancient Germanic people, for honey is an essential ingredient in the mead of poets, a drink which induces ecstasy,[85] and honey is to be found in nectar, the drink of immortality.[86] According to Paracelsus, honey means "the sweetness of the earth,"[87] which makes it an image of *Minne*, of immortality,[88] of an eternal bond,[89] and of ecstatic inspiration.[90] "Drink milk and honey before sunrise and there will be something divine in your heart" was written on an ancient Papyrus on magic.[91] Honey is also the food of the gods.[92] In India, honey, strangely enough, is also a symbol of the contact of all beings in the universe with the Self, the Anthropos ("*purusa*"). Thus, it is said in the *Brha-danyaka-Upanishad* II, 5[93] "This self is honey for all beings. And all beings are honey for this self. And in this self which is made up of the energy of light, from which the deathless *purusa* is made, and which is made up of *Atman*, i.e. which is made out of the energy of light, from which the deathless *purusa* is made, is the original atman of the deathless, of the *Brahman*. That is the cosmos." In this text, too, honey is an image of the loving contact of all living

---

[83] Cf *ibid.*, p. 245, footnotes 1 and 2.

[84] This had already been hinted at in the "Vision of the Three Visitors," in which Brother Klaus was challenged by the three men to "serve" them.

[85] M. Ninck, *Wodan und germanischer Schicksalsglaube*, p. 323.

[86] Cf K. Wyss, *Die Milch im Kultus der Griechen und Römer,* Giessen, 1914, p. 12, on milk and honey in the cult of Venus. On mead, *ibid.*, p. 19.

[87] M.-L. von Franz, *Aurora Consurgens*, p. 265.

[88] W. Robert-Tornow, *De apium mellisque apud veteres significatione et symbolica et mythologica,* Berlin: Weidmann, 1893, p. 121.

[89] See K. Wyss, *Die Milch im Kultus der Griechen und Römer,* pp. 26ff. on honey as a sacrificial offering to the dead, as a honey-milk mixture for the soothing delight of the souls of the dead.

[90] *Ibid.*; thus, the meaning of honey in Dionysian and other mystery cults.

[91] See also A. Dieterich, *Eine Mithrasliturgie*, p. 170f. (Trans.).

[92] Cf K. Wyss, *Die Milch im Kultus der Griechen und Römer,* p. 39, and W. Robert-Tornow, *De apium mellisque apud veteres significatione et symbolica et mythologica* (1891), p. 121.

[93] I.W. Hauer, '*Symbole und Erfahrung des Selbstes*', *Eranos-Jahrbuch 1934*, Zürich: Rhein Verlag, 1935, p. 71f. (Trans.)

creatures within the Self in its form of the macrocosmic Anthropos (*purusa*).

112 Seen from a psychological standpoint, the *Minne* in Brother Klaus's vision is, so to speak, the positive aspect of that threatening red colour which frightened Brother Klaus so terribly in the Liestal episode. For, as Jung wrote in "The Philosophical Tree,"[94] the "colour red" or "red tincture" of the alchemists psychologically represents a specific form of Eros, of being related through one's feelings, in which understanding is combined with love. This is in contrast to the collective, conventional Christian approach of loving one's neighbour as oneself, for it symbolises a more conscious, more individual and deeper relatedness between people, something which other mystics were seeking to develop at the time Brother Klaus lived.

113 Thus, we can surmise that upon the pilgrim's departure, Brother Klaus was left with a peculiar feeling of happiness. We are told: He felt so completely sated, that he desired nothing further, and that it seemed to him that the pilgrim had made known to him everything that was in heaven and on earth. It seems that the Berserker had about him a sphere of "absolute knowledge" which pointed towards a cosmic *Ulomelie* in which everything is connected to everything else.[95] Indeed, as Jung writes in his essay "Synchronicity: An Acausal Connecting Principle,"[96] it appears that the archetypes of the collective unconscious have a psychoid aspect to them which can

---

[94] C.G. Jung, CW 13, *Alchemical Studies*, §390f. Here, Jung discusses how according to which the alchemical lapis bleeds "rose-coloured" blood, which is "not natural or ordinary blood, but symbolic blood, a psychic substance, the manifestation of a certain kind of Eros which unifies the individual as well as the multitude in the sign of the rose and makes them whole. ... Goethe caught the mood of this Eros very well in his poem *Die Geheimnisse*. Such movements, as also the emergence of the idea of Christian charity with its emotional overtones, are always indicative of a corresponding social defect which they serve to compensate. In the perspective of history, we can see clearly enough what this defect was in the ancient world; and in the Middle Ages as well, with its cruel and unreliable laws and feudal conditions, human rights and human dignity were in a sorry plight. One would think that in these circumstances Christian love would be very much to the point. But what if it is blind and without insight? ... Love alone is useless if it does not also have understanding. And for the proper use of understanding, a wider consciousness is needed and a higher standpoint to enlarge one's horizon. ... Certainly love is needed ... but a love combined with insight and understanding. Their function is to illuminate regions that are still dark and to add them to consciousness—regions in the outside world as well as those within, in the interior world of the psyche. The blinder love is, the more it is instinctual, and the more it is attended by destructive consequences, for it is a dynamism that needs form and direction." In his "consultations," Brother Klaus demonstrated much of this type of understanding that is combined with Eros.
[96] *Ibid.*, Jung, CW 8, §§816–997.

also appear in physical events as ordering factors. The common denominator of both inner psychic and outer events is *meaningful coincidence.* The Chinese concept of Tao gives expression to this aspect of reality. Ch'uang-tse says of this,[97] "Outward hearing should not penetrate further than the ear; the intellect should not seek to lead a separate existence, thus the soul can become empty and absorb the whole world. It is Tao that fills this emptiness." And, to have insight, "you use your inner eye, your inner ear, to pierce to the heart of things, and have no need of intellectual knowledge." As Jung points out,[98] "this is obviously an allusion to the absolute knowledge of the unconscious, and to the presence in the microcosm of macrocosmic events." [This is] "not a knowledge that could be connected with the ego, and hence not a conscious knowledge as we know it, but rather a self-subsistent 'unconscious' knowledge which I would prefer to call 'absolute knowledge.' It is not cognition but, as Leibniz so excellently calls it, a 'perceiving' which consists—or to be more cautious, seems to consist—of images, of subjectless *simulacra.* These postulated images are presumably the same as my archetypes. ... Expressed in modern language, the microcosm which contains 'the images of all creation' would be the collective unconscious."[99] Contact with the latter often involves an experience of illumination in which a simultaneous, rather than a rational, realisation of all the world's secrets is conveyed.

Such considerations, which at first might seem peripheral, must be taken into consideration in our interpretation of Brother Klaus's vision because the pilgrim in the bearskin is, without doubt, an archetypal image which, psychologically speaking, must be seen as a personification of the Self. The latter is, however, the central content of the collective unconscious. Thus, it is obvious that the appearance of this content constellates, among other things, something of the "absolute knowledge" of the collective unconscious, which explains why Brother Klaus's experience of his encounter with

114

---

[97] *Ibid.,* §923.
[98] *Ibid.*
[99] *Ibid.,* §931.

the pilgrim is equivalent to the instant revelation of all that exists between heaven and earth.

Naturally, this pilgrim, as an image of the Self, is also a parallel figure for Christ[100] but one which completes, so to speak, the figure of Christ by including the lowly realm of the animals, along with the vastness of nature, thereby adding characteristics which the figure in the dogma does not possess so explicitly—at least not yet. The image of the pilgrim includes *Minne*, the secret power of the instinctive world and the above-mentioned element of "absolute knowledge." To some extent the Berserker has become incarnate in Brother Klaus for he himself wants to reveal the egoism in people, like "the spirit of Truth,"[101] and Brother Klaus often emphasised this ecstatic feeling of divine love which, apparently, he had inwardly experienced. For indeed, as he told a youth from Burgdorf who asked for his advice on meditation,[102] God knows how to make contemplation as appealing "as if one were dancing," and conversely, He can make it seem "as if one had to struggle with an adversary." Indeed, one of Klaus's prayers which has been handed down to us points in this direction:[103]

> *My Lord and my God, take from me everything that distances me from you.*
>
> *My Lord and my God, give me everything that brings me closer to you.*
>
> *My Lord and my God, detach me from myself to give my all to you.*

---

[100] As Jung has already pointed out.

[101] See the *Abt-von-Würzburg*-episode in R. Duerrer, *Bruder Klaus*, Vol. 1, pp. 346ff. (reported by Joan de Trittenheim), and Ch. Journet, *Saint Nicolas de Flüe*, p. 22.

[102] R. Duerrer, *Bruder Klaus*, 1: 407; Ch. Journet, *Saint Nicolas de Flüe*, p. 26f.; F. Blanke, *Bruder Klaus von Flüe*, p. 57.

[103] Ch. Journet, *Saint Nicolas de Flüe*, p. 28; for the history of the discovery of this prayer text, see *ibid.*, fn. 1.

Chapter 10
The Vision of the Fountain

The recently discovered handwritten manuscript found in Lucerne shows that the Berserker vision was followed by a second vision:[1]

"Through his suffering and by the will of God, Klaus's sleep was broken. And he thanked God for His sufferings and His martyrdom. And God gave him grace in which he found support and joy. Thereupon he laid himself down to rest and it seemed to him in his sleep, or in his spirit, that he came to a place which belonged to a community. There he saw a crowd of people doing heavy work. They were very poor. And he stood and looked at them and was amazed that, in spite of all their work, they were still so poor. Then, to his right, there appeared a well-built tabernacle in which he saw an open door and he thought to himself, 'You must go into the tabernacle and see what is inside, you must soon go in by the door.' Then he came to a kitchen which belonged to a whole community. On the right, he saw stairs going up—about four steps—and he saw some people climbing them, but only a few. It seemed to him that their clothes were sprinkled with white. And coming from the steps he saw a fountain out of which a stream was flowing down the stairs into a big trough and then on to the kitchen and it was composed of three substances: wine, oil and honey. This stream flowed as quickly as a flash of lightning and made such a loud noise that the place echoed, as if a horn were being played. And he thought, 'You must go up the stairs and see where the

---

[1] A. Stoeckli, *Die Visionen des seligen Bruder Klaus*, p. 18ff.

fountain comes from.' And he marvelled greatly that the people were so poor and that nobody went in to draw water from the fountain, which they could have done quite easily for it was common property. And he went up the stairs and came to a wide hall. And there, in the middle of the hall, he saw a large square box out of which the fountain flowed. And he went to the box and looked at it. And as he went to it he almost sank, as though he were crossing a swamp, and he drew up his feet quickly and came to the box. And in his spirit he realised that whoever did not walk quickly, lifting up his feet, would never get to the box. The box was reinforced on all four sides with strong iron[2] plates. And the fountain flowed through a pipe and sounded so beautiful in the box and in the pipes that he marvelled greatly. And the water of this stream was so clear and pure that one could have seen a hair lying at the bottom of it. And however strongly the water flowed, the box remained full and overflowing. And he relied in his spirit that however much flowed out of it, there was always more, and he saw how it trickled out through all the cracks. And he thought, 'Now you will go down again.' Then he saw great streams flow into the trough from all sides and he thought to himself, 'You will go out and see what the people are doing, why they don't come in to draw water from the fountain which has such a plentiful overflow.' And he went outside. And he saw the people working very hard, and yet they were very poor. And he watched what they were doing. And he saw that someone had built a fence through the middle of the courtyard and in the middle of the fence there was a latticed door which a man held closed, and he said he would let no one in or out unless they paid him a penny. And Klaus saw how someone turned a thumbscrew on one of the people, and how he said, 'That is to force you to give me a penny.' And he saw a piper who played for the people and who demanded a penny from

---

[2] Added by the author from the original text.

them. And he saw a tailor and a shoemaker and other craftsmen who all wanted pennies. And even though they did all this, they were still so poor they could hardly manage to pay. And he saw nobody go in to draw water from the fountain. And as he stood there and watched, the place was suddenly transformed into [a] dreary rocky slope like the place where Brother Klaus's church was and where he had his house, and he realized within himself, that the tabernacle was himself, Brother Klaus."

119   This time the tabernacle and the spring appear to the right of Brother Klaus—in the direction of consciousness.[3] Correspondingly, this vision is much closer to the conscious, or Christian, world view than the preceding vision was. In his rendition of this vision, Alban Stoeckli quotes a passage from a sermon by Johannes Tauler in which the latter speaks of turning inwards towards his own soul about which God observes: "and you will find 'it' there, gushing forth from the ground, as if from its own source … and the stream flows, wells up and grows."[4] Tauler calls this stream "the loving (*Minne*) intimacy of the Holy Ghost."[5]

120   From time immemorial Christ, too, has been seen as being one with "the inner rock" from which the water of life and mercy flows.[6] His body (the Church) forms the *fons vitae* for all mankind.[7] According to Basilius, the water that flows out of Christ, as the "pneumatic rock," is his visionary perception of God[8] and the experience of the *Logos Christi* within the mystic's own soul. And in this way, he himself becomes the "treasure house of living water."[9] Furthermore, as a parallel to Brother Klaus's vision, Charles Journet

---

[3] For more on the connection of consciousness to the right side and unconsciousness to the left side, see C.G. Jung, CW 12, *Psychology and Alchemy*, §287.

[4] A. Stoeckli, *Die Visionen des seligen Bruder Klaus*, p. 24.

[5] *Ibid.*, p. 25.

[6] See, e.g., Origenes, *Numeri-Homilie*, 12: 2, cited in H. Rahner, *"Flumina de ventre Christi,"* Biblica, Rome, 1941, Vol. 22, pp. 274ff.

[7] See, e.g., B. Ephraem Syrus, *Hymni et Sermones*, Lamy (ed.), Mechliniae, 1902, Vol. 1, p. 166 and Vol. 2, p. 130.

[8] See H. Rahner, *"Flumina de ventre Christi,"* Biblica, p. 285.

[9] Gregor v. Nyssa, in H. Rahner, *"Flumina de ventre Christi,"* Biblica, p. 286.

mentions some medieval illustrations in which this source of life is depicted.[10]

121   In these illustrations, the Blood of Christ is, for example, often caught in a smaller, four-sided vessel which is encircled by the four symbols of the evangelists or by the symbols of the four stations of Christ's life: His birth, His sacrificial death, His resurrection, and His ascension. Christ's redeeming blood flows out of this initial vessel into a large vessel in which mankind immerses itself to be cleansed of its sins.[11] The same motif is depicted in an altarpiece of Van Eyck's in the following manner:[12] The rays of divine grace descend upon a rectangular altar upon which the Lamb of God is standing. Its blood flows into a chalice after which it is divided through the seven channels of the sacraments, and from there it flows on into a larger vessel around which the figures of the old and new faiths are assembled.

122   Furthermore, the "four-cornered" box in Brother Klaus's vision can be compared to the "bowl-shaped altar" which the afore-mentioned alchemist, Zosimos of Panopolis, while pondering the nature of alchemical "water," saw in his dream vision.[13] In alchemy, water was thought to be the instrument of transformation, and in the vision of Zosimos, human beings were transformed into spiritual beings by means of this water,[14] just as in Brother Klaus's vision human beings apparently attain spiritual life.

123   As Jung emphasizes, the aim of all alchemy is to find the "miraculous" water, the *aqua divina* or *aqua permanens,* which is obtained through the agony of fire from the lapis, i.e., the *prima materia*. Water was the *humidum radicale,* which represented the *anima media natura* or *anima mundi,* the soul of the stone or metal, an *anima aquina* as it is also called.[15] "Altogether, the divine water possessed the power of transformation. It transformed the *nigredo*[16]

---

[10] Ch. Journet, *Saint Nicolas de Flüe*, p. 51.
[11] E. Mâle, *L'art religieux du XIIIe siecle en France,* Paris, 1919, p. 52, in Ch. Journet, *Saint Nicolas de Flüe,* p. 51.
[12] E. Mâle, op. cit., p. 236, in Ch. Journet, *Saint Nicolas de Flüe,* p. 51.
[13] C.G. Jung, CW 13, *Alchemical Studies,* §86 and C.G. Jung, CW 11, *Psychology and Religion,* §345.
[14] C.G. Jung, CW 13, *Alchemical Studies,* §86.
[15] *Ibid.,* §89.
[16] Blackness.

into the *albedo*[17] through the miraculous washing ... and therefore possessed the virtue of the baptismal water in the ecclesiastical rite."[18] In alchemy, the whitening (the *albedo*) mentioned above refers to the developmental stage in which the withdrawal of projections and the processing of unconscious contents[19] are in the foreground, i.e., a state of freeing oneself from being caught up in the world through one's projections. This explains why the colour white is a symbol of innocence in the allegory of the Church. The fact that, in Brother Klaus's vision, only very few people climb up to the water box in clothing sprinkled with white means that only very few chosen ones will take the path of total inwardness and will allow themselves to be redeemed by the water of the unconscious.

124   Psychologically speaking, the image points to a transformation of a perfectly natural, and therefore unconscious, person into a conscious being.[20] Within this context, water has a spiritual meaning[21] and symbolises the transforming power of the unconscious, i.e., the numinous experience of the individuation process, the psychic basis of which still remains a mystery right up to the present time. Thus, it would seem that it is not by chance that there are four "levels" (*Seigeln*) which lead up to Brother Klaus's water box, for the number 4 is often linked to all the natural symbols of the Self.[22] Interestingly enough, precisely the *uppermost* symbol, the box, is characterised by the number 4, whereas the lower symbol is characterised by the number 3 (the three pipes), as if the number 4 were superior to the number 3, which is the supreme number in Christianity. This emphasis upon the number 4 infers that we are dealing with *an immediate and individual experience of a natural symbol of wholeness,* and its elevation shows how individual contemplation had become of primary importance.

---

[17] Whiteness.
[18] *Ibid.,* §89.
[19] C.G. Jung, CW 14, *Mysterium Coniunctionis*, London: Routledge & Kegan Paul, 1963, §181.
[20] *Ibid.*
[21] *Ibid.,* §§180–181.
[22] I refer, for example, to C.G. Jung's explanation in CW 9/ii, *Aion*, §351–355. In their report, Woelflin and Salat transform the four steps into ten steps and relate them to the Ten Commandments. In contrast to this, the four steps of the original report are worth noting. See A. Stoeckli, *Die Visionen des seligen Bruder Klaus*, p. 22.

125   When the water flows down into the kitchen, it becomes three substances: wine, oil, and honey. These are three important spiritual, cultic essences, but the fourth, which is above them, is in its original state: It is pure water. In the vision, it is this pure water that is most highly esteemed at the place where it wells up within the soul, so to speak.

126   But a danger lurks around this box of "eternal water": The ground is muddy, and Brother Klaus must "walk over it quickly," as it were, in order not to sink into it. In so far as the box depicts both the container as well as what is contained within it, one can compare the box to the "*vas*" of the alchemists,[23] as a symbol of their *theoria— their symbolic understanding of the unconscious*. In Brother Klaus's vision, the box is overflowing, and thus he is surrounded by this mire which he must cross over. This overflowing water may refer to a part of spiritual life which is no longer symbolically "contained" and which therefore constitutes a sphere of dangerous unconsciousness. In the language of the Church Fathers, it would be the "swamp of sins."[24] Brother Klaus's crossing of the mire calls to mind the motif of the *transitus,* which both the Gnostic Peratics and the Church Fathers interpreted as a symbol of becoming conscious. According to the teaching of the Peratics, the crossing of the Red Sea which the Jews undertook during their exodus from Egypt signifies an exodus from their sinful existence and their temporal bodies into which the "ignorant" sink. On the other side of the sea, there is a place in which "the gods of those who are lost" and the "gods of salvation" are together. As Jung explains, "The Red Sea is a water of death for those that are 'unconscious,' but for those that are 'conscious' it is a baptismal water of rebirth and of transcendence. By 'unconscious' are meant those who have no gnosis, that is, are not enlightened as to the nature and destiny of man in the cosmos. In modern language it would be those who have no knowledge of the contents of the personal and collective unconscious. The personal unconscious is the shadow and the inferior function, in Gnostic terms the sinfulness

---

[23] On this concept, see C.G. Jung, CW 12, *Psychology and Alchemy*, §246 and §§338ff.

[24] Babylon, for example, was thought to be a *lacus inferior* and *confusio*; see R. Reitzenstein, *Das Iranische Erlösungsmysterium,* Bonn: A. Marcus & E. Weber, 1921, p. 77f. and p. 80.

and impurity that must be washed away by baptism. The collective unconscious expresses itself in the mythological teachings, characteristic of most mystery religions, which reveal the secret knowledge concerning the origin of all things and the way to salvation. 'Unconscious' people who attempt to cross the sea without being purified and without the guidance of enlightenment are drowned; they get stuck in the unconscious and suffer a spiritual death in so far as they cannot get beyond their one-sidedness. To do this they would have to be more conscious of what is unconscious to them and their age, above all of the inner opposite … "[25] Seen in the light of Jung's explanation, it appears that Brother Klaus was able to complete this dangerous transition and to avoid the danger of sinking into the unconscious which, for such a strict hermit, must have been a real danger. Brother Klaus overcame all these dangerous elements by means of his focused striving towards the centre, the four-cornered water-box, i.e., *the symbol of the Self.*

127 These three areas in Brother Klaus's vision (the courtyard, the kitchen, and the area with the well) also bring to mind the three-levelled fountain of wisdom mentioned in a sermon of Nicholas of Cusa: 1. the common trough out of which cattle drink, the *puteus sensibilis*; 2. Jacob's fountain out of which human beings drink, the source of rational philosophy; 3. the fountain of "redeeming wisdom" with its "metaphysical waters" out of which the "sons of the All-Highest, whom we call Gods" drink.[26] Here the "outsiders" would be the "brutish" people who drink from the three pipes and who correspond to rationalists. Only the mystic reaches the *aqua sapientiae* of the innermost room. This layering of the vision into three areas (the area of the "outsiders" who strive hard; the area of those who are in the kitchen where the three essences are dispensed; and the area of the water which Brother Klaus goes up towards) also calls to mind the gradation of the mystical viewpoint, as in the works of Heinrich Seuse and many other medieval mystics.[27] On an inner level, spiritual life can be determined on three levels: 1. the *via*

---

[25] C.G. Jung, CW 14, *Mysterium Coniunctionis*, §257.
[26] C.G. Jung, CW 16, *The Practice of Psychotherapy*, §485.
[27] Cf J. Buehlmann, *Christuslehre und Christusmystik des Heinrich Seuse*, Lucerne, 1942, p. 152f.

purificativa, which entails the mortification of the flesh and great suffering, that brings with it abandonment and hopelessness;[28] 2. the *via illuminative,* which includes the mysticism of the Holy Passion and the worship of the Virgin Mary;[29] and 3. Contemplation,[30] in which the sacred effect of holy grace takes place[31] and leads one to an immediate perception of the divine. This last level is a gift of wisdom.[32] While the second and third levels can easily be compared to the levels in Brother Klaus's vision, the first level appears to be different for the people at this level are not intentional ascetics, but rather pursue profit-making and thereby become all the more poverty stricken. In contrast to those who walk the *via purificativa,* their suffering has become mundane and meaningless. Therein, perhaps, lies an appeal to Brother Klaus who is asked in the vision to help these people to turn towards the "water of wisdom" once again. If anyone could help them, then surely it would be Klaus, who has experienced the meaning of willingly accepting his own suffering, and also because originally Klaus, too, had tried to break free and to live his life according to his own free will. The poor, hardworking people are in contrast to the centre: They are characterised by their self-interest, and they try to forcefully beg a penny from others and from Brother Klaus. As strange as it may seem, this calls to mind the request of the divine pilgrim for a penny in the preceding vision, and it is not by chance that a piper appears in the crowd next to the money collector and to the craftsmen. These collective people are, apparently, not aware of the secret of the fountain. They are the unawakened who have no knowledge of the source of the "divine water." They are split off from the centre, and the money collectors amongst them, i.e., the representatives of the profane municipal collective organisations, continue working towards the making of further laws and restrictions. It is an impressive mirroring of the spiritual development which took place

---

[28] This level corresponds to the *nigredo* in alchemy.
[29] This level corresponds to the *albedo* in alchemy.
[30] This differs from the vision.
[31] This partly corresponds to the *rubedo* in alchemy.
[32] Cf J. Buehlmann, *Christuslehre und Christusmystik des Heinrich Seuse,* p. 158, p. 83 and p. 17, and especially pp. 222ff., for more on Niklaus von Flüe.

during the Renaissance, i.e., an increase of the ego's own independence of mind and a loss of religious inner life. From a psychological standpoint, these people, however, must represent latent psychic tendencies within Brother Klaus himself, that is, those aspects within him which try to achieve their goal by means of their own effort rather than through inner devotion. Here, too, we see what becomes of the divine wanderer, Wotan, if he is not accepted: In this instance, *he multiplies himself into being a profane collective person* who, because he is not guided by an inner centre, only follows the whims of his own ego. Wotan has always been the one who stirs mass man into action, the creator of dangerous mass hysteria,[33] for everything that is not accepted by consciousness energetically reinforces the unconscious, i.e., the sphere of instinctual drives. This is why, as Jung pointed out, Wotan, the archaic god, is still the active figure behind the collective catastrophes of today.

128   The fact that the whole place suddenly transforms itself into the area where Brother Klaus lives is indeed a clear indication of the vision mirroring an event which takes place "on the spot," that is, within himself.

129   The people's desire for money shows that those who are excluded from the mystery are asking something of Brother Klaus, as if he were the right person to reconnect them to the centre. Indirectly, he has done this through his own "banal" reality, including the path of his religious development, for he is the embodiment of the spiritual, holy, and instinctual man who is utterly at one with nature. It is only within such a comprehensive totality that the profane excluded ones can be reintegrated.

130   This vision, too, became strangely real for later on, hundreds of petitioners and curious people surrounded the Ranft to ask Brother Klaus's advice so that, in the end, one had to have a pass issued by the parish to be allowed to go there. It is altogether impressive how his many characteristics which typify the "Anthropos" of his vision begin to shine through after Klaus's withdrawal to the Ranft. In the town council's meeting in Stans, he becomes the *mediator pacem*

---

[33] C.G. Jung, CW 10, *Civilisation in Transition*, §§371ff.

faciens inter inimicos, like the alchemical lapis. In his daily consultations, he is like the overflowing fountain of spiritual vitality. Furthermore, like the "Truth" in his Berserker vision, he often tore away the mask of those who consulted him and, with a mediumistic clairvoyance, revealed their secret thoughts and sins.

131   This second vision, more than the first, points towards an inner split of the opposites, and towards suffering and conflict—a contrast that is seen too narrowly if it is taken as a personal conflict between Brother Klaus the realistic farmer and Brother Klaus the mystic.[34] Rather, it is more the conflict of the time which is mirrored in this vision, a conflict which Klaus is also caught up in.

---

[34] See, for example, B. H. Federer, *Niklaus von Flüe* (Frauenfeld, 1928). Unfortunately, this otherwise excellent and impressive character sketch only covers the period up to Brother Klaus's "breaking away." Federer captures the atmosphere and the conditions of country life, the *genius loci* of Brother Klaus's life especially well.

<h1>Chapter 11</h1>
<h1>The Vision of the Heavenly Quaternio</h1>

132 During Brother Klaus's time of suffering and depression, his friend from Lucerne, Heiny am Grund, who was the local priest in Kriens at the time, tried to help[1] Klaus by giving him an illustrated text of the Passion of Christ to meditate upon. (Brother Klaus was almost illiterate.)[2] According to this text, one had to mediate upon the seven canonical hours of prayer, for example, the third and the ninth, etc., each one being a Station of the Cross of Christ's suffering.[3] Brother

---

[1] R. Duerrer, *Bruder Klaus*, Vol. 1, p. 39f. See also, F. Blanke, *Bruder Klaus von Flüe*, p. 13f. and especially p. 77 and, for further reading, the literature cited there, especially W. Oehl, "*Bruder Klaus und die deutsche Mystik*," *Zeitschrift für Schweizer Kirchengeschichte,* Stans, 1917, Vol. 11. pp. 161–174. See also R. Duerrer, *Bruder Klaus*, Vol. 1, p. 38f. on Brother Klaus's great awe of the priesthood. See also Ch. Journet, *Saint Nicolas de Flüe*, p. 23, fn. 2. Cf *Oeuvres mystiques du bienheureux Henri Suso,* Thiriot, Paris, 1899, Vol. 2, pp. 194ff.

[2] R. Duerrer, *Bruder Klaus*, Vol. 1, p. 65. Cf F. Blanke, *Bruder Klaus von Flüe*, p. 79. Brother Klaus was probably able to read letters. See K. Vokinger, *Bruder-Klausen-Buch* (Stans, 1936), p. 245f.

[3] R. Duerrer, *Bruder Klaus*, Vol. 1, p. 39: "He [Klaus's trusted friend, probably Heiny am Grund] responded to this with some helpful suggestions intended to free me of my temptation, but I told him that I had already tried what he suggested as well as other similar solutions, but I had found no comfort in them and nor were they of any assistance to me whatsoever. Only then did he add the best and most helpful suggestion, namely, devout contemplation on the sufferings of Jesus Christ. Greatly relieved, I replied that this was unknown to me. ... So he instructed me in understanding the Stations of the Cross of Christ's suffering through the seven canonical hours. Whereupon I began to contemplate and performed the exercise daily and with the mercy of our Redeemer, I began to make some progress in my impoverishment, and because I was caught up in many business and worldly activities, I saw that I was not able to be fully devout. Which is why I often withdrew to this secret place nearby to continue my devotions on Christ's suffering, and nobody knew my whereabouts except my wife, and she came to know of it purely incidentally. And thus I stayed for two years ... " See also the following for more on meditational literature of that time: J. Buehlmann, *Christuslehre und Christusmystik des Heinrich Seuse*, p. 82, fn. 15. F. Blanke (*Bruder Klaus von Flüe*, p. 14f.) believes that the *Speculum humanae salvationis* is the basis of the exercises which Heiny am Grund gave to Brother Klaus, and he reconstructs it in the following manner: "At vespers, at 6.00 pm Klaus offers thanks to the Lord for love, the love he showed in the washing of the feet and at the holy Last Supper. At *complin* at 9.00 pm, he thanks our Redeemer for suffering and sweating blood out of love for him [Klaus], and he asks Him to free him from the bonds of evil. Shortly after midnight, Klaus says the prayers of *lauds*: 'I thank you, Lord, for showing me such great love that on my behalf you were mocked and ridiculed in the house of Caiaphas. For the outrage of your ill-treatment I ask You to forgive me the outrage of my sins." Klaus rose early for *prime*. He gives thanks for the love "that You accepted the ridicule of Herod and his soldiers on my behalf. Through Your mercy, help me achieve the same patience in all temptations." At 9.00 am Klaus says the prayers of the *tierce*. He thanks the Lord that, out of His love for him [Klaus], He allowed Himself to be scourged and Klaus asks Him for the privilege of being scourged while on earth so that he will be spared this punishment in eternity. At *sext* (at noon) he offers thanks for Christ allowing Himself to be nailed to the Cross on Klaus's behalf, and at *nones* (at 3.00 pm) Klaus thanks the Lord for

Klaus did this and felt some relief from his state, even if the problem was only later resolved after he "broke away" from his relations and retreated to the Ranft. Perhaps these devotional exercises are connected to the vision of the fountain, but they are most definitely connected to the following vision, which is listed as the third vision in the newly found Lucerne text:[4]

133 "Through his suffering and by the will of God Klaus's sleep was interrupted, and he thanked God for His suffering and for His martyrdom. And God gave Klaus grace so that he found support and joy in it. Thereupon he laid himself down to rest. And when his rational mind was constrained, though he believed himself to not yet be asleep, it seemed to him that someone came in by the door and stood in the middle of the house and called out to him in a strong clear voice and asked him what his name was, and said: 'Come and see your Father and see what He is doing.'

134 And it seemed to him that he arrived at the target quickly (he covered the distance that an arrow travels), that is, a beautiful tent in a great hall. He saw people who lived there and the man who had called to him was at his side and acted as his intercessor. And although this man spoke, yet Niklaus did not see him and did not even wonder about it, and he spoke for him and said: 'This is the man who lifted up and carried your son and came to his help in his fear and distress. Thank him for it and be grateful to him.'

135 There a handsome majestic man came through the palace. His face was like a shining light and he wore white robes like a priest's alb. He laid both arms on Niklaus's shoulders and pressed him close and thanked him fervently for having stood by his son and helped him in his need. And Niklaus was downcast and felt most unworthy and said, 'I do not know that I have ever done your son a service.' Then the man left him and Niklaus did not see him again.

His death 'for having died for me on the Cross.'" Blanke describes how these meditations helped Brother Klaus to free himself of an egocentric attitude towards suffering. (Trans.)

[4] A. Stoeckli, *Die Visionen des seligen Bruder Klaus*, p. 20f.

136   And then a beautiful majestic woman who was also clothed in white came through the palace.[5] And Niklaus saw clearly that her robe was freshly laundered. And she laid both arms on his shoulders and pressed him warmly to her heart with overflowing love, because he, Niklaus, had stood so faithfully by her son in his need. And Niklaus felt unworthy and said, 'I do not know that I have ever done your son a service except that I came here to see what you were doing.' Then she left him and he did not see her again.

137   And then Niklaus looked round and saw the son sitting in a chair beside him and he saw that he was also dressed in the same way and that his clothes were spotted with red, as if they had been sprinkled with blood. And the son leaned towards Niklaus and thanked him profoundly for having helped him in his need. Then Niklaus looked down at himself and saw that he, too, was dressed in white sprinkled with red, like the son. And that surprised him very much for he had not known that he was dressed like that. And then he suddenly found himself in the place where he had lain down so that he thought he had not slept.

138   This vision, too, has motifs that are common to those of other mystics. Alban Stoeckli draws attention to a parallel in a sermon by Tauler:[6] "Thus spoke the Lord: 'Dearly beloved, I thank you and I am pleased with you for thanking Me for my suffering and for having helped Me to carry the heavy burden of My cross by your afflictions which you have endured. And behold, now I shall be with you once again.'" And at a different point in the same sermon: "Here God gives Himself abundantly to the soul beyond all the soul's desires. When God finds the soul in a state of inconsolable misery, He is just, for, as is written, when King Assuerus's dearly beloved Esther stood helplessly before him with her pale face, and fell to the ground, he immediately offered her the golden sceptre, arose from his royal throne, embraced her, kissed her and offered to share his kingdom with her. This Assuerus is the Heavenly Father. So, when He sees His beloved soul in front of Him with her sorrowful face

---

[5] *Ibid.* (Trans.).
[6] *Ibid.*, p. 27f.: preached on the fifth Sunday after Pentecost: *Estote misericordes*; a medieval German text, *Die Predigten Taulers*, F. Vetter (ed.) (Berlin: Weidmann, 1910), Vol. II, pp. 150ff.

unconsoled by all things, and when her spirit is broken and she stands bent over before Him, He offers her His golden sceptre, rises from His throne, metaphorically speaking, enfolds her in His arms and raises her above her illness through His divine embrace."

139   Similarly, in Brother Klaus's vision, the *unio mystica* with God is also mentioned, but it takes on further unexpected forms: First of all, an invisible being calls Brother Klaus with a "strong clear voice" to attend to his father and see what he is doing, and then the voice speaks to God on his behalf, like an intercessor. Of course, one thinks of the Paraclete who is an advocate for mankind before God. But what appears to be strangely dreamlike and illogical is that the Paraclete asks Brother Klaus to firstly see what God is doing, but later, he does not do this at all. Rather, God is asked to thank Brother Klaus. Perhaps this compensates too great a respect and distance which Brother Klaus feels towards the Godhead so that the Holy Ghost exhorts him to perceive God without any inner barrier. But it is just as strange that the Holy Ghost must insist that God thank Brother Klaus, as if He would not do this of His own accord—which is quite different from the Mother of God who spontaneously comes to him.

140   Elevating the Virgin Mary to the level of being God's beloved companion was more or less sanctioned four hundred years later in the "*Declaratio Solemnis*" of Pope Pius XII, which brought the discussion as to whether or not the vision was heretical almost to a halt.[7]

141   Brother Klaus always had a very special relationship to the Mother of God. At the time when he was struggling so strongly with the devil, he said he "always found comfort in the dear woman." She once appeared to him in the crown of an apple tree at the spot where

---

[7] C.G. Jung, CW 11, *Psychology and Religion*, §486: "It is clear that this is a vision of God the Father and Son, and of the mother of God. The palace is heaven, where 'God the Father' dwells, and also 'God the Mother.' In pagan form they are unmistakably God and Goddess, as their absolute parallelism shows. The androgyny of the divine Ground is characteristic of mystic experience. In Indian Tantrism the masculine Shiva and the feminine Shakti both proceed from brahman, which is devoid of qualities. Man as the son of the Heavenly Father and Heavenly Mother is an age-old conception which goes back to primitive times, and in this vision the Blessed Brother Klaus is set on a par with the Son of God. The Trinity in this vision—Father, Mother and Son—is very undogmatic indeed. Its nearest parallel is the … Gnostic Trinity: God, Sophia, Christ. The Church, however, has expunged the feminine nature of the Holy Ghost, though it is still suggested by the symbolic dove."

the lower chapel in the Ranft now stands. For Brother Klaus, Mary was the earthly representative of the *Sapentia Dei*, and he once said to a pilgrim that Mary is the *Queen of Heaven and Earth* and that she had been anticipated through divine wisdom. The *Sapientia Dei* had surrounded Mary at the very moment God thought of her conception. This is why Mary was conceived more in the mind of the Highest God rather than in her mother's womb ... the power of the Almighty had gone out and enveloped her and thus she was imbued with the Holy Ghost.[8] Proof of Mary's secret identity with the *Sapientia Dei* was, for Brother Klaus, her immaculate conception—a concept he adhered to even though it was still being debated by theologians at the time.[9] The later developments in Catholic dogma confirmed all these views of Brother Klaus and the title *Queen of Heaven and Earth* is even now officially recognised.

142   The new dogma of the *Assumptio Mariae* has, as Jung emphasises,[10] a very widespread psychological significance. In his Apostolic Constitution, *"Munificentissimus Deus,"* Pope Pius XII draws special attention to the opinion of the Church Fathers that the star-woman of the Apocalypse who was taken up to heaven is a prefiguration of the Assumption.[11] Thus, as Jung goes on to say,[12] Mary is not only the symbolic vessel for the incarnation of God in Christ, but she is also the redeemer of whom the Apocalypse foretells. Psychologically speaking, however, this new redeemer is a symbol of a further incarnation of God, namely, in an ordinary *"creaturely man."*[13] But, as Brother Klaus's vision so beautifully shows, the latter is raised to the level of being a Brother of Christ. This can

---

[8] A. Stoeckli, *Die Visionen des seligen Bruder Klaus*, p. 41f.; "This refers back to the pilgrim's second question on the immaculate conception of the Virgin Mary. Brother Klaus, who accepted the affirmative standpoint of the pilgrim, presents a new argument here for the same theory. His proof, apparently, is based upon the words in the paper *"Dominus possedit me in initio viarum suarum, antequam quicquam faceret a principio"* (Proverbs 8:22) ["The Lord possessed me in the beginning of his way, before his works of old." KJV], which the Church applies to the Virgin Mary ... ". (Trans.).

[9] See F. Blanke, *Bruder Klaus von Flüe*, p. 100.

[10] C.G. Jung, CW 11, *Psychology and Religion*, §744.

[11] *Constitutio Apostolica 'Munificentissimus Deus'* (31): *"Ac praeterea scholastici doctores non modo in veteris testamenti figuris, sed in illa etiam muliere amicta sole, quam Joannes Apostolus in insula Patmo* (Rev. 12:if.) *contemplatus est, Assumptionem Deiparae Virginis significatam viderunt."* C.G. Jung, "Answer to Job," in CW 11, *Psychology and Religion*, §744, fn. 5.

[12] *Ibid.*, §744.

[13] *Ibid.*

only mean that "creaturely man" becomes the birthplace of a total incarnation of the divine. Such a realisation of the divine had otherwise been the special concern of the alchemists who, as Jung shows, were intent upon becoming an "unspotted vessel" for the Paraclete themselves, thereby realizing "the *idea* [of] 'Christ' on a plane far transcending a mere imitation of Him."[14] But the latter appears as an archetypal spiritual reality within the soul and has already revealed itself to Brother Klaus in the star, in the stone, in the Berserker, and, here, in the motif of the heavenly *quaternio* within which Brother Klaus is encompassed as a twin-brother of Christ. In retrospect, we can also better understand the promise of the three noblemen when they said that they would leave the cross for Brother Klaus to bear during his life. Until his death, Klaus would have to bear the burden of the dead wood of the Cross because he did not understand his election as Christ's brother (and not just His "imitator"), but that after Klaus's death, as the flag-bearer of the bear's paw, he would be able to realise his spiritual wholeness and thereby his brotherhood with Christ, that is, his immediate relationship to the Anthropos (that is, to the Self).

143   The symbol of the new redeemer in Revelations or the elevation of an ordinary man to being the double of Christ suggests the drive towards individuation,[15] the goal of which is both to heal and make man's fragmentary self whole.[16] But, for men, this requires the integration of the anima, which is why the figure of the star-woman, that is, the Virgin Mary, is given increasing importance, as Brother Klaus's vision clearly shows. As Jung emphasises,[17] the dogmatisation of the Assumption thus means "a renewed hope for the fulfilment of the yearning for peace which stirs deep down in the soul, and for a resolution of the threatening tension between the opposites. Everyone shares this tension and everyone experiences it in his

---

[14] C.G. Jung, CW 14, *Mysterium Coniunctionis*, §27.
[15] Jung, "Answer to Job," op. cit., §745.
[16] *Ibid.*, "Whatever man's wholeness, or the self, may mean *per se*, empirically it is an image of the goal of life spontaneously produced by the unconscious, irrespective of the wishes and fears of the conscious mind. It stands for the goal of the total man, for the realization of his wholeness and individuality with or without the consent of his will. The dynamic of this process is instinct, which ensures that everything which belongs to an individual's life shall enter into it …". Cf also, §751f.
[17] *Ibid.*, §754f.

individual form of unrest ..." Brother Klaus had also been gripped by such a restlessness. This is mirrored in the image of the unredeemed people at work in the outer courtyard of the tabernacle in his vision of the fountain. The existence of such a restless, rootless crowd within himself is what forces Klaus to climb up the four steps to the source of the fountain within the unconscious, i.e., to the Self, and which also pushes modern man into the process of individuation. As a result, however, each individual is forced to see that the inner divine opposites are within himself, for him to suffer and to unite. Thus he becomes a "Son of the Highest" and, simultaneously, the shadow-brother of Christ, so to speak, and thereby is included in the Holy Trinity as its fourth component.

144   Brother Klaus's last vision clearly shows *that the unconscious is not concerned with destroying the Christian symbol but rather is only concerned with supplementing it with a feminine element and that of the common man, thereby enriching it.*[18]

145   Apart from the elevation of the feminine, the theme which the lysis of this vision aims at is the establishment of the *quaternio* within which Brother Klaus is represented as Christ's twin-brother.[19] However, the invisible Holy Ghost is, like the spirit Mercurius of the alchemists, the one who unites all four as the *quinta essentia*, of which He is a part Himself. That the Holy Ghost is one with God the Father and God the Son needs no proof: He is connected to the Mother of God through the conception of Christ and to Klaus, through his "being filled with the Holy Ghost" and through His

---

[18] Cf. Jung's letter of 12 October 1959 to Pfarrer Uhsadel: (On Niklaus) ... "the unconscious attempts to compensate a strict Catholic faith in terms of how it evolves. The latter harms the figure of Christ, whereas the former enriches it or—to put it more clearly—tries to amplify it ('enrich it') with archaic natural symbolism in the sense of the Germanic use of the word *Christus—der Christ* [the Christ (trans.)] and the Christians, as opposed to the Roman usage of *chrétian, cristiano* etc., thus, like the antique word *Christos* and *Christianus*. In the case of the former, the faithful become 'Christ,' in the case of the latter, one becomes a follower—a successor, an imitator." (Trans.)

[19] C.G. Jung, "Answer to Job," in CW 11, *Psychology and Religion*, §713 where, on the matter of this prediction of such a far-reaching incarnation of God in the vision of Revelations says the following about the son of the star-woman: "What is meant here cannot be the return of Christ Himself, for we are told that He would come 'in the clouds of heaven', but not be *born* a second time, and certainly not from a sun-moon conjunction. ... The fact that John uses the myth of Leto and Apollo in describing the birth may be an indication that the vision, in contrast to the Christian tradition, is a product of the unconscious. But in the unconscious is everything that has been rejected by consciousness, and the more Christian one's consciousness is, the more heathenishly does the unconscious behave, if in the rejected heathenism there are values which are important for life." (This 'second Son' is the total human being, consisting of the totality of the psyche.)

continued effect upon those chosen by Him. His "clear, joyful voice" is an echo of the figure in the bearskin and the "spirit of Truth" in his previous vision[20] that now makes its goal clear, namely, *the creation of a divine quaternio.*[21] Brother Klaus is, as it were, chosen to play the role of Christ's human double,[22] that means, to realise this role both in himself and through himself.[23] The red and white robe which both Brother Klaus and Christ wear points towards the alchemical *rubedo* and *albedo* as the unification of the opposites. By suffering the clash of the opposites within himself rather than outside of himself, he makes visible the *homo altus*, or *teleios rtifexn*, the "totality of man" or the lapis of alchemy, which the alchemists thought of as being the *Analogia* of Christ. For, as Jung points out,[24] the alchemist "does not dream of identifying himself with Christ; on the contrary, it is the coveted substance, the *lapis,* that alchemy likens to Christ. It is not really a question of identification at all, but of the hermeneutic *sicut*—'as' or 'like'—which characterizes the analogy. ... Without knowing it, the alchemist carries the idea of the *imitatio* a stage further and reaches the conclusion we mentioned earlier, that complete assimilation to the Redeemer would enable him, the assimilated, to continue the work of redemption in the depths of his own psyche. This conclusion is unconscious. ... The artifex himself bears no correspondence to Christ; rather he sees this correspondence to the Redeemer in his wonderful stone. From this point of view, alchemy seems like a continuation of Christian mysticism carried on in the subterranean darkness of the

---

[20] The Holy Spirit is the 'Spirit of Truth', and the Berserker was referred to as the 'Truth.'

[21] See *Ibid.,* §727.

[22] The alchemical idea of the stone is compared to an earthly *analogia Christi.*

[23] *Ibid.,* §739: "Ever since John the apocalyptist experienced for the first time (perhaps unconsciously) that conflict into which Christianity inevitably leads, mankind has groaned under this burden: *God wanted to become man, and still wants to.* That is probably why John experienced in his vision a second birth of a son from the mother Sophia, a divine birth which was characterised by a *coniunctio oppositorum* and which anticipated the *filius sapientiae,* the essence of the individuation process. See also §748: "In order to interpret this event, one has to consider not only the arguments adduced by the Papal Bull, but the prefigurations in the apocalyptic marriage of the Lamb and in the Old Testament anamnesis of Sophia. The nuptial union in the *thalamus* (bridal-chamber) signifies the *hieros gamos,* and this in turn is the first step towards incarnation, towards the birth of the saviour who, since antiquity, was thought of as the *filius solis et lunae,* the *filius sapientiae,* and the equivalent of Christ. When, therefore, a longing for the exaltation of the Mother of God passes through the people, this tendency ... means the desire for the birth of a saviour, a peacemaker, a *mediator pacem faciens inter inimicos.*"

[24] C.G. Jung, CW 12, *Psychology and Alchemy,* §§451–2.

unconscious—indeed some mystics pressed the materialization of the Christ figure even to the appearance of the stigmata. ... Had the alchemist succeeded in forming any concrete idea of his unconscious contents, he would have been obliged to recognize that he had taken the place of Christ—or, to be more exact, that he, regarded *not as ego but as Self*, had taken over the work of redeeming not man but God. He would then have had to recognize not only himself as the equivalent of Christ, but Christ as a symbol of the Self. This tremendous conclusion failed to dawn on the medieval mind."

146

But precisely this same unconscious development, that reaches even greater depths than medieval mysticism does, would appear to be reflected in Brother Klaus's vision. Brother Klaus was to pay heed to God ("to see what He is doing") and to acknowledge himself as being the twin-brother and helper of Christ. If we ask what kind of conscious attitude could most readily be compensated by such a vision, we could suppose that Brother Klaus was exceptionally humble and that he was deeply impressed by his inner distance to God and by his own shadow, and that he was searching for meaning in his suffering of his shadow. *Then* his vision could be taken as an answer, as a statement of the unconscious telling him that all this dark turmoil within himself is God's will and that it has individuation, the process of *God becoming incarnate in an ordinary man*, as its goal.

147

As Jung has shown in "Answer to Job," this conflict of the second part of the aeon of Pisces is anticipated in the Revelation of John.[25] "At first, God incarnated his good side in order ... to create the most durable basis for later assimilation of the other side. From the promise of the Paraclete we may conclude that God later wants to become *wholly* man; in other words, to reproduce himself in his own dark creature (man not redeemed from original sin).[26]... The incarnation in Christ is the prototype which is continually being transferred to the creature by the Holy Ghost,"[27] and this clearly

---

[25] C.G. Jung, CW 11, "Answer to Job," *Psychology and Religion*, §739.
[26] *Ibid.*, §741.
[27] *Ibid.*: "This disturbing invasion [i.e. St. John's vision] engendered in him [i.e., St. John] the image of the divine child, of a future saviour, born of the divine consort whose reflection (the anima) lives in every man—that child whom Meister Eckhart also saw in a vision. It was he who knew that God alone

shows that, according to his vision, *Brother Klaus is one of those who was chosen to be a vessel for such a continuing incarnation.*[28]

148   It is no coincidence that in this vision, the elevation of the Mother of God is represented side by side with Klaus becoming the twin-brother of Christ for, as Jung emphasises,[29] "The dogmatization of the *Assumptio Mariae* [which sanctions her elevation] points to the *hieros gamos* in the pleroma, and this in turn implies ... the future birth of the divine child, who, in accordance with the divine trend towards incarnation, will choose as his birthplace the empirical man. The metaphysical process is known to the psychology of the unconscious as the individuation process."[30] In so far as Klaus is called upon to individuate and to offer, by all the means available to him, his consciousness as a natural, willing vessel for the individuation process, he is simultaneously raised to the *typos* of that second redeemer. But the Mother of God is therefore the mother of this all-embracing totality, so to speak. Thus, we can understand Klaus's special devotion to her. That she appeared to him in the crown of an apple tree is, perhaps, not without symbolical meaning for the tree is an analogy to the Tree of Knowledge. Furthermore, the tree is generally a symbol of the individuation process as a *natural* process of unfolding and becoming conscious.[31] Here, Mary appears as a heathen tree numen, that is, in complete unity with nature, and while appearing in this form, she "heals" the estrangement of a certain profane Christian conscious attitude towards nature which, at that time, was increasingly being felt to be inadequate.

---

in his Godhead is not in a state of bliss, but must be born in the human soul. ... *The incarnation in Christ is the prototype which is continually being transferred to the creature by the Holy Ghost.*" (Author's italics).

[28] *Ibid.*, §744: "... the Pope has recently announced the dogma of the *Assumptio Mariae*. ... Mary as the bride is united with the son in the heavenly bridal-chamber, and, as Sophia, with the Godhead. This dogma is in every respect timely. In the first place it is a symbolical fulfilment of John's vision. Secondly, it contains an allusion to the marriage of the Lamb at the end of time, and, thirdly, it repeats the Old Testament anamnesis of Sophia. These three references foretell the Incarnation of God. The second and third foretell the Incarnation in Christ, but the first foretells the Incarnation in creaturely man."

[29] *Ibid.*, §755.

[30] *Ibid.*

[31] C.G. Jung, CW 12, *Psychology and Alchemy*, §§418ff. There was already a comparison of the *Sapientia Dei* to a tree in the Bible, and Mary is an earthly image of divine wisdom.

149   From what is said in certain passages in the *missale*, it seems that Brother Klaus connected Mary to the figure of the *Sapientia Dei*, and he interpreted the latter as being the prefigurative form of Mary, as predestined by God. As Jung so impressively outlines in "Answer to Job,"[32] the *Sapientia* represents God's all-knowingness and self-reflection and, through His approximation to her, a *new creation*,[33] which is brought about through God's desire "to regenerate Himself in the mystery of the *heavenly nuptials*."[34] Furthermore, Klaus's devotion to the figure of the *Sapientia* is possibly connected to his last vision, which, as we know, is of the "terrifying countenance of God," a shattering experience which he was forced to grapple with for a long time. Mary, in her divine wisdom and with her benevolence towards man, must have helped him in his struggle.

---

[32] See in particular C.G. Jung, CW 11, *Psychology and Religion*, §609 and §617.
[33] *Ibid.*, §625.
[34] *Ibid.*, §624.

Chapter 12

The Vision of the
Terrifying Face of God

150 Brother Klaus had his terrifying vision between the years 1474 and 1478, that is, somewhere from thirteen to nine years before his death (1487).[1] Woelflin reports that, after the vision, Brother Klaus's visitors were filled with terror when they looked at him. On the origins of this fear, Klaus himself said that it had come about when he saw a *piercing light resembling a human face*. At the sight of it he feared *that his heart would burst into little pieces* and, overcome with terror, he turned his face away and *fell to the ground*.[2] Because of what he had seen, his face had become terrifying (*horribilem*) to others.[3] The humanist Karl Bovillus describes the same vision in 1508:[4] "… a vision appeared to him in the sky, on a night when the stars were shining and he stood in prayer. He saw the head of a human figure with a terrifying face, full of wrath and threats."[5] As Jung points out,[6] a comparison was quickly made between this image and the image of the avenging Christ of Revelation I:13.[7] And, as Jung goes on to show,[8] this vision of light is connected to the star

---

[1] F. Blanke, *Bruder Klaus von Flüe*, p. 37 and pp. 92–95, where these problems of dates are discussed and secondary literature is given.

[2] Author's italics.

[3] C.G. Jung, CW 9/i, *Archetypes and the Collective Unconscious*, §14f. See F. Blanke, *Bruder Klaus von Flüe*, p. 37 who goes on to say: "When Woelflin maintains that all Brother Klaus's visitors felt frightened at his appearance, he is exaggerating. For, of all the pilgrims to the Ranft that we know of, only Bonstetten had this impression. It seems to me that Brother Klaus's frightening appearance, reflecting his terrifying vision of God, has its origins in the comparison of Bonstetten's and Woelflin's statements. One is reminded of Moses whose countenance was so changed by his encounter with God on Mount Sinai that his own people were afraid to approach him (2 Moses 34: 30). Between the laughing Brother Klaus of 1474 and the terrifying Brother Klaus of 1478 lies Klaus's terrifying vision."

[4] C. G. Jung, CW, Vol. 9/i, *Archetypes and the Collective Unconscious*, §14 and §15.

[5] A. Stoeckli, *Die Visionen des seligen Bruder Klaus*, p. 34 (also in R. Duerrer, *Bruder Klaus*, 1: 560). In, C.G. Jung, CW 9/i, *Archetypes and the Collective Unconscious*, §14.

[6] C.G. Jung, CW 9/i, *Archetypes and the Collective Unconscious*, §14.

[7] See also the comments of M.-B. Lavaud that Jung cites in *ibid.*, p. 10, fn. 17.

[8] C.G. Jung, CW 11, *Psychology and Religion*, §479.

which Brother Klaus saw before his birth and to the light which he saw in Liestal. If we compare the three visions of light, then we see that there is a development in the sequence of the motifs: First is the remote star, far out in the cold cosmos; then the radiant light (which stabs and wounds Klaus in the stomach, the seat of emotions); and finally, the radiant light with the terrifying face in it which turns into a primordial experience of the divine in which God reveals Himself as a *person* with a *human face*.

151 However, no mention is made of this last big vision in the parish register of Sachseln. But, as Alban Stoeckli quite rightly emphasises, this does not refute the truth of the other reports.[9] Rather, it more than likely means that Brother Klaus was more reticent about this vision than he was about his other visions.

Face of God Image

---

[9] A. Stoeckli, *Die Visionen des seligen Bruder Klaus*, p. 32f.

152   The biographer Woelflin knows nothing of the wheel image connected to this vision, whereas Bovillus does, and the latter's aforementioned report goes on to say[10] St. Niklaus saw

153   "a face and on the head was a threefold or papal crown, in the middle of which was the small sphere of the world, and on this sphere there was a cross. The face bore a long three-pronged beard. Six sword blades without handles appeared to go out from the face in different directions. One went upwards from the forehead and penetrated the sphere and cross, with its broad end stuck in the forehead and its narrow end pointing upwards. Two other blades emanated from each eye respectively, with their pointed end in the eyes and their broader end pointing upwards. Two sword blades emanated from the nose with their broader end in the nostrils. The sixth sword blade emanated from the mouth with its broad end pointing upwards and the tip of the sword in the mouth. All of these sword blades appeared to be the same. Brother Klaus had this vision painted in his hermitage. I [Bovillus] saw it and my soul comprehended it and it was etched into my memory. As its true meaning has remained hidden from me (although, through its terrifying nature it suggests that mankind is not threatened by small thunderbolts), perhaps you [Heiny am Grund] can better explain what it means ..."

154   Apparently, Bovillus mistook the spokes of the wheel for swords. Nevertheless, it is apparent from his report that these "spokes" (which he called "swords") were connected to the terrifying face in this *single* image and that it is this image which Klaus had painted in his cell.[11] According to Gundolfingen, however, the painting was

---

[10] R. Duerrer, *Bruder Klaus*, Vol. 1. p. 560f. (Trans.).

[11] Stoeckli adds: "The Witwyler report of 1571 according to which 'the above-mentioned original was found in his home in the Ranft' should accordingly be given more importance than Duerrer (R. Duerrer, *Bruder Klaus*, p. 744, fn. 9) supposes." (Trans.) A. Stoeckli, *Die Visionen des seligen Bruder Klaus*, p. 35, fn. 1.

to be found in the Ranft chapel.[12] Compared with Woelflin's report quoted above, in the reports of Bovillus and Gundolfingen mention is at least made of the terrifying vision somehow underlying the image of the wheel.[13] Jung therefore reasoned that the image of the wheel represents, so to speak, an attempt on Brother Klaus's part "to get his original experience into a form he could understand."[14] It was necessary for him to assimilate this terrifying original experience "to fit it into the total structure of the psyche and thus restore the disturbed psychic balance. Brother Klaus came to terms with his experience on the basis of dogma, then firm as a rock; and the dogma proved its powers of assimilation by turning something horribly alive into the beautiful abstraction of the Trinity idea."[15] By electing to live in seclusion and by turning inwards, Brother Klaus saw so deeply into himself "that the wondrous and terrible boon of original experience befell him. In this situation the dogmatic image

---

[12] *Ibid.*, p. 35, suggests several copies existed. See also C.G. Jung, CW 11, *Psychology and Religion*, §476: "Did he not likewise learn in that High School of the Holy Ghost the representation of the wheel, which he caused to be painted in his chapel, and through which, as in a clear mirror, was reflected the entire essence of the Godhead?"

[13] Lately, this has been disputed; see F. Blanke, *Bruder Klaus von Flüe*, pp. 95ff. I, however, agree with C.G. Jung, CW 9/i, *Archetypes and the Collective Unconscious*, §9f., that the picture of the wheel represents a kind of labour of assimilation of his 'terrifying vision.' Jung (*ibid.*, §16) says, "Traditionally, this great vision was brought into connection with the Trinity picture in the church at Sachseln, and so, likewise, was the wheel symbolism in the so-called 'Pilgrim's Tract.' Brother Klaus, we are told, showed the picture of the wheel to a visiting pilgrim. Evidently, this picture had preoccupied him for some time. Blanke is of the opinion that, contrary to tradition, there is no connection between the vision and the Trinity picture. This scepticism seems to me to go too far. There must have been some reason for Brother Klaus's interest in the wheel. Visions like the one he had often cause mental confusion and disintegration (witness the heart bursting 'into little pieces'). We know from experience that the protective circle, the mandala, is the traditional antidote for chaotic states of mind. It is therefore only too clear why Brother Klaus was fascinated by the symbol of the wheel. The interpretation of the terrifying vision as an experience of God need not be so wide of the mark either. The connection between the great vision and the Trinity picture, and of both with the wheel-symbol, therefore seems to me very probable on psychological grounds."

[14] *Ibid.*, §12.

[15] Jung continues (*ibid.*, §17): "But the reconciliation might have taken place on a quite different basis provided by the vision itself and its unearthly actuality—much to the disadvantage of the Christian conception of God and no doubt to the still greater disadvantage of Brother Klaus himself, who would then have become not a saint but a heretic (if not a lunatic) and would probably have ended his life at the stake. This example demonstrates the use of the dogmatic symbol: It formulates a tremendous and dangerously decisive psychic experience, fittingly called an 'experience of the Divine,' in a way that is tolerable to our human understanding, without either limiting the scope of the experience or doing damage to its overwhelming significance. The vision of divine wrath, which we also meet in Jakob Böhme, ill accords with the God of the New Testament, the loving Father in heaven, and for this reason it might easily have become the source of an inner conflict. That would have been quite in keeping with the spirit of the age—the end of the fifteenth century, the time of Nicholas Cusanus, whose formula of the *complexio oppositorum* actually anticipated the schism that was imminent. Not long afterwards, the Yahwistic conception of God went through a series of rebirths in Protestantism. Yahweh is a God-concept that contains the opposites in a still undivided state."

of divinity that had been developed over the centuries worked like a healing draught. It helped him to assimilate the fatal incursion of an archetypal image and so escape being torn asunder."[16] This process of assimilation that Jung is referring to here is also reported in the so-called "Pilgrim's Tract," a document written by an unknown pilgrim whom Brother Klaus visited and who later wrote a devotional tract that has survived in three different editions from the fifteenth century.[17] This pilgrim cannot be identified with any certainty but is most probably Ulrich from Nuremberg whose commentaries formed the basis of the parish register of Sachseln.[18] In his tract, the pilgrim reports,[19]

155   "And he [Brother Klaus] began to speak and said to me, 'I would like to let you see my book which I am studying and whose teaching I am trying to understand.' He showed me the drawing of a wheel with six spokes as shown and he said, 'Do you see this figure? The Divine Being is in the centre, and that is the undivided Godhead in which all saints find joy. The three points which point towards the inner circle are the three persons of the Trinity, and they emanate from the one Godhead and embrace heaven and the whole world over which they have power. And just as they emanate from this

---

[16] Jung continues (*ibid*, §§19–21): "Angelus Silesius was not so fortunate; the inner conflict tore him to pieces, because in his day the stability of the church that dogma guarantees was already shattered. Jakob Böhme, too, knew a God of the 'Wrath-fire,' a real *Deus absconditus*. He was able to bridge the profound and agonizing contradiction on the one hand by means of the Christian formula of Father and Son and embody it speculatively in his view of the world—which, though Gnostic, was in all essential points Christian. Otherwise he would have become a dualist. ... Dogma takes the place of the collective unconscious by formulating its contents on a grand scale. The Catholic way of life is completely unaware of psychological problems in this sense. Almost the entire life of the collective unconscious has been channelled into the dogmatic archetypal ideas and flows along like a well-controlled stream in the symbolism of creed and ritual. It manifests itself in the inwardness of the Catholic psyche. The collective unconscious, as we understand it today, was never a matter of 'psychology', for before the Christian Church existed there were the antique mysteries, and these reach back into the grey mists of Neolithic prehistory. Mankind has never lacked powerful images to lend magical aid against all the uncanny things that live in the depths of the psyche. Always the figures of the unconscious were expressed in protecting and healing images and in this way were expelled from the psyche into cosmic space."
[17] According to A. Stoeckli, *Die Visionen des seligen Bruder Klaus*, p. 36: The first and oldest came from the office of Peter Bergers of Augsburg, without a date, and both of the others were printed by Markus Ayrer of Nuremberg, the first one bearing the date of 1488.
[18] On the probable confusion of this name with Ulrich im Moesli with Eichhorn, see A. Stoeckli, *Die Visionen des seligen Bruder Klaus*, pp. 36–38.
[19] Cited in A. Stoeckli, *Die Visionen des seligen Bruder Klaus*, p. 41f. (Trans.).

Vision Wheel

divine power, so do they return to it and are at one and are indivisible with this everlasting power. That is the meaning of this figure. [...][20] As you can see, within this wheel there is great breadth, from the inward-turning point of the inner circle that ends as a small point.

156 The meaning and form of the spokes corresponds to almighty God ... who, in the form of *a little child*, entered and emerged from the most exalted Virgin without violating her virginity. He has given us this same delicate body as a victual to partake of the indivisible Godhead. As you can see by this spoke which is broad where it meets the inner circle and narrow where it meets the outer circle, the greatness of the all-powerful God is in the *small substance of the host*.[21] Now observe a further spoke of the wheel which is broad where it meets the inner circle and narrow where it meets the outer, that is *the meaning of man's life*, which is small and accessible. In this short time we are able, through God's love, to earn inexpressible joy without end. That is the meaning of my wheel." After making further statements,[22] the pilgrim finishes up by saying, "Thus, as Father

---

[20] There follows a passage on God's anticipation of Mary through His divine wisdom.

[21] Author's italics.

[22] It is about the six medallions as acts of mercy and six keys. On how this is the pilgrim's idea and not Klaus's, see A. Stoeckli, *Die Visionen des seligen Bruder Klaus*, p. 42ff.

Brother Klaus has taught me, you should pay close attention to the inner circle of the aforesaid wheel, and understand it as being the clear *mirror of the true living God.*"

157   The pilgrim's comments omit any clear connection to the face in the vision. Gundolfingen's report, however, supplements them and, along with the "Pilgrim's Tract," is the oldest surviving testimonial.[23] "Did he [Klaus] not likewise learn in that High School of the Holy Ghost the representation of the wheel, which he caused to be painted in his chapel, and through which, as in a *clear mirror*, was reflected the entire essence of the Godhead?"[24] Three rays[25] point towards the divine countenance within the inner circle. The Trinity's three supreme effects emanate from this radiant divine countenance: the creation, the passion of Christ and the annunciation of the Lord from the ear, eye and mouth respectively, and all point in the direction of the broader outer circle, thus embracing both heaven and earth. And just as the scope of the Trinity moves outwards from the points of these rays, so, too, does their scope reverse from the broad end of the three other rays and moves inwards, into the mirror of the divine. Indeed, through our recognition of *perceivable things and the responses they evoke within us,*[26] we can, through logical thinking, come to a recognition of the incomprehensible Divine. The three rays that have their pointed ends touching the mirror of the divine indicate this, for indeed, our intellect moves along the broader path, that is, through our perception of things, towards the essence of the divine which is both fine and pointed. The outer ends of the rays correspond to the essence of the incarnation of the divine in man with its all-embracing and widespread redemption ... " There follows a commentary on the outward-pointing rays which basically corresponds to the "Pilgrim's Tract." These profound pictorial elaborations by Brother Klaus would seem to have been partly inspired by an illustrated tract "*Spiegel menschlicher Behältnis*,"

---

[23] See *ibid.*, p. 43f.
[24] Author's italics. C.G. Jung, CW 11, *Psychology and Religion*, §476.
[25] "Rays" instead of "spokes," according to the pilgrim!
[26] Author's italics.

printed by Anton Sorg in Augsburg in 1476,[27] which, however, is more concerned with the medallions that, as is mentioned above, have nothing to do with Brother Klaus. This tract has relevance as a model for Brother Klaus's wheel picture only in so far as it depicts the Godhead as a three-faced Godhead which Klaus could have seen in one of the many books of Ulrich im Moesli. Indeed, it would seem that Klaus, too, owned such an illustrated booklet.[28] Be that as it may, these sparse materials were the only outer help Brother Klaus had at his disposal to help him understand his vision. In none of them, however, was there an image of a wheel. *The latter would seem to have arisen largely from within Brother Klaus himself.* It gave him, so to speak, a "structural" framework to connect his vision to the images in devotional books and to the descriptions he had given of his vision. Generally speaking, the motif of the wheel is the "ordering principle" par excellence[29] for it is a mandala, a symbol in which the function of creating order is inherent.[30] Here, as Jung points out, it serves to clarify what has been experienced.[31] "Just as a stone, falling into calm water, produces wave after wave of circles, so a sudden and violent vision of this kind has long-lasting after-effects, like any shock. And the stranger and more impressive the initial vision was, the longer it will take to be assimilated, and the greater and more persevering will be the efforts of the mind to master it and render it intelligible to human understanding. Such a vision is a tremendous 'irruption' in the most literal sense of the word, and it has therefore always been customary to draw rings round it like those made by the falling stone when it breaks the smooth surface of the water."[32] … "When we consider that the mental attitude of that age, and in

---

[27] It refers to the "*Speculum humanae salvationis*" (translated 1324). For more, see A Stoeckli, *Die Visionen des seligen Bruder Klaus*, p. 46ff. On the function of the wheel as a symbol, see too F. Weinhandl, *Ueber das aufschliessende Symbol* (Berlin, 1924). The author shows very nicely the symbol's function as a mediator that transports contents to consciousness.

[28] See A. Stoeckli, *Die Visionen des seligen Bruder Klaus*, pp. 47ff and p. 51.

[29] M. Frischknecht, who adopted Jung's interpretation (without stating clearly enough that he was doing so, in my opinion) fills in more detail and shows how this wheel, which was at first a circle, represents an attempt to ward off some kind of spell: M. Frischknecht, "*Das schreckliche Gesicht des Klaus von Flüe,*" *Theologische Zeitschrift*, Universität Basel, 1946, Vol. 1, pp. 23ff.

[30] For this, see C.G. Jung, CW 9/i, *Archetypes and the Collective Unconscious*, §634.

[31] C.G. Jung, CW 11, *Psychology and Religion*, §477.

[32] See Seuse's picture (cited in A. Stoeckli, *Die Visionen des seligen Bruder Klaus*, p. 48 and pp. 56ff.).

particular that of Brother Klaus, allowed no other interpretation than that this vision represented God himself, and that God signified the *summum bonum,* Absolute Perfection, then it is clear that such a vision must, by its violent contrast, have had a profound and shattering effect, whose assimilation into consciousness required years of the most strenuous spiritual effort."[33] ... "Brother Klaus's elucidation of his vision with the help of the three circles (the so-called 'wheel') is in keeping with age-old human practice, which goes back to the Bronze Age sun-wheels (often found in Switzerland) and to the mandalas depicted in the Rhodesian rock-drawings. These sun-wheels may possibly be Palaeolithic; we find them in Mexico, India, Tibet, and China. The Christian mandalas probably date back to St. Augustine and his definition of God as a circle. Presumably Henry Suso's notions of the circle, which were accessible to the 'Friends of God'[34] were derived from the same source. But even if this whole tradition had been cut off and no little treatise with mandalas in the margin had ever come to light, and if Brother Klaus had never seen the rose-window of a church, he would still have succeeded in working his great experience into the shape of a circle, because this is what has always happened in every part of the world and still goes on happening today."[35] Mandalas are indeed "instruments of meditation, concentration, and self-immersion, for the purpose of realizing inner experience ... [and] they serve to produce an inner order." Thus, "they express the idea of a safe refuge, of inner reconciliation and wholeness."[36] In conjunction with this fundamental symbol of inner order which Brother Klaus placed over

---

[33] C.G. Jung, CW 11, *Psychology and Religion,* §478. A little further on (§483) Jung says, as just mentioned: "Brother Klaus's vision was a genuine primordial experience, and it therefore seemed to him particularly necessary to submit it to a thorough dogmatic revision. Loyally and with great efforts he [Klaus] applied himself to this task, the more so as he was smitten with terror in every limb so that even strangers took fright. The unconscious taint of heresy that probably clings to all genuine and unexpurgated visions is only hinted at in the Trinity Vision, but in the touched-up version it has been successfully eliminated. All the affectivity, the very thing that made the strongest impression, has vanished without a trace, thus affording at least a negative proof of our interpretation."

[34] *Ibid.,* §484. See A. Stoeckli, *Die Visionen des seligen Bruder Klaus,* p. 56. This statement comes to us from Alanus de Insulis in medieval scholastic literature and is originally an hermitic citation; cf W. Oehl, "*Bruder Klaus und die deutsche Mystik,*" *Zeitschrift für schweizerische Kirchengeschichte,* Stans 1917, p. 161 and in particular pp. 241ff.

[35] See the evidence and discussions of C.G. Jung, CW 11, *Psychology and Religion,* §484.

[36] C.G. Jung, CW 9/i, *Archetypes and the Collective Unconscious,* §710.

the image that had erupted within his soul, in an attempt, so to speak, to hold it at bay, he also formulated the explanations outlined above, the historical significance of which Stoeckli has already detailed.

158   It seems to me that the fact that Brother Klaus's symbol of the circle is a *six*-spoked wheel is of particular significance. In traditional number symbolism, six is considered to be a perfect number because it is equal to the sum of its divisors. One side of a hexagon within the circle corresponds precisely to the radius. This is why six plays a special role in the cyclical measurement of time (60 minutes, 60 seconds, etc.). Thus, the hexagonal division of the circle has especially to do with time. This aspect of six, consisting of two sets of three, is given special emphasis in number symbolism. Allendy says[37] that the *Ternarius* represents creative logos. But, in the number six, the living creature *reacts* to it, so that six represents the opposition of the living creature to its creator in an uncertain equilibrium. In antiquity, six was the number of Aphrodite and of marriage and, in the Christian tradition, it is a symbol of harmony and perfection.[38] Nevertheless, the latter seems to me to have been understood as being above all *a dynamic phenomenon*, as an action-reaction, that is, as a dynamic inter*action* of two principles. I consider this dynamic aspect to be essential for in Brother Klaus's own explanation, the *effects* of God and his creation, the in*going* and the out*going* of the divine, is particularly emphasised. *Thus Klaus's wheel represents a process rather than a goal*, which in turn lends significance to a further aspect of the wheel as a symbol, namely, the idea of *motion*. Rhys Davids says that, in India, the wheel was thought of as a symbol of becoming.[39] A victorious king, for example, was referred to as "the wheel-turner" because his victorious campaigns extended throughout the entire world. Its meaning is positive in the sense of progressive becoming but negative in the sense of not getting anywhere. This same dynamic aspect can be found in the ἴυγξ symbol of late antiquity. The latter is a "magical

---

[37] René Allendy, *Le symbolisme des nombres*, Paris: Chacornac Freres, 1948, p. 149f.
[38] C.G. Jung, CW 16, *The Practice of Psychotherapy*, §236, fn. 7.
[39] Cf R. Davids, "*Zur Geschichte des Rad-symbols*," *Eranos-Jahrbuch*, Zürich: Rhein Verlag, 1934, p. 162.

wheel" which was used to enchant one's beloved, or even as a synonym for ardent desire.

159   Thus, when Brother Klaus uses the wheel to keep the image of the terrifying divine countenance at bay, it is, in my opinion, an attempt on his part to understand this divine being as *an experiential process,* not, as it were, "in itself," but rather in the *effect* it had upon him. In this context, a further fact draws our attention: The concept of motion is inherent to the wheel. But here the wheel is still, and the dynamic events which Brother Klaus describes take place within the wheel itself, as an interaction between the flowing movement of the spokes. Psychologically speaking, this would seem to point towards an intense introversion of psychic energy within which is the power to heal. This is what is required to make the shock of the terrifying vision easier to bear.

160   In this respect, M.-B. Lavaud has pointed out that this terrifying primordial image of the divine can also be understood from the standpoint of the Christian tradition.[40] He cites Seuse who in his *"Horologium Sapientiae"* (I, VII) says, *"quod divina sapientia amabilis sit pariter et terribilis."*[41] Daniel and Job were also terrified by the countenance of God,[42] as was John in the Revelation of St. John (Rev. 1:17). St. John had an experience of this dark, angry, and vengeful God when he was an old man, about which Jung says,[43] *"In confinio mortis* and in the evening of a long and eventful life a man will often see immense vistas of time stretching out before him. Such a man no longer lives in the everyday world ... but in the sight of many aeons and in the movement of ideas as they pass from century to century."* Thus it happens that "the spirit of God itself ... blows through the weak mortal frame and again demands man's *fear* of the unfathomable Godhead." Apparently, this is precisely what happened to Brother Klaus, too, in his solitude. Although the "terrifying countenance" can be readily understood in connection with the Judaeo-Christian tradition,[44] in my view, it also seems to be related

---

[40] M.-B. Lavaud, *Vie profonde de Nicolas de Flüe,* p. 101f.
[41] That divine wisdom is loving and, at the same time, terrifying.
[42] Holy Bible (KJV), Daniel 7: 9–10; Job 4:15; see also Jeremiah 20:11.
[43] C. G. Jung, *CW,* Vol. 11, *Psychology and Religion,* §717.
[44] Here one could draw a comparison with Jacob Böhme's reference to God's dark, fiery rage.

to the motifs of the dreams and events that preceded it. For this vision seems like a final, powerful self-revelation of that unknown god who had previously become manifest in such Germanic and Wotanlike ways. This terrifying face is indeed the face of the same god who appeared at Brother Klaus's baptism as the unknown old man, who was suggested in the star and glowing light and, finally, who was revealed in the "Berserker" and the "Truth" which the people could not bear. The word "Wotan" is connected to the old-Nordic root word "*othr*" which, as an adjective, means "raging, raving, violent." Added to this is the Gothic word "*wods*" (possessed, insane). As a noun with the same etymological root, it means "gifted poet," "poem," "soul," "mind/spirit," and "intellect." Related to this is the modern Norwegian word "*oda*" or "*ode*" (storm, courage, hot-headedness, lust, sperm)[45] in which the motif of "ecstatic courtly, intimate love" resonates once more.

161   This terrifying element is so central to the god Wotan that a German glossary explains the word "*daemon*" (god) as "terrifying mask." "To have the helmet of terror in one's eye," in Icelandic, means something like "to look at with piercing, flashing eyes." The German word "*Drache*" (dragon) is related to "*derkein*" (to look with flashing eyes).[46] Thus, terror, light, and the terrifying countenance are all mythologically intimately connected. The "Glow of Terror" is what a Nordic skald calls his sword, and we recall that in Brother Klaus's first vision of light, he was so filled with pain, as if his stomach were being slit open with a knife. Thus, we can, then, quite literally talk of an "incisive" experience. Brother Klaus's experience brings to mind Nietzsche's poem "The Lament of Ariadne,"[47] which, as Jung has shown,[48] is, in point of fact, dedicated to the god Wotan:

---

[45] See M. Ninck, *Wodan und germanischer Schicksalsglaube*, p. 31.
[46] *Ibid.*, p. 152: "The dragon *Fafnir* says of itself, 'I wore the helmet of terror to protect myself against humans while I was lying on the gold …'. (Trans.) In Iceland, right up to the present time, the expression 'to have the helmet of terror in his eyes,' in the sense of 'having piercing eyes' is in use. In the south, the old High German masculine names of '*Egihelm*,' '*Agihelm*,' and '*Uogihelm*' have their roots in a similar idea. The German word '*Daemon*' means *egisgrimolt* or '*Schreckensmaske*' (mask of terror)." (Trans.)
[47] Friedrich Nietzsche, *Also sprach Zarathustra*, Leipzig: Alfred Kröner, 1923, Kaufmann, trnas. p. 365.
[48] C.G. Jung, CW 10, *Civilisation in Transition*, §381.

162
Stretched out, shuddering,
Like a half-dead thing whose feet are warmed,
Shaken by unknown fevers,
Shivering with piercing icy frost arrows,
Hunted by thee, O thought,
Unutterable! Veiled! Horrible one!
Thou huntsman behind the clouds.
Struck down by thy lightning bolt,
Thou mocking eye that stares at me from the dark!
Thus I lie,
Writhing, twisting, tormented
With all eternal tortures,
Smitten
By thee, cruel huntsman,
Thou unknown – God!

163   Nietzsche quite rightly felt that this divine figure which he called Dionysus[49] was meant as a *Deus absconditus*, whose claim on modern Christian man we can hardly grasp, but about whom we could perhaps say *one* thing: He appears to represent *a psychic image of God and of wholeness that extends into the cosmos.*[50] This spontaneous aspect of extending into and being within nature is essential. It can be seen as a compensation for the onset of our European uprootedness, along with our alienation from nature that has come about through technology, as well as our loss of Christian faith. The breakdown of a tradition is, as Jung says,[51] "always a loss and a danger; and it is a danger to the soul because the life of instinct—*the most conservative element in man*[52]—always expresses itself in traditional usages. Age-old convictions and customs are deeply rooted in the instincts. If they get lost, the conscious mind becomes

---

[49] *Ibid.*, §383.
[50] *Ibid.*, §394, "At all events, the Germanic god represents a totality on a very primitive level, a psychological condition in which man's will was almost identical with the god's and entirely at his mercy."
[51] C.G. Jung, CW 16, *The Practice of Psychotherapy*, §216.
[52] Author's italics.

severed from the instincts and loses its roots, while the instincts, unable to express themselves, fall back into the unconscious and reinforce its energy." This can, among other things, lead to the destructive mass phenomena which we are experiencing today[53] and which was personified in the image of the "outsiders" in Brother Klaus's fountain vision. The individuation process, however, is a compensation which nature has apparently brought about in response to such a profanity.[54] It is expressed in Brother Klaus's visions in, for example, the figure of the Berserker and in all Klaus's repeated experiences of light. Perhaps we are now better able to understand the fact that the Self (the four lights) seems to ask of Brother Klaus that he be tied down to *one particular place*. That the Self demands a committed relationship to others, indeed, often to particular people, is an empirically provable psychological fact.[55] But here this required individual relationship is extended to include nature. It seems to me that here we have the answer to the question that was touched upon at the beginning, namely, how are we to view the seemingly pagan Germanic aspects in Brother Klaus's visions? To assume, on the one hand, that we are simply dealing with surviving remnants of pre-Christian paganism or, on the other hand, with a regression into paganism, is, in my view, not convincing. The whole context of the visions speaks against this; for example, the motif of the three divine visitors burdening Brother Klaus with the task of being the *bearer of the cross*; the fact that in one vision the "spirit of Truth" appears as a person wearing a bearskin, while in the next vision Klaus is introduced to the *Christian* kingdom of heaven, etc. Thus, one explanation is perhaps more readily to be found in some facts which Jung pointed out to me, namely, that the image of Wotan as a god has two characteristics which Yahweh does not have:

---

[53] C.G. Jung, CW 10, *Civilisation in Transition*, §463.
[54] C.G. Jung, CW 16, *The Practice of Psychotherapy*, §219, "But at this point a healthful, compensatory operation comes into play which each time seems to me like a miracle. Struggling against that dangerous trend towards disintegration, there arises out of this same collective unconscious a counteraction, characterized by symbols which point unmistakably to a process of centring. This process creates nothing less than a *new centre of personality*, which the symbols show from the first to be superordinate to the ego..." (author's italics).
[55] *Ibid.*, §444.

firstly, *an intense relationship to cosmic nature;* and secondly, *the practice of casting of sticks or bones and the throwing of the runes,* a realm Wotan is master of, in other words, *his alignment with the principle of synchronicity.*[56] These two characteristics are almost completely missing in the figure of Yahweh, yet they are, apparently, a part of a complete god-image which would seem to encompass not only darkness and evil, but also cosmic nature and its meaningful manifestations in synchronistic events. It is only when these aspects are taken into account that an individual encounter with the divine *hic et nunc* is possible in which the *genius loci* and *nature that surrounds it come together in a meaningful way within the psychic realm of an individual,* allowing him to perceive everything as being part of the *one* cosmos.[57] However, psychologically speaking, this represents *a tremendous increase in the value placed upon the meaning that is found in each individual's life*—an increase which brings him to the brink of deification and places supreme importance upon both his conscious understanding and his ethical behaviour.

164 The relationship Brother Klaus had to nature, which was constellated through invasive archetypal contents, meant that he represented not only a typical Christian saint, but that he simultaneously embodied the ancient image of the primitive medicine man, the Nordic shaman and the prophet. It is as if an ancient "pattern" of the individuation process had returned, but on a higher level, so that it might be reconciled with the spiritual development of Christianity, thereby broadening the latter to include this new dimension of nature. Accordingly, Brother Klaus's inner experiences and his lonely effort to realise them map out the individuation process of modern man. His visions, however, reveal with impressive clarity certain basic tendencies of the collective unconscious that strive to further develop the Christian religious

---

[56] Yahweh is indeed present at the burning of the thorn-bush, but as the ruler of the heavenly host of stars he allows rain to fall upon the just and unjust alike. In comparison, however, to the other Mediterranean pre-Christian religions, Yahweh's relationship to nature plays a much less important role. As Dr. Siegmund Hurwitz has pointed out to me, while oracles were used in the Jewish religion to determine God's will, it was, nevertheless, only a latent characteristic and did not dominate.

[57] Compare what Jung has said about the *unus mundus* in C.G. Jung, CW 14, *Mysterium Coniunctionis,* §§759–775.

symbol. Thus, they act as points of reference that show us where we stand and where the unconscious psyche wants to bring us, namely, to a deeper realization of the problem of the opposites and thereby to both a greater nearness to God and to a greater fear of Him.

Book 2

The Passion of Perpetua: A Psychological Interpretation of Her Visions

◊

Original Editor's Foreword

The substance of this book, originally written in German and published in 1951 with C.G. Jung, is Marie-Louise von Franz's discussion and interpretation of the dreams—sometimes referred to as visions—of St. Perpetua, an African Christian martyred in A.D. 203. As Dr. von Franz notes in her introduction, her study grew out of a book report she undertook as a member of a seminar led by Jung.

This material was first published in an English translation by the late Elizabeth Welsh in the journal *Spring 1949* under the title "The Passio Perpetua." In 1980, it was published by Spring Publications in its Jungian Classics Series. The text presented here is based on the 1980 Spring edition. I added the appendix, chose the illustrations and compiled the bibliography. Some references have been added or updated. The sources for some quoted material could not be found.

There are perhaps many readers who have never heard of St. Perpetua (patron saint of mothers in the Catholic pantheon) but who nevertheless have this book in hand because they appreciate the psychological understanding that Dr. von Franz brought to everything she focused on—alchemical texts, fairytales, dreams, Jung's model of typology, and much, much more.

I think they will not be disappointed.

Daryl Sharp

◊

Introduction

¹⁶⁵ The present essay originated in Professor C.G. Jung's seminar at the Eidgenossische Technische Hochschule (ETH), being the outcome of a report on a book which contained the visions of St. Perpetua. These visions made such an impression on me that I attempted their psychological interpretation.

¹⁶⁶ One might well question both the sense of applying a modern form of psychological interpretation to this series of visions and the extent to which it is justifiable from the historical point of view. For such a method cannot fail to reveal connections which lie neither within Perpetua's own spiritual range nor within that of her time.

¹⁶⁷ Perpetua actually interpreted her own visions, as the text shows. For instance, to her, the dragon of the first vision was the devil, whose aim it was to deter her from going the way of her martyrdom, while the shepherd who gave her the sweet-tasting food represented Christ. Her interpretations were accepted by the nascent Church of her day, and also later. Even today, their message remains compatible with Church teachings and meaningful for many.

¹⁶⁸ Nevertheless, it seems to me that an attempt at an interpretation based on the scientific hypotheses of C.G. Jung's school of analytical psychology might throw light on some new and perhaps important factors.

¹⁶⁹ The divine hypostases in the Christian conception of the world are accepted as absolute metaphysical reality in the dogma. They did not reveal themselves in some place outside the human sphere (which would be a contradiction in itself, inasmuch as revelation implies the human being who receives the message); thus, we must conclude that these realities were experienced as a living totality— that is, by the human *soul* (the psyche). In fact, it was only in this way that such realities were able to become the formulated content

of a creed—thanks to the testimony of human beings. It was the record in the Gospels and the witness of St. Paul that built up the image of Christ as we know it.

170   At the same time, it was above all the experiences of single individuals in visions and dreams (like those of St. Perpetua) which confirmed the collective faith—that is to say, the conviction that God had really become man in Christ. These individual experiences gave real foundation to the doctrine.

171   Dreams and visions are statements made by the human soul in a realm where consciousness and its conceptions are excluded. If we consider these spontaneous unconscious statements of the soul, we are able to perceive the Christian conception of the world originating in them as a phenomenon in itself. We can leave aside all that a philosophical knowledge, derived from the already existing cultures of antiquity, contributed to it, as well as all that was added by the theological interpretations and the theoretical and political deliberations of the ecclesiastical councils.

172   It is true that these additions were creative acts of human consciousness which gave meaning and reality to the soul's spontaneous statements, but at the same time these additions caught and imprisoned the statements of the soul in a formulation which was dependent on the historical situation, and consequently transitory. Therefore, we are justified, I think, in attempting a new and wider formulation of the same phenomena from a modern psychological standpoint, though we are fully aware that this new interpretation must also be transitory.

173   Viewed from this perspective, it would be inadmissible to look upon the dragon of Perpetua's first vision simply and solely as the dogmatic figure of the devil. According to our scientific working hypothesis, we must take the dragon simply as it appears—that is to say, as a dream-image of a dragon and, inasmuch as it occurs frequently in myths and dreams, as the archetype of the dragon.

174   In this case, the interpretation has to be reached through amplification, that is, by recalling similar images of dragons for comparison, a method which may not allow us to define the psychic

meaning of the image by means of an abstract concept but will enable us to describe it in a way which at least throws light upon the underlying energic processes.

175   For instance, the a priori interpretation of the dragon as the devil excludes every positive element in this figure, while the psychological way of considering it reveals quite unmistakably a positive as well as a negative aspect—a duality in the image of the dragon which throws a completely new light on the whole vision.

176   Naturally, the same argument applies to all the images and motifs appearing in the visions. As most of these are archetypal—which means that there exists a practically inexhaustible store of comparative material—I have confined myself principally to material from Perpetua's time and have endeavored to show how these images appeared to people of that era in their conscious minds, and even more in spontaneous manifestations of the unconscious which welled up quite regardless of the consciously held creed.

177   This may perhaps lead to a new understanding of that significant epoch, inasmuch as the unprejudiced eye will then be able to perceive the birth of the Christian faith at its very source: in the soul of the human being at that time.

◊

Chapter 14
The Text

178   The text of the "Passio Perpetuae et Felicitas," which describes the last days of the African martyrs Perpetua and Felicitas and their fellow sufferers, was discovered about the middle of the 17th century by Lukas Holsten among manuscripts coming from Monte Cassino. It was edited by P. Poussines and soon afterward—in the year 1668— was included in the *Acta Sanctorum.* A Greek version was found in Jerusalem in 1889 and published the following year.

179   Opinion is still divided as to which is the original text, but most scholars are inclined to look upon the Greek version either as an independent text or as a translation.[1]

180   A great number of noted theologians attribute the account to the Father of the Church, Tertullian. (The visions, on the other hand, are recorded by the martyrs themselves.) The proofs given by J.A. Robinson in his stylistic examination of the text are, to my mind, convincing evidence in favor of Tertullian's authorship.

181   Actually, Tertullian's claim is disputed mainly because, when making mention of the visions in his later writings, he says that Perpetua met only martyrs in the next world. This led to the conclusion that he had confused her visions with the vision of Saturus (a fellow martyr whose mandala vision is also recorded in the "Passio Perpetuae").[2] In my opinion, however, this refers—as Robinson points out—to the many people clad in white whom Perpetua, in her first vision, meets in the World Beyond.

---

[1] For the history of the text, see, among others "The Passion of St. Perpetua," in J.A. Robinson, *Texts and Studies: Contributions to Biblical and Patristic Literature,* vol. 1; and P. Franchi de Cavalieri, *La Passio SS. Perpetuae et Felicitatis.*

[2] See Tertullian, *de Anima* 55, 4. [For English, see A. Roberts and J. Donaldson, eds. *The Ante-Nicene Fathers: Translations of the Writings of the Fathers Down to A.D. 325,* vol. 5. Saturus's vision is given here in an appendix.—Ed.]

182   In any case, Tertullian was in close connection with the martyrs whose sufferings are described in the text. Perpetua, Felicitas, and their fellow martyrs (Satuminus, Secundulus, Renovatus, and Saturus) were all put to death in Carthage in A.D. 203, during the time that Tertullian was its bishop.

Chapter 15
The Problem of the Orthodoxy
of the Martyrs

183 Theologians have always differed on whether or not the martyrs belonged to the sect of the Montanists, which Tertullian himself joined about A.D. 205-207, a step which led to his break with the Church.[1]

184 Indeed, the author of the text appears to have had fairly strong Montanist leanings, but we do not know if the martyrs were of the same persuasion. The Montanist movement, which was by no means unimportant in Africa at that time, goes back to Lucius Montanus, a Phrygian from Pepuza who had presumably been a priest of Cybele before his conversion to Christianity.[2] We hear of him first about the middle of the second century. In fits of frenzied ecstasy accompanied by ravings and convulsions (as was customary in the Great Mother cults of Asia Minor), he poured forth new revelations in the name of the Paraclete or even in the names of God the Father and God the Son. He proclaimed himself to be the founder of a new "Church of the Spirit."

185 Among his female followers, Maximilla and Prisca were particularly conspicuous, chiefly for spreading prophecies concerning the coming end of the world. In fact, the whole attitude of Montanism was closely bound up with this expectation. The movement was called "New Prophecy" and claimed that its oracles (imparted by the Spirit) marked a new era of revelation comparable to those of the Old and New Testaments.

---

[1] [For a psychological perspective on Tertullian and his association with the Montanists, see Edward F. Edinger, *The Psyche in Antiquity, Book 2: Gnosticism and Early Christianity*, pp. 105ff.—Ed.]

[2] See P. de Labriolle, *La Crise Montaniste.*

186   The Montanists divided history into three periods corresponding to the three hypostases of the Trinity—that of the Father, that of the Son, and that of the Holy Ghost. Tertullian, for instance, says:

187   So too, righteousness—for the God of righteousness and of creation is the same—was first in a rudimentary state, having a natural fear of God; from that stage it advanced, through the Law and the Prophets, to infancy; from that stage it passed, through the Gospel, to the fervor of youth; now, through the Paraclete, it is settling into maturity.

188   Thus, the new revelation takes place through the Paraclete, whose coming after his death Christ had promised:

189   And I will pray the Father, and he shall give you another Comforter [Paraclitum], that he may abide with you for ever; even the Spirit of Truth; whom the world cannot receive, because it seeth him not, neither know him: but ye know him; for he dwelleth with you, and shall be in you.

   (John 14: 16-17)[3]

190   The author of the "Passio Perpetuae" also emphasizes the approaching end, inasmuch as he refers to the Acts of the Apostles:

191   And it shall come to pass in the last days, saith God, I will pour out of my Spirit upon all flesh: and your sons and daughters shall prophesy, and your young men shall see visions, and your old men shall dream dreams. (Acts 2:17)

192   He further admits that he recognizes later visions besides the prophecies of the Old and New Testaments as sources of revelation, by which he proves himself to be a Montanist. In view of the approaching second coming of Christ, the Montanists urged the observance of unusually severe penitential exercises and rigorously strict habits, and in this also, Tertullian supported them. They called

---

[3] [Biblical references throughout are to the Authorized King James Version.—Ed.]

themselves *Pneumatikoi,* in contrast to the Catholic *Psychikoi,* and claimed, in opposition to the Catholic bishops, that they constituted the true spiritual Church of which only those who accepted the Paraclete could be members.

193   There were already Montanists in Rome about the year A.D. 200 (Their principal representatives were Proclus and Aeschines.) Judging by the papal decrees issued against the Montanists, the sect must have survived well into the eighth century. In spite of the movement's dogmatic orthodoxy, the Church opposed it on account of its wildly ecstatic and all too rigorous elements, its complete denial of the world, and the consequent danger that, on the ground of individual revelations, it might destroy the unity and temporal order of the Church—but above all, because it recognized the right of women to teach. There is obviously a connection here with the orgiastic Great Mother cults of Asia Minor, and it would seem that the spirit of the latter must unconsciously have found its way into Montanism.

194   The Church itself, it is true, has never denied the possibility of divine Revelation through dreams and visions, but these acquired far greater importance with the Montanists, for they regarded them as the most evident manifestation of the Paraclete. In their religious ardor, and true to the spiritual attitude which led them to shun the world, they often sought a martyr's death of their own accord. We are inclined, therefore, to assume that the martyrs whose ecstatic behavior is particularly striking must have belonged to the Montanists, but it is just as probable that they had only been influenced by them and had not yet gone far enough in this direction to be in conflict with the Church.

195   The psychological importance of the visions recorded in the "Passio Perpetuae," which is our chief concern, lies above all in the fact that they enable us to gain a deep insight into the unconscious spiritual situation of the time. We find archetypal images constellated in them which we also encounter in the literature of that epoch, when the *Weltanschauung* of antiquity was dissolving and the Christian conception of the world was breaking through. They

appear here spontaneously in an unusual person, at an unusually tragic moment of her life, and lay bare the whole deep conflict of that time.

196   This record of an ancient series of four visions or dreams, occurring within a relatively short space of time (about 14 days), is also quite exceptional. Usually, the dreams handed down to us from antiquity—for instance by Artemidorus and Synesius—contain only single examples, and if there is any account of the conscious situation of the dreamer, it is always insufficient.

◊
Chapter 16
The Life of St. Perpetua

197   Where St. Perpetua is concerned, fortunately we are in possession of some facts. She came of a wealthy family, the Vibii, and at the time of her execution was twenty-two years of age. Her parents were still living, and her father—who was not a Christian—fought desperately up to the very last in hopes of prevailing upon his daughter to give up her resolve and recant.

198   Perpetua married quite young and had a son, whom she was still nursing and who was brought to her several times in prison. Strangely enough, her husband is never mentioned. She had two brothers, one of whom was likewise a catechumen.[1] A third brother, Dinocrates, who features in her second and third visions, had died a pagan at the age of seven.

199   Perpetua herself was baptized only twenty days before her death. She is reported to have said at the time:

200   I was inspired by the Spirit not to ask for any other favor after the [baptismal] water but simply the perseverance [suffering] of the flesh.[2]

---

[1] [One who is being taught the principles of Christianity.—Ed.]
[2] Herbert Musurillo, trans., "Perpetua," in *The Acts of the Christian Martyrs,* p. 109.

◇

Chapter 17
The Visions of St. Perpetua

201 Whereas the facts of her life and the description of her martyrdom are contributed by another hand, the visions—or rather dreams—are recorded by Perpetua herself. She had the first vision in prison after a visit from her brother. The text runs as follows:[1]

202 My brother then said to me: "Sister, thou hast already traveled so far on the Christian road that thou canst now ask for a vision, and it shall be shown thee whether the passion awaits thee, or thy release."[2] And, mindful that I was in the habit of holding converse [colloquies] with God, who had so abundantly blessed me with his favors, and strong in faith and trust, I promised to report it to him [my brother] on the morrow. And I called [for the vision] and the following was shown to me:

203 I beheld[3] a ladder of brass, of miraculous size, which reached up to Heaven, and was so narrow that it could only be ascended *singly*. On either side of the ladder, all manner of iron implements were fastened— swords, lances, hooks, daggers and spears—so that anyone who was careless, or who did not hold himself erect while climbing, was torn to pieces and remained hanging. Beneath the ladder was a gigantic dragon, lying in wait for the climbers and frightening them away.

---

[1] I have rendered the text of the visions myself from various sources, including W.H. Shewring, *The Passion of SS. Perpetua and Felicity*; E.C.E. Owen, *Some Authentic Acts of Early Martyrs;* and Roberts and Donaldson, eds.. *The Ante-Nicene Fathers,* vol. 5, pp. 700ff.

[2] ["Passion" here refers to martyrdom, an archaic use of the word.—Ed.]

[3] Literally, "I behold." Perpetua uses the present tense of this verb both here and in the following visions.

204 Saturus, however, went up before me (just as he later chose to be put to death first, for love of us, because he it was who had taught us, but afterward was not with us when we were thrown into prison). And he reached the top of the ladder and, turning to me, spake: "Perpetua, I am holding thee, but see that the dragon does not bite thee." And I answered: "He shall not harm me, in the name of Jesus Christ." And the dragon slowly lifted his head out from under the ladder, as if in fear of me, and I trod on it, as though I were treading on the first rung of the ladder, and ascended to the top.

205 And I beheld a vast garden and, seated in the center of it, a tall white-haired man, in shepherd's dress, who was milking sheep, and round about him were many thousands of people clad in white. And he raised his head, looked at me, and spake: "It is well that thou art come, child!" And he called me to him and gave me also a morsel of the cheese which he was milking, and I received it with folded hands and ate. And all who stood round said, "Amen."

206 And at the sound of this invocation I awoke, and was aware that I was still eating something sweet, I know not what. And I immediately reported the vision to my brother, and we understood that it meant the coming passion. And from that time we began to put no more hope in this world.

207 The second vision, following her condemnation, goes like this:

A few days later, as we were all praying, a word suddenly burst from my lips, in the middle of the prayer, and I said, "Dinocrates!" And I started, for he had never entered my mind before, and I was pained at the recollection of his fate. And I knew immediately that I was held worthy to pray for him, and I began to intercede for him, and prayed at great length, lifting up my voice in lamentation.

208   And forthwith, in the same night, the following was shown to me: I beheld Dinocrates, coming forth from a dark place, where there were many other people, glowing with fever and thirsty, his face dirty and pale, and showing the wound in it which he had when he died. This Dinocrates had been my own brother, who succumbed to a cancer of the face at the age of seven in the most frightful circumstances, so that his death was a source of horror and dismay to everybody. It was for this child that I had prayed; and between myself and him there was a great distance, so that we could not reach one another.

209   In the place where Dinocrates stood there was also a *piscina* [basin], filled with water, whose rim was higher than the boy, and Dinocrates reached up as if to drink. But I was pained at the thought that the *piscina* was full of water, and yet that he could not drink on account of the height of its rim. And I awoke, and knew that my brother was in need, but I was confident that I would be able to help him in his need, and I prayed for him daily till we were taken over to the prison of the Proconsular palace; for we were to fight in the amphitheater. That was [just] the time of Caesar Geta's birthday. And I prayed for [Dinocrates], groaning and weeping night and day, that fulfillment might be granted me for his sake.

210   Here is Perpetua's third vision:

  The day that we remained in the prison I was shown the following: I beheld the same dark place which I had seen before (now quite light) and Dinocrates, with a clean body and well clothed, was refreshing himself.

211   And where the wound was, only a scar was to be seen; and the *piscina* which I had perceived before had lowered its rim to the height of the boy's navel, and he drank from it without ceasing, and on its edge stood a golden flask filled with water,

and Dinocrates went up to it and began to drink out of it and it never became empty.

212   Content and happy, he then went off to play as children do—and I awoke. Then I understood that he had been removed from the place of punishment.

213   The fourth vision follows:[4]

On the day before we were to fight [with the beasts], I saw the deacon Pomponius, in a vision, come to the prison door and knock violently. I went out and opened to him, and he wore a white festive toga, without a girdle, and manifold [elaborate] shoes, and he spake to me: "Perpetua, we are awaiting thee, come!"

214   And he took my hand, and we began to walk through a rough and pathless country. Toiling and panting, we came at length to the amphitheater and he led me into the middle of the arena and spake to me; "Fear not, I am here with thee and shall fight with thee," and departed.

215   I beheld a huge crowd tense with expectation. And as 1 knew that I was to be brought before the beasts, I marveled that they were not let in. [Instead] an Egyptian of horrible appearance came out with his attendants to fight against me. Fair young men, my attendants and friends, came to me also and I was undressed and changed into a man.

216   My attendants began to rub me with oil, as was the custom before an *agon;* whereas I saw the Egyptian rolling himself in the dust. And there then came forth a man of miraculous size, so that he almost towered above the whole amphitheater, wearing a festive tunic, without a girdle, with a purple undergarment, which appeared across the middle of his chest between two other purple stripes falling from his shoulders and manifold shoes made of gold and silver.

---

[4] In this account, I have followed the translation in Shewring, *The Passion of SS. Perpetua and Felicity.*

217 He carried a rod, like a trainer of gladiators *[lanista]*, and a green bough, on which hung golden apples. And he called for silence and spake: "This Egyptian here, if he is victorious, will kill her with the sword, and if she vanquishes him, she will receive this bough." Thereupon he withdrew.

218 And we fell upon each other and began to deal blows with our fists. He endeavored to seize me by the feet. But I trod upon his face with the soles of my feet and I was lifted up in the air and began to trample him as if I myself no longer touched the ground. But when I saw that I was getting no further in this way, I clasped my hands together and seized his head, then he fell upon his face and I trod upon his head. And the people began to shout and my assistants to jubilate.

219 I, however, went up to the *lanista* and received the bough. And he kissed me and spake: "Daughter, peace be with thee." Then, wreathed in glory, I began to go toward the gate of the pardoned *[porta sanavivariaj]*.

220 And I awoke and understood that it was not with the beasts, but against the devil that I should have to fight, but I knew the victory would be mine.

221 The main facts of the actual ensuing martyrdom, which were contributed by yet a third hand, are as follows.

222 When Perpetua was led into the arena, she and the others sang psalms in ecstatic exaltation. She was immediately knocked down by a mad cow, which was let loose upon her so that her dress tore, whereupon she tried anxiously to hide her nakedness and to put up her hair, which had fallen loose. Then, she gave her hand to her fellow martyr Felicitas in order to help her rise.

223 The crowd could not help being impressed by such a scene and pardoned her to the extent that she should be put to death by the sword. The gladiator, who was a novice, thrust

the sword into her ribs with an unsteady hand and hit bone. Perpetua groaned aloud, and according to an eyewitness, took the trembling hand of the young gladiator and guided it to her throat. ... It was as though so great a woman, feared as she was by the unclean spirit, could not be dispatched unless she herself were willing.[5]

---

[5] Musurillo, trans., "Perpetua," in *Acts of the Christian Martyrs*, p. 131.

Chapter 18
Interpretation of the First Vision

224   That is the account of the "Passio Perpetuae." Concerning the genuineness of the visions, which is occasionally, if rarely, a subject of controversy,[1] the general impression they give seems somehow to banish any thought of their being a literary fiction.

225   Moreover, considered from a psychological point of view, they contain not a single purely Christian motif; rather, they contain only archetypal images common to the pagan, Gnostic, and Christian worlds of that time. Had the visions been invented for the sake of edification, the author would most certainly have made use of exclusively Christian motifs. As it is, Christian authors have not known what to make of, for instance, Perpetua's transformation into a man in the last vision.

226   One would hardly, moreover, invent such an incident as that of Dinocrates's name suddenly jumping into Perpetua's mind—her second vision—when she should have been attending to her prayers, to say nothing of her dream, or fourth vision, the following night.

227   In addition, a psychological interpretation reveals a connecting inner thread running through all four visions, a thread that is by no means evident in the outer motifs. It only comes to light through the interpretation and, therefore, could not possibly have been invented by a person of that time.

228   Perpetua had the first of the visions or dreams as an answer to a definite question that had arisen in her consciousness: Was she destined to suffer martyrdom or not? It was by no means uncommon at that time to call for or invite visions in this way; indeed, it was a generally widespread custom in both the pagan and Christian

---

[1] See Joh. J. Zitntnermann, *Disquisitiones Historicae et Theologicae, de Visionibus.*

worlds. In the so-called incubation oracles, it was customary to call upon the Deity for dreams in answer to definite questions. This practice, moreover, was not limited to the sacred places, and thus numerous prescriptions for bringing about true dreams have been preserved in the magic papyri.[2] Perpetua was confident of receiving an answer because, as she said, she "often held converse [conversations] with God."

229   The vision granted to her on the following night clearly states her psychological situation; she stands before a narrow ladder at the foot of which lies a dragon. This ladder leads up to a heavenly Garden of Eden. At first glance, the picture immediately recalls Jacob's ladder, which "reached to heaven" (Gen. 28:12), but the conception itself appears originally to have been old Egyptian, figuring in the Egyptian mysteries as a stair with seven gates or seven steps, symbolizing the seven planetary spheres through which the soul had to ascend to God after death. A *klimax heptapylos*— expressing the idea of ascending out of the different metals belonging to the planets (lead, tin, iron, mercury, an alloy for Venus, silver, gold) by means of a stair with seven gates—was likewise associated with the Mithraic mysteries.[3]

230   The *heptaporos bathmis* (stair of seven steps) of the Chaldean oracles or the 80 steps of punishment in the cult of Mithras, mentioned by the mythographer Nonnos, were similar conceptions.

231   A further parallel is to be found in the visions of the philosopher Zosimos; he likewise sees in a dream an altar in the shape of a shallow bowl to which 15 steps lead up.[4] There, he perceives the place of the *askese,* or punishment, where people are cooked in boiling water in order that they may become *pneumata* (spirit beings).

232   The stair or ladder, therefore, has the meaning of a process of spiritualization, a development in the form of steps, leading to a

---

[2] [The so-called magic papyri are a collection of magical spells, formulas, hymns, and rituals from Greco-Roman Egypt, second century B.C. to fifth century A.D. See Hans Dieter Betz, ed. *The Greek Magical Papyri in Translation: Including the Demotic Spells*— Ed.]

[3] See F. Cumont, *Textes et monuments figures relatifs aux mystères de Mithra,* II: 27.

[4] See "The Visions *of* Zosimos," *Alchemical Studies,* CW 13, pars. 85ff. [CW refers throughout to *The Collected Works of C.G. Jung*]

Jacob's Ladder by William Blake

higher state of consciousness.[5] Thus, for instance (as Professor Jung has brought to our notice), an alchemist, Blasius Vigenerus, says that "through the symbols, or signs, or attributes of God," which originate in the visible world, we "should be lifted up, as on a Jacob's ladder or Homer's golden chain, to the knowledge of the spiritual and intelligible things."[6]

233   This ascending process of transformation was sometimes dangerous and a real torture, as may be seen in the Zosimos visions. In Perpetua's vision, there are iron implements fastened to the ladder to tear the unwary climber to pieces. Added to this, the ladder can only be climbed singly, and there is no turning back. This picture undoubtedly contains a suggestion of her coming martyrdom. For instance, a contemporary source describes how the martyrs built, as it were, a ladder leading up to the gates of Heaven out of the steps of their sufferings, the instruments of their torture. It is surely for this reason that Perpetua's dream represents martyrdom in the form of a ladder, in order to convey that, seen from the psychic level, it has the meaning of a *transitus* to a higher state of consciousness; thus, the dream enables her to perceive the inner meaning of the event, the realization of which prepares her to meet her imminent fate.

234   The fact that the ladder can only be climbed singly shows that this road to higher consciousness is an individual path which ultimately must be trodden alone. The necessity of looking ahead—and on no account glancing back—is surely founded on the knowledge that when once the possibility of attaining a higher state of consciousness has arisen, one cannot return to a condition of unconsciousness without imperiling the soul. Indeed, the undertaking is fraught with such difficulties that a single backward glance (as in the cases of Lot's wife and of Orpheus) suffices for a weak nature to be again overpowered by the tremendous force of the unconscious.

235   The idea that climbing upward on the ladder means a progression to a higher state of consciousness—and at the same time

---

[5] See *Psychology and Alchemy*, CW 12, par. 80.
[6] "Tractatus de Igne et Sale," in *Theatrum Chemicum*, VI:31.

a painful *transitus*—is also expressed by the Syrian poet Jacob of Batnae, in regard to Sarug's singular conception of Jacob's ladder as a prefiguration of Christ's death upon the cross:

236   The cross is set up as a wonderful ladder upon which mankind is in truth led up to heaven. ... Christ arose upon earth as a ladder of many steps, and raised Himself on high, so that all earthly beings might be exalted through Him. ... In the ladder, Jacob truly perceived the crucified one. ... On the mountain. He [the Lord] made fast the mysterious cross, like a ladder, set Himself on the top of it and from thence blessed all the nations. ... At that time, the cross was set up as a guiding ideal, as it were a ladder, and served all peoples as a path leading up to God.[7]

237   Saturus, later Perpetua's fellow martyr, now ascends before her (in the dream) and endeavors to instill courage into her. In reality, this Saturus had not been imprisoned at the same time as Perpetua, Felicitas, and their other fellow martyrs, but he subsequently behaved toward the authorities in such an aggressive way that he likewise ended up in prison. He did this deliberately in order to be able to help the others spiritually and strengthen them in their faith. So, he was one of those who sought a martyr's death passionately and of their own free will. That is the reason why Perpetua interprets her dream—in this respect—objectively, as an anticipation of the real event, just as the instruments of torture attached to the ladder led her to conclude that she would have to face martyrdom.

238   Undoubtedly, the whole vision has a "prognostic" value, but when we compare the entire proceeding in it with the actual fulfillment, it becomes evident that it has been transferred to the mythological level. For instance, martyrdom is not represented as such but as a ladder leading up to heaven; and it is a dragon—in other words a purely mythological figure—that tries to hinder Perpetua's ascent. It is as though the dream were intent on representing the real and deeper meaning of the event threatening the dreamer in the outer world in order thereby to prepare her for

---

[7] My translation, from "Die Vision Jakobs von Beth-El," in P.S. Landesdörfer, ed., *Ausgewahlte Schriften der syrischen Dichter,* p. 87. As Professor Jung brought to my notice, the Virgin Mary was also described as *scala efferens a terra in coelum.* (Pitra, *Analecta sacra.* 1, p. 264)

her inescapable fate. Therefore, it displays the archetypal background of this fate.

239   In such an inner connection, Saturus also becomes a symbolic image: He represents the Christian spiritual attitude of the fanatical believer, or in other words a Christian animus figure in Perpetua herself.

240   As the unconscious consists in the first place of all the parts of the personality which—mainly for reasons of outer adaptation—have not been integrated into consciousness, its character is specifically complementary to that of consciousness. It is therefore usually embodied in an archetypal figure of the opposite sex which transmits the contents of the collective unconscious. Hence, by "animus," we mean the personification of all the masculine components of a feminine personality, a woman's unlived traits which have remained in the unconscious background.

241   In the case of a man, the anima embodies chiefly his affects, feelings, and emotions, while a woman's animus represents rather an a priori opinion or conviction of a collective nature which arises from the unconscious. A conviction of this kind can indeed take possession of a woman with such demonic and passionate force that it is capable of completely destroying her feminine existence. But the animus also possesses creative power: It is the *logos spermatikos* (the spermatic Word) which transmits new contents from the unconscious.[8]

242   Inasmuch as Perpetua—judging from the slender knowledge we possess of her personal life—had lived a thoroughly feminine existence as a wife and mother, all her traditionally masculine traits such as courage, determination, the power to stand unflinchingly by a conviction even in the face of death—traits which break through to a striking extent in her martyrdom—are chiefly embodied in the unconscious animus figure and are projected onto Saturus, who, we are told, first converted her to Christianity.

---

[8] See "Anima and Animus," *Two Essays on Analytical Psychology,* CW 7, par. 336; also Emma Jung, "On the Nature of the Animus," in her *Animus and Anima.*

243   In other words, she experiences and sees in Saturus these qualities which he evidently actually possessed to a high degree. Hence, it becomes apparent through the dream that Perpetua's Christian spiritual attitude was not mainly a consciously integrated one, acquired through the Christian teaching (which was indeed unlikely, seeing that the latter had been of such very short duration). It was rather a passionate conviction which arose from the unconscious, a spiritual state of emotional possession which took hold of her completely and drew her fatefully into the collective problem of her time—the problem to which her individual existence was destined to succumb.

244   When the dream depicts Saturus ascending the ladder before her, it shows precisely—on the subjective level—that this masculine spiritual attitude in Perpetua herself, which had hitherto remained unconscious, has now taken over the lead. The unconscious thus parallels consciousness and supports it in the fulfillment of a new type, that of the Christian.

245   At the foot of the ladder, however, lies a dragon which endeavors to prevent her from climbing. In Christian imagery, the dragon, or serpent, has become a symbol for the devil, as "leviathan … the dragon that is in the sea" (Isa. 27:1), or as the tempter in the Garden of Eden. In most dualistic religious systems, the dragon generally plays the role of a chthonic, wicked demon, the enemy of light, usually of a feminine nature. As a cold-blooded animal, however, with a very small development of the cerebrum, the serpent chiefly signifies the system of reflexes (the basal ganglia and the spinal cord), the instinctive psyche or "nature-spirit," or simply the unconscious. As far back as the teaching of the Gnostic sect of the Perates, the serpent was identified with the cerebellum and the spinal cord. In the macrocosm, the Father corresponded to the cerebrum, but the cerebellum was associated with the Son, the Redeemer—that is, with the serpent (as Logos). The serpent conveyed the pneumatic substance to the spinal cord, which in turn brought forth the seed of all creatures.[9]

---

[9] Hippolytus, *Elenchos* V, 17, pp. 1 Iff.

246   In pre-Christian antiquity, in Gnosticism, and also in its medieval continuation, alchemy, the serpent signifies not only an ambiguous and concealed Deity but also a sacred demon dispensing blessings—a true Redeemer. Thus, the Perates also say that the all-encompassing serpent (that is, the Ouroboros, tail-eating dragon), which as Oceanus surrounds the earth like a ring, is the wise Logos of Eve, the *mysterium* of Eden, the river that flows out of Eden (Eden is the brain) and divides into the four origins. And as "the serpent of brass," which Moses "put upon a pole" (Num. 21:9), it becomes a symbol of Christ, the *Soter*-serpent. In Egypt also, the dragon was principally worshipped as a serpent of salvation, as the outward form of the god of revelation, Hermes, as the *Agathodaimon*, or as Osiris, "lord of the Egyptian earth" and husband of Isis.

247   In the Roman catacombs, in the so-called Balbina *coemeterium*,[10] there is a remarkable fresco which is looked upon as an illustration of Perpetua's vision: a human figure is ascending a ladder under which lies a serpent. The ladder rises out of a cornfield consisting of single tall ears of corn. So here, the serpent represents the earth spirit connected with the cornfields. This points even more clearly to the Egyptian *Agathodaimon* that was worshipped as "cornfield head" and *Pantokrator*.

The Ouroborus as crowned dragon (left) and winged and wingless serpents[11]

---

[10] See Fernand Cabrol, ed., *Dictionnaire d'Archéologie Chretienne el de Liturgie,* vol. 2, col. 151, and also under "Balbina."
[11] [From Eleazar, *Uraltes chymisches Werk* (1760), part 2, nos. 4 and 3 (Mellon Coll., Yale University Library).—Ed.]

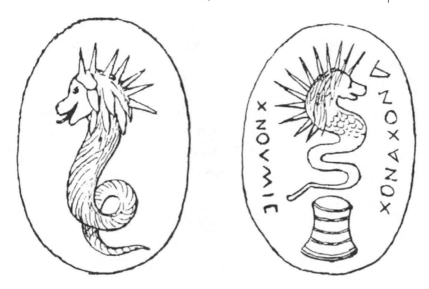

Agathodaimon on Gnostic gem and amulet[12]

248   The Gnostic Ophites also interpreted the ear of corn which was shown in the Eleusinian Mysteries as the Logos which rules the world. It is a symbol for all the dying and resurrecting vegetation gods such as Attis, Osiris, Adonis, the Phrygian Papas, and so forth.

249   In this connection the dragon is clearly a symbol for an "unconscious nature-spirit," "the wisdom of the earth." Therefore, seen from the Christian standpoint, it also represents the pagan conception of the world in which experience of the Deity, or of the spirit, was projected into the material reality of the world. In antiquity, one experienced divinity through a feeling of being gripped and moved by the phenomena of nature—in the rustling of the Dodonean oaks, in the murmuring of a fountain, in the starry heavens, and the glow of the rising sun. These were the manifestations of the highest power. This form of experience, however, had obviously become unsatisfying, even destructive, and it had to be surmounted rather than overcome.

250   The process of withdrawing the projection of the gods from nature had actually already begun in the Stoa. They interpreted the Olympians as the embodiment of specific psychic characteristics,

---

[12] [From Charles William King, *The Gnostics and Their Remains: Ancient and Medieval*, plate 3, figs. 7 and 2.—Ed.]

but only again in favor of a "subtle material" conception of the spirit, as having a fiery, ethereal nature—the all-pervading and all-ruling *Nous*. But it was Christianity which first took the real step toward a purely spiritual, extramundane conception of God. It is the realization of this fact which is represented in Perpetua's ascent over and beyond the dragon to a heavenly place. Consequently, in the vision, the dragon stands for the danger of slipping back into the old pagan spiritual attitude, out of which the ladder shows the way to higher consciousness.

251   As a feminine and chthonic being, however, the dragon also means Perpetua's own instinctive soul, her will to live, and her feminine reality which she tramples underfoot and disregards as she steps beyond.

252   In the *Shepherd of Hermas*, we also find—as J.A. Robinson has pointed out—the image of a gigantic animal symbolizing the anti-Christian power. It is a beast resembling a sea monster, about a hundred feet in length with a head like an earthenware vessel. This recalls the demonic angel Amnael in the old alchemical text, *Isis to Horus*. On his head, as a *semeion* (sign or symbol), he carries just such a vessel, containing the alchemical secret substance Isis is seeking.[13] The motif of the vessel as the head itself, or even as *on* the head, points to a feminine *mysterium,* so these parallels confirm what is already clear to us—namely, that Perpetua rejects her own feminine instinct in order to attain spiritual transformation. In so doing, she treads on the dragon's head. This is a well-known gesture of triumph and, as St. Augustine (who often refers to the "Passio Perpetua" and appears to have been very much impressed by it) already recognized,[14] probably is also an allusion to Genesis 3:15:

253   And I will put enmity between thee and the woman, and between thy seed and her seed; it shall bruise thy head, and thou shalt bruise his heel.

---

[13] See M. Berthelot, *Collection des Anciens Alchimistes Grecs.*
[14] Germ. 280. See Jacques Paul Migne, ed., *Patrologiae cursus completus,* Latin series, vol. 38, col. 1282.

254   The trampling of the dragon, according to Psalms 91:13—"the young lion and the dragon shalt thou trample under feet" *(et conculcabis leonem et draconem)*—was also frequently looked upon at that time as a sign of martyrdom and as victory over the devil.

255   On reaching the top of the ladder, Perpetua finds herself in a garden, in the center of which a gigantic shepherd, clad in white, is milking sheep. As this garden lies in Heaven above, it can be no other than the celestial garden, Paradise, the Heavenly World Beyond; and this is also the reason why, immediately on waking, Perpetua interprets the dream as a premonition of her approaching death. It is in the garden that she is received into the bright company of the Blessed, robed in white.

256   The idea that Paradise should again become the abode of humanity after death is already foreshadowed in the Apocryphal Books of the Old Testament. Perpetua's vision, and especially Saturus's vision of Paradise, included further on in the "Passio Perpetuae," in which he enters into a heavenly garden with cypresses and roses, facing the east, are among the earliest known Christian conceptions of Paradise.

257   Curiously enough, the idea of Paradise led to a long, dogmatic discussion. According to prevailing opinion at the time, it is a *locus corporalis,* a material place occupying a definite space where the souls abide, in contrast to the extramundane Heavenly kingdom, the "Father's Mansion," for which it is a preliminary stage. According to the Church Father Hippolytus, it exists on earth toward the east.[15] Another conception, however, places Paradise beyond the cosmos. In the *Passio SS. Montani et Lucii,* for example, Christ appears—in the figure of a boy with a shining countenance—to a fellow martyr named Victor and promises him eternal life. When the latter asks where Paradise is to be found, Christ answers: *"Extra mundum"* (beyond the world). Indeed, Origen had to refute a conception according to which Paradise "is only an immaterial world, existing merely in the fantasies of the mind and in thought."[16] Philo was

---

[15] Hippolytus, *Hexaemeron,* in Migne, ed., *Patrologiae,* Greek series, vol. 10, col. 585.
[16] Origen, *de Principiis,* 1, II, chap. 3. For English, see Roberts and Donaldson, eds., *Ante-Nicene Fathers.*

already familiar with this interpretation and himself held that Paradise is a symbol of God's wisdom.

258 The localization of Paradise outside the cosmos is explained by the idea that its four rivers, with their purifying and fertilizing properties, had their origin in the division of "the waters which were under the firmament from the waters which were above the firmament" (Gen. 1:7). These celestial waters very early on in the patristic literature became a symbol for the Holy Ghost. From this primordial place the power of God created the four rivers of Paradise, so that the latter were somehow regarded as identical with them.[17]

259 Since Perpetua does not journey over the face of the earth toward the east, but rather climbs up a ladder to Heaven, the Paradise of her vision must be the extramundane Paradise. In psychological language, the higher level of consciousness which she seeks to attain is thus revealed as a spiritual reality beyond the material world and the cosmos. In this reality, ideas exist in themselves and are no longer experienced as projected into the universe.

260 The curious uncertainty concerning the material position of Paradise in space no doubt comes from the fact that Christianity did not recognize that its own conception of God and its most important dogmas primarily reside within the soul as psychological realities (which indeed was quite impossible to realize at the time, as is proved by Origen's refutation mentioned above). Instead, they were projected as absolutes in a space beyond the world—with the result that these ideas again acquired a peculiar substantiality.

261 In Perpetua's vision, in the middle of the garden the "Good Shepherd" receives the Saint and gives her "a morsel of the cheese which he was milking." The figure of the shepherd as a guiding spirit, a *Paredros* and Redeemer, was an archetypal concept common to the pagan and Christian worlds of that time.[18] In the pagan world, he was called the Poimandres, "shepherd of men" (an aspect of Hermes), who leads them to enlightenment and redeems them. He

---

[17] [For further elaboration of the psychological significance of the four rivers, see Edward F. Edinger, *The Aion Lectures: Exploring the Self in C.G. Jung's Aion*, pp. 139ff.—Ed.]

[18] See R. Reitzenstein, *Poimandres*.

became the prototype for the shepherd in the Christian text, the *Shepherd of Hermas,* which Robinson—quite rightly, it seems to me—looks upon as the source of the text under discussion.

262 The text entitled *Poimandres* begins with the following description of the ecstatic vision of a Hermetist:

263 Methought there came to me a Being of overwhelming and boundless proportions, who called me by name and spake: "What do you wish to hear and see and know by thought?"

264 "Who are you?" I said.

265 "I," said he, "am the Poimandres, the Spirit of Truth *[ho tes authentias nous].*[19] I know what you wish, for indeed *I am with you everywhere.*"

266 "I would fain learn," I said, "the things that are, and understand their nature and acquire knowledge of God." He answered me: "Keep in mind all you desire to learn, and I will teach you!" When he had thus spoken, he changed his semblance, and forthwith all things were opened out in a moment, as by a sudden turn of the scale [rope], and I beheld a boundless vision, I saw all creation as a most mild and joyous light.[20]

267 It is not only in the Hermetic writings that this God of Redemption and leader of souls appears as a symbol of *Nous,* or Logos, in the form of a shepherd. Attis, who is interpreted as *Anthropos* and Logos in the Sermon of the Naassene, is a "shepherd of the shining stars." In like manner, the Phrygian Zeus or Papas was pictured by the Gnostics as a goatherd. They interpreted the Greek word *Aipolos* (goatherd) as *Aeipolos* (the ever-rotating one); that is, the all-transforming and generating Logos.

---

[19] Scott endeavors to prove that *authentia* means sovereignty, omnipotence, but from my point of view, the meaning of genuineness or truth is nearer the sense in this case. Perhaps the nearest rendering would be Spirit of Absoluteness.

[20] My own rendering of the Greek text in *Corpus Hermelicum,* book 1, in W. Scott, ed., *Hermetica.*

The Poimandres, shepherd of men. (Museum of the Acropolis, Athens)

268   The same applies to the Egyptian God Anubis, and to the Egyptian sun-god, Horus. In the *Egyptian Book of the Dead*, the latter is the "good shepherd" who rules over the "four human races," which form his flock.

269   The shepherd is a cosmic figure and, at the same time, is generally also considered the first man, the *Anthropos*.[21] As a text says, he is "the son of God, who can do everything and become everything as he will [and] appears to any one as he will." He extends

---

[21] Therefore in Perpetua's vision, as in the *Poimandres*, he is of supernatural stature.

throughout the universe and is the redeemer from the compulsion of the stars, the *heimarmene.*

270   But why should just the image of the shepherd have been chosen for this conception of God and as a symbol of *Nous?* Philo of Alexandria endeavors to explain it as follows:

271   The role of shepherd is such an exceedingly good one, that it is not only ascribed to kings and wise men, and to the souls which have been purified through initiation, but also, and rightly, to God himself, the leader of the universe. For, as if in a meadow or pasture, the Shepherd and King-God, with justice and law, leads his great flock: the earth and the water, the air and the fire, and all that in them is, plants and living beings, mortal and immortal, and also the nature of the heavens, and the circlings of sun and moon, and the rhythmic dances of the stars. He sets over them his upright Word [Logos], his first-born Son, who will receive the charge of this holy flock as the vice-regent of the Great King.[22]

272   Thus, the shepherd was a symbol of the ordering mind of God, the Stoic *Nous* or Logos, which pervades the whole universe. Therefore, he carries the staff of king and judge, with which he rules. He is a "*pneuma* reaching from heaven to earth."

273   At that time, humanity looked upon the laws of nature chiefly as the effects of an indwelling semimaterial and divine spirit. But this spirit had now "become man"; it was no longer merely the power of nature but also a *daimon paredros,* personally experienced by each individual. Numerous prayers in the pagan *Magic Papyri* are addressed to this spirit which pervaded and ruled the cosmos; for instance:

274   Hail, thou who comest forth from the four winds, Pantokrator, thou who breathest the life-giving *pneuma* into

---

[22] Philo, *de Agricultura,* 50. My rendering of the Greek text. [For English, see F.H. Colson and G.H. Whitaker, *Philo with an English Translation.*—Ed.]

man . . . whose eyes are the sun and moon, shining in the pupils of man . . . thou are the Agathodaimon, who generates everything and nourishes the inhabited earth.[23]

275   Or again:

Thou who sittest on the head of the cosmos, and judgest everything, surrounded by the circle of truth and faith. Thou who bearest on thy head the golden crown, and in thy hand the staff with which thou sendest forth the gods.[24]

276   He was usually represented as a beggar with staff and knapsack, as the power that holds the cosmos together and as the "shepherd of the stars," that is, the center of all the innumerable celestial constellations. From the psychological point of view, this primordial image of the shepherd represents the Self, whence all the other archetypal images of the collective unconscious receive their invisible regulation.

277   Christ as the Good Shepherd and *Pantokrator* has taken over all the functions of the pagan god. He is a liberator from the *heimarmene;* as *Kosmokrator,* he likewise extends throughout the universe. He is called the all-powerful Logos of God, "who walking on earth, touches the heavens." In contemporary art, he often figures as a kind of Hermes, a lamb on his shoulders, over his head the seven planets, on either side of him, sun and moon, and at his feet, seven lambs, representing the seven nations. On an epitaph in the Domitilla *coemeterium,* he is even depicted as Attis with a shepherd's staff and pipe. The *Martyrium Polycarpi* (chapter 19) calls him "the shepherd of the Universal Church which extends all over the world," and in the Alberkios inscription, he is "the holy shepherd, who feeds his flocks of sheep on mountains and plains."

278   In a saying such as the opening verses of Psalm 23—"The Lord is my shepherd; I shall not want"—which St. John in the New

---

[23] Karl L. Preisendanz, ed.. *Papyri Magicae Graecae*, vol. 1, p. 107.
[24] *Ibid.*

Testament applies to Christ (John 10:11-16), he is still quite definitely thought of as a kind of *daimon paredros*—that is, as a personal guardian spirit that accompanies each individual, just in the same way as the Poimandres declares, "I am with you everywhere." In the *Martyrium Polycarpi* (chapter 19), he is even called "the shepherd, the savior of our souls and *the guide of our bodies.*"

279   Thus, he is, so to speak, a nonpersonal guiding spirit, yet also in some way connected with the ego, almost in the sense of an apparition, which means that, at that time, the unconscious no longer appeared as a power projected into nature, but rather as a daimon accompanying man. This is shown most impressively in the appearance of the shepherd described by Hermas:

280   While I was praying at home, seated on my bed, there entered a man of lordly appearance, *in shepherd's garb,* clad in a white goat skin, his pack on his shoulders and a staff in his hand; and he greeted me, and I returned the greeting.

281   Forthwith he sat down by me, saying: "I am sent by the highest angel, that I may dwell with thee all the remaining days of thy life."

282   I suspected that he had come to tempt me, and asked: "Who art thou?

283   For I know into whose keeping I was given."

284   He said to me: "Dost thou not know me?"

285   "No," I replied.

286   Then he declared: "I am the shepherd into whose care thou hast been given." And while he was still speaking he changed his semblance, and I knew that he was the one into whose keeping I had been given.[25]

---

[25] My rendering of the text in Reitzenstein, *Poimandres,* p. 11.

287 The shepherd then undertakes the function of strengthening Hermas in his faith and instructing him.

288 As we shall see, something of the same kind takes place in Perpetua's vision when, in a scene which recalls the Holy Communion, the shepherd gives her a morsel of cheese and she receives it with folded hands. This scene in particular has been looked upon as a proof that the martyrs were Montanists, for a special group among them, the so-called Artotyrites—from *artos* (bread) and *tyros* (cheese)—are said to have celebrated their Eucharist not with wine but with bread and cheese. In any case, the manner in which the cheese is dispensed in the vision is entirely modeled on the partaking of the Holy Communion.

289 Some writers have also seen a certain connection in this passage with the *Passio Montani*, which describes the passion of "a certain Montanus" and his followers. As a result of the death of the proconsul, these martyrs were doomed to linger a considerable time in prison. Several of their visions which have been recorded are not unlike St. Perpetua's. For instance, a woman named Quartillosia had the vision of a young man of supernatural stature who fed the prisoners with two bowls of milk that never became empty and promised them a third, after which he disappeared through the window.

290 The singular picture in the St. Perpetua vision of the shepherd milking cheese (which moreover could occur only in a genuine dream) probably comes from the fact that two conceptions overlap: the idea of the Holy Communion, the receiving of the Host, as something "made by the hand of man," something solid; and, on the other hand, the idea of bestowing a drink in the form of milk.

291 In the Phrygian mysteries, for instance, the mystic abstained from eating meat, "and moreover he fed on milk as one newly born." This is important inasmuch as Montanus himself was a Phrygian. Milk and honey were also looked upon as stimulating and inspiring, much the same as wine. In a magic papyrus, we read: "Drink milk and honey before sunrise, and in thy heart there will be something divine." Milk also stood for spiritual teaching in the Christian world:

"As newborn babes, desire the sincere milk of the word *[logikon]*, that ye may grow thereby: if so be ye have tasted that the Lord is gracious" (1 Pet. 2:2). And:

292   Ye have need that one teach you again which be the first principles of the oracles of God; and are become such as have need of milk, and not of strong meat. For everyone that useth milk is unskillful in the word of righteousness; for he is a babe. (Heb. 5:12-13; also 1 Cor. 3:2)

293   St. Paul described himself and his followers as "children in Christ" *(nepioi en Christo),* and Clement of Alexandria even calls the Christians directly *galaktophagoi* (milk-drinkers). Milk, too, stands for an emanation of the Deity. In the so-called *Odes of Solomon,* we read:

294   A cup of milk was offered to me; and I drank it in the sweetness of the delight of the Lord. The Son is the cup, and He who was milked is the Father: and the Holy Spirit milked him: because his breasts were full, and it did not seem good to Him that His milk should be spilt for nought; and the Holy Spirit opened her bosom and mingled the milk from the two breasts of the Father; and gave the mixture to the world [literally, "aeons"], without its knowing it; and they who receive [it] are in the perfection of the right hand [literally, "on the right hand in the *Pleroma*"].[26]

295   As Reitzenstein doubtless rightly interprets it, the drink of milk denotes the beginning, and the draught of wine, on the other hand, the complete fulfillment of man's divinity.[27] According to the rules of the Church instituted by Hippolytus, the neophytes first received a cup of water, then a mixture of milk and honey, and finally wine and water as the real Eucharist.

---

[26] J.H. Bernard, ed., *The Odes of Solomon,* in J. A. Robinson, *Texts and Studies,* vol. 8, no. 3, Ode 19.
[27] *Hellenislische Mysterienreligionen,* p. 330.

296   The sweet-tasting morsel which Perpetua receives at the hands of the shepherd is thus a kind of spiritual food, or teaching, through which she is admitted to the bright company of the Blessed (those who stand around robed in white and say "Amen"), the company in the Beyond, whence—in the fourth vision—comes the deacon Pomponius, in festive garb, to fetch her away. It also has the meaning of a *cibus immortalis,* an immortal food, inasmuch as those "who worship God in spirit and in truth have a share in his glory and are immortal with him in that they are partakers of eternal life through the Logos." The Holy Ghost was indeed a life-giving breath.

297   If the gods of antiquity were already dead—that is, if the highest value bestowing life and giving it meaning had sunk at that time into the unconscious and become dissolved—this value had risen again in a changed form in the figure and teaching of Christ, the God become man and mediator. The unconscious life force streamed forth from the new teaching, enabling life to progress on a fresh course and bringing about a step forward in culture.[28]

298   The first of Perpetua's visions describes this process in archetypal images. It is true that the complex meaning in their deeper connections could hardly have been accessible to her consciousness, but they did give her the inner feeling of a meaning in her destiny. Thus, they enabled her to accept her martyrdom.[29]

299   Although the dream represents the Christian teaching as the highest value and as a new source of life, one can hardly assume that the unconscious intended to drive Perpetua into martyrdom. The obstructing factor in itself, for instance, is by no means exclusively characterized as a power of evil, although Perpetua interprets it as the devil. The dragon may also represent the unconscious animal side which seeks to hinder Perpetua's ascent and which she tramples underfoot. Quite objectively, the dream simply lays before our eyes the inner process which is taking place.

---

[28] For the problem of the death of the god, see "Psychology and Religion," *Psychology and Religion,* CW 11, pars. 145ff.

[29] [This is, after all, in the nature of archetypal images which, as anyone who has undergone depth analysis can attest, impinge on consciousness at times of deep personal strife.—Ed.]

300   The suprapersonal imagery is the language of the collective unconscious. The impressive power and depth of the images can no doubt be explained by the fact that they were called forth as a vital reaction of the unconscious to the fate threatening the dreamer in the outer world.

Chapter 19

Interpretation of the
Second and Third Visions

301   Perpetua's second vision contains a piece of the more personal side of her problem in a language that is more accessible to her conscious world, although it touches upon the same basic motifs that appeared in the first vision.

302   This is the dream of the little brother, Dinocrates, in the underworld. The Roman Catholic Church takes such visions very concretely and uses them as a basis for its doctrine of the intercession of saints, which has the effect of succoring the souls in Purgatory. (Perpetua herself seems to have interpreted the dream in this sense.)

303   If, however, we consider the dream on the subjective level—that is, in the first place as an inner event—Dinocrates (like Saturus in the first vision) undoubtedly embodies a spiritual content in Perpetua herself. His suffering, as portrayed in the dream, is in some way identical with her own painful condition. This suffering should therefore be understood as the inner need that caused her to yearn for the "fountain of living water," the baptismal water.

304   To Perpetua, this little brother who died in early childhood, together with all the memories which are linked with him, represents a piece of her own past, something childlike, a spirit in herself as yet unbaptized for whom the redeeming truth, symbolized by the water, is literally "too high." This is shown by the fact that the edge of the *piscina* (pool) is beyond the child's reach. Between Perpetua and this little brother there is a "great distance,"[1] which means that

---

[1] See Luke 16:26.

consciously she is far removed from this childish spiritual attitude, though it still clings to her. And this is also corroborated by the fact that she tells us she had not thought of him for a long time.

305   This childish piece of paganism in Perpetua—the dream figure Dinocrates—is suffering from a cancer; that is to say, he is subjected to a state of inner decay which cannot be arrested. Thus, the dream points to a regression, or rather to a difficulty which has arisen in Perpetua's inner development, which is perhaps the danger of allowing herself to be influenced by her father, who strove with all his might and all the authority he possessed to have her recant her faith. (This is probably why her resistance to the Christian attitude is represented as a "child in the family.") Apparently, a more childish unconscious spirit is still alive in Perpetua, one threatened with decay, one for whom the Christian truth is out of reach so that she yearns in vain for its redeeming effect.

306   Franz Josef Dölger, in his essay on the Dinocrates vision, points out that this picture of the underworld coincides exactly with the pagan concept of Hades rather than with the Christian notion of Purgatory. Thus, the pagan in Dinocrates is even more clearly emphasized.[2] It also recalls the description of the underworld in the *Book of Enoch* (chapter 22), as divided into a dark place for sinners and a light place, in the middle of which there is a "bright spring of water."

307   The idea that the dead suffer from thirst in the underworld is again an ancient and widespread idea that is also found in the third vision of the *Shepherd of Hermas*. Dölger goes on to prove that the vision here refers to the belief, prevalent in antiquity, that those who had died before their time or had suffered a violent death, underwent particular torment in Hades and could only be delivered through the prayers of the living.[3]

308   Looked at from a psychological point of view, this idea is the symbolic representation of the fact that contents of the unconscious, which are split off and unable to live fully in reality, become negative

---

[2] See *Antike Parallelen zum leidenden Dinocrates ub der Passio Perpetuae, Antike und Christentum,* vol. 2, pp. 1ff.
[3] *Ibid.*

and appear as ghosts seeking release, so to speak. In other words, they cause psychological disturbances, as seems to be the case here where just such a split-off content belonging to Perpetua's childhood is concerned.

309 When the pagan attitude in Perpetua is represented as a child, the dream may possibly be alluding to the fact that pagan consciousness is relatively infantile when compared to the Christian attitude. Rufinus, at all events, has expressed this view:

310 He [a saint] taught all men that they should direct their minds away from the visible and material things to the invisible and immaterial. "It is indeed time," he said, "that we turned to an occupation of this kind, for we cannot always remain boys and children, but must now once for all rise to the higher spiritual things and become grown men."[4]

311 In the third vision, shortly before Perpetua's death. Dinocrates again appears to her, transfigured and redeemed by the water of life. The decaying wound on his face is healed over, and he "went off to play as children do." Thus, he had become the image of one reborn *in novam infantiam* and, as such, his fate also represents a forecast of Perpetua's own situation and development.[5] For, whereas in the second and third visions she experiences everything in the person of Dinocrates or as an onlooker, in the fourth dream she herself is confined in the dark prison and has to take up the fight with the spirit of darkness in order to receive the bough of the tree of life.

312 A modern dream should be mentioned here, one which contains the same symbolism in a most striking way, and which, moreover, arose out of a situation similar to Perpetua's.[6] It is the dream of the Roman Catholic student Sophie Scholl, a girl of 21 who was

---

[4] [The source for this passage could not be found, but the Rufinus referred to is probably Tyrannius Rufinus of Aquileia, a fourth-century associate but later antagonist of St. Jerome. See this Web site: www.ocf.org/OrthodoxPage/reading/St.Pachomius/Xrufin.html.—Ed.]

[5] Concerning the anticipatory character of the child archetype, see Karl Kerenyi and C.G. Jung, *Essays on a Science of Mythology*, pp. 83f

[6] For this material I am indebted to Hildegard Nagel. [Miss Nagel was a regular participant in Jung's early seminars.—Ed.]

guillotined in Munich for spreading anti-Nazi propaganda. In prison the night before her death, she dreamed that on a beautiful sunny day she was carrying a child in a long white robe to its christening. The way to the church led up a steep mountain, but "firm and safe" she carried the child in her arms. Suddenly, without warning, a crevasse opened in front of her. She had only enough time to lay the child safely down before she crashed into the depths.

313   In reality, Sophie died with immense courage. She herself interpreted her dream in the sense that the child's white robe stood for the idea for which her own death prepared the way. The steep path up to the church recalls the ladder of Perpetua's first vision, which represented the difficult way of individuation. The fate of the child that has not yet been christened points to Dinocrates. The abyss is an image of the "jaws of death" which swallow up the mortal side, whereas the Divine Child—the Self in the process of becoming—lives on.

314   One can hardly help being deeply moved and impressed by the way in which the unconscious reacts: Without the faintest sentimentality but with unerring certainty, it represents the real, significant inner process and conveys symbolically the absolute knowledge which provides real support.

315   The pitiful condition of little Dinocrates in Hades and his redemption recall most vividly the contemporary alchemical concepts of those "bound in Hades" who yearned for the divine water, the *hydor theion*. In the *Treatise of Comarius to Cleopatra,* for instance, we read that the holy waters descended from on high to visit the dead—prostrate, chained, and crushed in the darkness of Hades—and that the *pharmakon zoes* (medicine of life) penetrated them and revived them; and he (the spirit) clothed them in divine and spiritual glory, and they came out of the earth. And it was said:

316   They array themselves in light and glory; in that they had increased in accordance with nature, and their figures had been transformed, and they had arisen from sleep, and had come forth from Hades. The body of the fire had given them

birth. [Compare Dinocrates' feverish heat *(aestus)!]...* and as they came forth from it they clothed themselves in glory, and it [the body of the fire] brought them complete oneness, and the image was fulfilled through body, soul and spirit, and they became one.[7]

317 Dinocrates drinks the water from a golden flask, which also strikes one as a remarkably alchemical motif. It recalls the vessel of Hermes *(vas Hermetis)* which was in some way imagined to be consubstantial with its contents. In the Hermetic treatise *The Krater,* we read that after God had created the universe, he filled a vessel, a kind of baptismal font (compare the *piscina),* with *Nous* and sent it down to earth, so that people who dipped themselves in it should receive a share of *ennoia* (consciousness, enlightenment).[8]

318 We find another Christian vision which parallels Perpetua's in the *Passio SS Mariam et Jacobi.* A martyr named Marianus found himself transported in a dream to a heavenly grove of pines and cypresses:

319 In the middle there stood the overflowing basin of a pure and transparent fountain, and there Cyprianus [a martyr who in reality had already died] took a phial which lay at the edge of the fountain and drank; then replenishing it anew, he handed it to me and I drank with joy and, as I said, *"Deo gracias,"* I awoke at the sound of my own voice.

320 Water, as Jung says, "is an excellent symbol for the living power of the psyche."[9] It is also spiritual and as such is often of a fiery nature.

321 The quickening influx of energy from the unconscious may well be looked upon as the effect of the Christian faith, and the water of the *piscina* is here an intimation of a kind of baptismal water, a symbol of Christ or of the Holy Ghost. Thus, for instance, Justin Martyr says:

---

[7] Berthelot, ed., *Collection des Anciens Alchimistes Grecs,* vol. 2, p. 297.
[8] See Scott, ed., *Hermetica,* vol. 1, pp. 149ff.; also *Psychology and Alchemy,* CW 12, pars. 408f.
[9] *Psychology and Alchemy,* CW 12, par. 94.

322   As a spring of living water from God, in the land of the heathen barren of all knowledge of God, has this Christ gushed forth, who appeared also to your people, and healed them that from their birth and in the flesh were blind, dumb and lame.... Also he awoke the dead. ... This he did in order to convince those are ready to believe in him that, even if a man be afflicted with any bodily infirmity and yet keeps the commandments given by Christ, he shall be awakened at the second coming with an uncrippled body, after Christ has made him immortal and incorruptible and without sorrow.[10]

323   In the first Dinocrates dream, Perpetua had felt herself to be inwardly cut off from this living spiritual effect of the Christian teaching, entangled in unconsciousness and overpowered by the weight of outer events. But the following dream—her third vision—which she had in prison shortly before her death, shows her little brother cured of his ills and happy, playing in the Beyond.

324   This clearly implies that in the meantime, as a result of her intercession—that is, through being consciously concerned with the problem which Dinocrates embodies—she has grown both inward and upward; she has attained an attitude in which the Christian truth becomes a real inner source of strength and in which her childlike side also actively participates. At the same time, this effect must be understood as an unconscious one, for it proceeds from the Beyond (depicted as Paradise or the Underworld).

325   Between the first Dinocrates vision and the preceding one, there is indeed no outward connection of motifs, but the inner structure certainly reveals a very striking parallel. This is an important argument in support of the fact that we are dealing with a genuine series of dreams and not with a fabrication. In both visions, an obstructing element comes into play: in the first, the dragon, as the reaction of the instincts; in the second, Dinocrates, representing Perpetua's own childishness.

---

[10] Quoted by Jung in *ibid.*, par. 475, note 141.

Alchemical image of the fountain of life.
(*Rosarium philosophorum*, 1550)

326   In both cases, it is a matter of reaching something higher: the ascent of the ladder to an extramundane place and Dinocrates reaching up to the *piscina*, which is too high for him. Both visions depict the attainment of a symbol of the living spirit and communion with it by means of the milk as heavenly food and through the draught from the fountain of life. Finally, in both the second and third visions, there is an allusion to rebirth: on the one hand, in the partaking of milk as food of the reborn and, on the other, in a dramatization of the process in the figure of little Dinocrates, who goes off to play "as children do."

327   Although the problem has undoubtedly come somewhat nearer to the dreamer's consciousness in the second vision, through being connected with a personal content (Dinocrates), Perpetua still projects the inner conflict into the figure of her pagan little brother, from whom, the vision says, she is separated by "a great distance." This means that consciously she is far removed from its realization. In the third vision, however, she is quite personally and actively drawn into the problem. (It may be argued that in the first vision she also played an active part, but there the dream only pointed to the path she was beginning to follow, and there was no actual drama.)

♦

Chapter 20

Interpretation of the Fourth Vision

328 Perpetua's fourth and last vision begins with her in prison, waiting to appear before the beasts. At first sight, this is simply a statement of the dreamer's conscious situation. By this, the dream implies that the ensuing conflict, depicted in the course of the vision, is actual reality. Nevertheless, we are bound to look upon this imprisonment, figuring among the events of the dream, as referring to an inner situation.

329 In the mysteries of Isis and Serapes, there existed a curious custom, that of the so-called *katochoi* (prisoners) of the Deity. *Katoche* principally means arrest or imprisonment, and consequently, *katochos* means prisoner. On the other hand, however, the verb *katechesthai ek theou* (used in conjunction with *theophoreisthai* or *korybantian* and with the idea of Bacchic ecstasy) denotes a condition of ecstatic raving; *katochos* then similarly means possessed by a god, and *katoche* a state of possession. (Compare Perpetua's state of trance during her martyrdom.)

330 Such *katochoi* existed as early as the second century before Christ, for instance in the Serapium of Memphis, a sect in which the state of imprisonment was one of free choice to which laymen voluntarily submitted, as novitiates, prior to their initiation into the priesthood. The *katochoi* also called themselves "slaves" or "servants of God." Some of them even wore chains and often did not leave the outer court of the temple for years. Others went about begging and lived a life of the most rigorous self-imposed asceticism. Many of them interpreted their own dreams and took them very seriously. Their period of imprisonment often lasted till such a time as the novice, and an already initiated mystic had the same dream on the

same night. This would admit the novice to initiation. It might occur suddenly, or after waiting many years, or sometimes never. The novice also occasionally chose the spiritual father who initiated him.[1] Whoever attempted initiation without being "called" was doomed to die. And only the man whom Isis had appointed in a dream might enter the *adyton* of the goddess.

331   All these ancient customs may undoubtedly be looked upon as the first steps leading to the Christian institution of monachism, which originated in Egypt.[2] It is also noteworthy that St. Paul should speak of himself as "a prisoner *[desmios]* of Jesus Christ" (Eph. 3:1) or of being "in the bonds of the Gospel."

332   The psychological meaning of such a confinement is unmistakable. Imprisonment under whatever circumstances implies restricted freedom of action and isolation from the surrounding world. It is a sequestration, a voluntary or involuntary state of introversion, which in certain cases may be brought about by a state of possession—that is, by being fascinated with an unconscious content. This is how the unconscious images (therefore the dreams) which formed the initiation process of the mysteries were activated. That is why the prison is often an initial symbol of the process of individuation in contemporary dreams.

333   In the ancient mysteries the initiation took place under the guidance of a spiritual leader. On parallel lines, in Perpetua's vision, the deacon Pomponius knocks at the prison door. He wears a festive garment and manifold shoes. He takes her by the hand and leads her through dark and devious paths to the arena.

334   At that time, a deacon was an assistant to the bishop in his diocese, a kind of parochial aide. Here, we are dealing with a real personality known to Perpetua. By means of bribery, he was able to bring about some alleviation in the conditions of her captivity, and he was also a spiritual support to her. In the dream, Pomponius has evidently taken upon himself the function of a Christian animus figure (which is natural, seeing that Perpetua, who had been

---

[1] See Reitzenstein, *Historia Monachorum und Historia Lausiaca*, pp. 107ff.
[2] [Monachism, according to the American Heritage Dictionary, is an archaic term for monasticism.—Ed.]

baptized only 20 days before, in all probability projected her Christian attitude onto the deacon of the place). He is now the leader of her soul (he takes her by the hand) and her spiritual father, a symbol of her Christian faith.

335 The function that Pomponius fulfills is similar to that of Saturus in the first vision. Should there be any difference in their roles, it would mainly consist in the fact that Saturus seems rather to embody her temperamentally courageous inner attitude in the face of her martyrdom, whereas Pomponius is more of a teacher—that is to say, he stands more for the Christian faith as a spiritual doctrine.[3] In the dream he is characterized as one who is already initiated (which clearly does not reflect his position in real life and proves the projection); he wears a festive garment and manifold shoes.

336 In the ancient mysteries, the festive garment plays an important role, as the celestial garment of the glorified celestial body, which the mystic puts on. Thus, before his third initiation, Apuleius was exhorted in a dream to be initiated anew in order to attain further enlightenment, as he could no longer wear "the garment of the Goddess which he had put on in the province and had then laid aside in the sanctuary there."[4] In Egypt, the resurrected one wore the headdress of the sun-god Ra, a sun-diadem. The Mithraic mystics received a garment on which animals were embroidered. It signified the glorified resurrection after death, the state of full enlightenment through the Gnosis and of becoming one with the Deity; at the same time, it meant a *metasomatosis,* a complete transformation.

337 In the Christian concept of Paradise, the Blessed are robed in white—as a symbol of joy and innocence, according to one of the Fathers of the Church. Here, the deacon Pomponius is likewise an already fully enlightened mystic, a spirit from the Beyond—that is, a figure arising from the unconscious. At the same time, he is a symbol of Perpetua's own coming development. He says: "Perpetua, we are awaiting thee, come!" From the World Beyond, Paradise or

---

[3] See Emma Jung, *Animus and Anima,* pp. 5ff.
[4] Apuleius, *Metamorphoses,* XI. [For English, see W. Adlington, trans., *The Golden Ass of Apuleius,* pp. 299f.—Ed.]

the land of the dead, he brings her the message that they are expecting her there. He is also the one whose office it is to usher her into this place.

338   The animus is indeed the figure that transmits the contents of the collective unconscious; he is a psychopomp. The words he addresses to her in the amphitheater where he leaves her ("Fear not, I am here with thee and shall fight with thee") show that he stands much less for a concrete figure than for an unconscious, spiritual power. In the dream, however, he disappears, and in his place enters a gigantic *lanista*, who promises her the bough of the Tree of Life if she wins the battle. Thus, in the function he fulfills, he evolves, as it were, into this bigger, more archetypal figure which (as we shall see) is clearly a symbol of both an absolute faith and a positive attitude.

339   At first, Pomponius leads Perpetua through a rough and pathless country, and it is only with great effort that they reach the amphitheater. Such straying about on tortuous paths recalls the plight of her little brother Dinocrates in Hades, described in her second vision. A disorientation has obviously set in at this point, a condition of perplexity and distress resulting from the state of introversion symbolized by the prison. Perpetua is evidently assailed by doubts and resistances at the thought of her martyrdom. In the midst of this disorientation of her consciousness, the deacon becomes her guiding Christian animus—that is to say, a symbol of the Christian faith.

340   Pomponius takes her to the amphitheater/arena. Its shape recalls a magic circle, or mandala. As a symbol of the Self, which embraces the totality of the conscious and unconscious sides of the psyche, the amphitheater naturally includes both the opposing attitudes and the conscious portion of the personality. These are personified by the pagan Egyptian and the Christian assistants and by Perpetua herself, with the *lanista* symbolizing the value of the Self.

341   In the ritual mandala, the circular boundary surrounding the center always has the purpose of preventing an outburst or a disintegration, as well as preventing any interference from the outside. It is inside this enclosure that the final contest now takes

place. Inasmuch as the ritual mandala also aims at reconciling the opposites, the very appearance of this symbol is already an intimation of a possible solution of the conflict. This doubtless consists in the fact that Perpetua will be "withdrawn" into the suprapersonal meaning of the process to such a degree (compare her trance during her martyrdom) that she will be able to endure the destruction of her individual existence.

342   Historically, the amphitheater was actually a circular building devoted to a cult, and the games that took place there were religious ceremonies in honor of the gods. Therefore, Tertullian rightly called it "the *temple* of all demons."[5] It is here that the crowd in the vision now gathers to witness the fight between the Saint and the Egyptian. One might say that the Christian inner guiding principle leads to a concentration of the conflict in Perpetua herself, around which stand the formerly dissociated forces of the collective unconscious (the people). All the various parts of the personality collect around a suprapersonal center, where the final conflict between the opposites will be decided.

343   At first, Perpetua expects the wild beasts to be let in. Interpreted on the subjective level, this means that she believes the fight is to be waged against the unconscious in the form of the animal world of the instincts. These are the same forces she has already encountered in the guise of the dragon. But the dream shows that, in reality, the conflict is far more complicated: A gigantic Egyptian of horrible appearance comes toward her with a sword.

344   This Egyptian is a remarkably complex embodiment of her situation. In late antiquity, Egypt meant the land of ancient wisdom. It was looked on in much the same way that the modern European looks upon India. As far back as Herodotus, Egypt and her priests held this meaning. Plato, for example, was wont to give out his most important ideas and myths as the secret wisdom of the Egyptian priesthood. According to Hekataios of Miletus, the Egyptians were the oldest and most religious people in the whole world.

---

[5] Tertullian, *de Spectaculis,* 12. [For English, see Roberts and Donaldson, eds, *Ante-Nicene Fathers,* vol. 3.—Ed.]

345   The Greeks projected their own unconscious onto Egypt, and, as a result, it became the source of all secret revelation, the land where an archaic religious attitude was still to be found, which their own enlightened consciousness had lost. Thus, in a satire, Apuleius's Lucian (whom we know also from Apuleius's *Golden Ass)* says:

346   The oldest philosophers were the Hindu Brahmans, or Gymnosophists. Philosophy went direct from them to the Ethiopians, from thence to the Egyptians.[6]

347   The Cynics especially saw the realization of their ideals in these Indian and Egyptian sages. Egypt was therefore the site par excellence of all dark magic, and the cult of the animal that was practiced there made a particularly deep impression upon the Greek philosophers and sophists. In the "Treatise Asclepius III" of the *Corpus Hermeticum,* Hermes says:

348   Do you know, Asclepius, that Egypt is an image of heaven, or, to speak more exactly, in Egypt all the operations and powers which rule and work in heaven have been transferred to earth below? Nay, it should rather be said that the *whole Kosmos dwells in this our land* [Egypt] *as in its sanctuary.*[7]

349   If the pagans thus looked to Egypt as the land of the great mysteries, the most religious land of ancient wisdom and magic, in the eyes of the Christians it was bound to become the prototype of all that was evil, and especially of the "clouded, obscure, misleading Pagan spirit."[8]

350   For the Gnostic Perates, however, Egypt also meant the transitory world, the passage through the Red Sea, the way to immortality. In their allegorical interpretation of the Bible, the Fathers of the Church very soon explained the exodus of the Israelites from Egypt as an exodus out of spiritual darkness. (Such

---

[6] See Reitzenstein, *Hellenistische Wunderzählungen,* pp. 41ff.
[7] Scott, ed., *Hermetica,* vol. 1, pp. 340f.
[8] *Ibid.*

things can hardly have been unknown to Perpetua, who came from an educated family.)

351 In a certain sense, the Egyptian in Perpetua's fourth vision also constitutes an analogy to the dragon in the first vision, since both—as Hugo Rahner so beautifully demonstrates[9]—became images of the devil in the patristic symbolic language. The Fathers of the Church found support for this in the passages in Ezekiel where God causes the Egyptian Pharaoh to be addressed as "the great dragon that lieth in the midst of his rivers" (29:3), and "as a whale [dragon] in the seas" (32:2). Thus, the Egyptian king (drowned in the Red Sea) also becomes an image of the devil.

352 From the psychological point of view, on the other hand, there is a difference between the image of the devil as dragon and as Egyptian, inasmuch as the latter embodies a more spiritual content which is closer to consciousness. Accordingly, Perpetua's fourth vision reveals that the central conflict does not consist solely in overcoming the animal instincts but also implies a fight against the spirit of paganism, against the experience of the spirit projected into nature, against the spirit of the most ancient tradition and against the spirit of the earth from which the Christians endeavored to free themselves.

353 In this connection, the four visions show a gradual development of the pagan counterattitude in the unconscious: At first, it is embodied in a lower, cold-blooded animal (the dragon); then, it appears in human form, as an ill child (Dinocrates); and lastly as a full-grown warrior (the Egyptian). So, the conflict is continuously being brought nearer to consciousness, and at the same time, the menacing factor grows increasingly important, appearing in ever more spiritual terms. It is in this last form that paganism proved most dangerous to the Christian faith. Therefore, St. Paul says:

354 Put on the whole armor of God, that ye may be able to stand against the wiles of the devil.

---

[9] Rahner, "Antenna Crucis II," in *Zeitschrift für Kathol. Theologie*, p. 111.

355   For we wrestle not against flesh and blood, but against principalities, against powers [*archas kai exousias,* i.e., the domination of the spirits of the planets], against the rulers of the darkness of this world, against spiritual wickedness in high places [*pros ta pneumatika tes ponerias en tois epouraniois*]. (Eph. 6:11-12)

356   By this, he means the *pneuma* projected into the cosmos and into nature, the pagan experience of the spirit.

357   The Christian devil is in truth none other than the *Agathodaimon* of the pagans, once worshipped as lord of the black Egyptian earth and husband of Isis. Referring to this scene, we also read in a sermon ascribed to St. Augustine: "How art thou fallen from heaven, O Lucifer, son of the morning!" (Isa. 14:12) This is clearly an allusion to the bright, spiritual side of this divine opponent of Christ.

358   The fact that the Egyptian in Perpetua's vision wallows in the dust and that Perpetua, as she conquers him, treads him into the earth stresses precisely the earthly quality, the state of being imprisoned in the earth, which is characteristic of this *pneuma*.[10] According to Philo of Alexandria, the kingdom of the air, against whose demons St. Paul fights, is black;[11] in the *Epistle of Barnabas* (IV: 10, XX: 1) the devil is already called the black one. Besides this, the blackness of the Egyptians—and particularly of the priests of Isis who were imported into Rome to celebrate the mysteries and whose dark complexions were singularly striking there—strengthened the conception of the devil as an Egyptian, a symbol of the dark, chthonic mysteries of departing antiquity.

359   In the event of defeat, Perpetua was to be killed by the sword of the Egyptian. But it is she who conquers him and then treads on his head, which again points to the mental function of this enemy. During the fight, he endeavors to lay hold of her feet. Psychologically, this means that he is seeking to undermine her

---

[10] See Tertullian, *de Pallio,* 3. (For English, see Roberts and Donaldson, eds., *Ante-Nicene Fathers,* vol. 3.) Rolling in the dust is also a trick that the wrestler uses in order to make it difficult for his opponent to lay hold of him.

[11] *De Opificio Mundi,* 7.29. (For English, see F.H. Colson and G.H. Whitaker, eds., *Philo with an English translation.)*

standpoint, to make her doubt her convictions, and thus cause her to waver. A passage in the writings of Origen, who calls the pagan attitude a "spiritual Ethiopian," also points to the character of this dark Egyptian, who is at the same time a figure parallel to the serpent:

360   He who partakes of the supernatural bread, and strengthens his heart thereby, will become the son of God. But he who partakes of the dragon is himself no other than the spiritual Ethiopian, in that by the snares laid for the dragon, he is himself transformed into the serpent.[12]

361   (Perpetua treads on the Egyptian's head, just as in the first vision she stepped on the head of the dragon.)

362   When the Egyptian throws himself at Perpetua's feet, the dream seems to suggest a connection with Perpetua's father. The latter never ceased to pursue her with entreaties to recant her Christian faith, and his exhortations appear to have affected her deeply, for upon one occasion she said: "I thank God, and recovered when he had departed."[13] Among the many arguments he used, he once pleaded with her as follows:

363   Daughter ... have pity on my grey head—have pity on me your father, if I deserve to be called your father, if I have favoured you above all your brothers, if I have raised you to reach this prime of your life. Do not abandon me to be the reproach of men. Think of your brothers, think of your mother and your aunt, think of your child, who will not be able to live once you are gone. Give up your pride! You will destroy all of us!

364   None of us will ever be able to speak freely again if anything happens to you.[14]

---

[12] Origen, *Peri euches*, 27:12. (For English, see Roberts and Donaldson, eds., *Ante-Nicene Fathers*.)
[13] Musurillo, trans., "Perpetua," in *Acts of the Christian Martyrs*, p. 112.
[14] *Ibid.*, p. 113.

365 Perpetua goes on to say:

> This was the way my father spoke out of love for me, kissing
> my hands and throwing himself down before me. With tears
> in his eyes he no longer addressed me as his daughter but as
> a woman *[domina]*. I was sorry for my father's sake, because
> he alone of all my kin would be unhappy to see me suffer.[15]

366 This moving passage sheds a profound light on the way her family
affected Perpetua's fate. Her relation to her father appears to have
been a particularly close one. In the case of a woman, the father
stands for the first image of man in general, the first embodiment of
the animus, and, as such, he determines her spiritual temperament
and her relation to spiritual contents generally. Therefore, through
her relation to her father, Perpetua seems to have been in great
measure fated to suffer the conflict and to come to terms with the
religious problems of her day.

367 Perpetua's father, on the other hand, appears to have been just as
unusually attached to her. (He addresses her "as a woman.") On one
occasion, when she turns a deaf ear to his entreaties, he falls upon
her, screaming, and moves as if to tear her eyes out. Since Perpetua
is very closely bound to him, his arguments against Christianity
wound her very deeply. Once, when he leaves her after a scene such
as the one just described, she says that "he departed, vanquished
along with his diabolical arguments *[cum argumentis diabolis]*.[16]

368 So, there is some justification for drawing a certain psychological
parallel between the Egyptian who throws himself at Perpetua's feet
and upon whom she looks as the devil, and the figure of her father.

369 St. Augustine likewise recognizes this connection and therefore
says that the devil made use of the father, instructing him with
deceiving words in order to bring about Perpetua's downfall by
appealing to her feeling of filial piety. It is the spirit of her father—
that is, the spirit of tradition—in Perpetua herself which rebels

---

[15] *Ibid.*
[16] *Ibid.*, p. 108.

against the new creed. When the dream substitutes the more general figure of the Egyptian for that of the father, it expresses the fact that the fight is not only against the individual father, but against that which he means to Perpetua in an inner sense: a fight against a universal spirit, a pagan animus, which must be overcome. The Egyptian's threat is to pierce her with his sword—that is, to enter her, penetrate her spiritually; and when he throws himself at her feet, it is not with the intention of entreating her, as in the case of her real father, but of bringing about her fall, of destroying her standpoint.

370   Then, in the fourth vision, Perpetua is surrounded by fair youths who befriend her; they unclothe her and massage her body with oil, as for a Greek *agon* (contest). And she is transformed into a man.

371   This unveiling of her masculine nature, so to speak, at this particular time, appears to be in some measure connected with personal considerations. About the year A.D. 200, the persecutions of the Christians in Africa were of a local character and very much encouraged by the aggressive attitude of the Christians themselves. Perpetua, as a young woman of 22 with a tiny son, would hardly have had to suffer such a fate had she not adopted the strong, masculine spirit of the believer and thrown herself actively into the spiritual battle. It is also obvious that she sought a martyr's death to demonstrate her faith, as is shown by her remark at the time of her baptism:

372   I was inspired by the Spirit not to ask for any other favor after the [baptismal] water but simply the perseverance [sufferings] of the flesh.[17]

373   Perhaps one may therefore be justified in looking upon her prison (*katoche*) as a state of possession. In any case, the dream shows that in the conflict which now breaks out, she adopts a masculine, warlike attitude and identifies completely with the Christian animus figures that had appeared only as unconscious parts of her personality in the earlier dreams. She becomes a *miles Christi*, a soldier of Christ, just as also in the pagan world the initiation into

---

[17] *Ibid.*, p. 109.

the mysteries was frequently interpreted as a *sacramentum* (military oath). In the mysteries of Mithras, for instance, the initiates of a certain degree were called *milites* (soldiers). Their service was a military service dedicated to the god, and the Pauline conception of the *militia Christi* likewise grew out of these ideas. St. Paul describes himself as a *stratiotes* (soldier) and speaks of the "armor of light" (Rom. 13:12).

374   But the laying off of Perpetua's garment has a still deeper meaning. In the *Corpus Hermeticum*, we read:

375   Seek for yourselves one who, holding you by the hand, leads the way [here it is Pomponius] to the gates of the Gnosis, where the shining light, clear of all darkness, is to be found; where no one is ever drunk, but where all are sober, looking into their hearts toward Him who wishes to be seen.

376   For He cannot be heard, nor read, nor yet is He visible to the eyes, but only to the spirit and the heart.

377   First, however, thou must rend the garment which thou wearest, the web of unconsciousness *[to hyphasma tes agnosias]*, the stronghold of wickedness, the bonds which thou bearest, the daric veil, the living death, the visible corpse, the surrounding grave. ... [For this is] the hostile garment, which narrows thee down to thyself, so that thou canst not raise thine eyes above to the beauty of truth.[18]

378   Therefore, in order for the mystic in this initiation to receive the glorified celestial garment of light, he must first remove and tear up his garment of earthly materialness *(soma—sema)* and the *agnosia* (unconsciousness).

379   In the apocryphal *Odes of Solomon*, which were influenced by Gnosticism, we likewise read:

---

[18] Scott, ed., *Hermetica*, VII, S 2, 3.

380 I forsook the folly which is cast over the earth; and I stripped it off and cast it from me: and the Lord renewed me in His raiment, and possessed me by His light.[19]

381 And further: "I put off darkness and clothed myself with light."[20] And again: "I was clothed with the covering of thy Spirit, and thou didst remove from me my raiment of skins."[21]

382 So, this laying aside of the garment means stripping away unconscious animal nature, the state of imprisonment in illusion, and, under certain conditions, even earthly material existence. Thus, Perpetua becomes, so to speak, entirely a spirit (hence her masculinity).

383 In the *Excerpta ex Theodoto,* quoted by Clement of Alexandria, we likewise read that the masculine always unites directly with Logos, but that the feminine, after a process of becoming masculine, enters the *Pleroma* together with the angels. That is why it is said that woman is transformed into man and the earthly Church into angels.[22] This means the redemption of the "psychical" through its transformation into the "pneumatical." The belief that, in the Beyond, the sexes cease to exist as opposites and are united is also alluded to in a *logion* transmitted by Clement of Alexandria:

384 When ye shall have trodden underfoot the cloak of shame [compare the laying aside of Perpetua's garment] and when the two will have become one, and the outer like the inner, and the masculine like the feminine, neither masculine nor feminine.[23]

385 This idea is based on the supposition that the two sexes are united within the human being not only physiologically but also as a psychological totality, seeing that the unconscious invariably contains the opposite qualities of each individual. Hence, in

---

[19] Bernard, ed., *Odes of Solomon,* Ode 11.
[20] *Ibid.,* Ode 21.
[21] *Ibid.,* Ode 25.
[22] See Robinson, "The Fragments of Heracleon" in *Texts and Studies,* 1:57, note 28.
[23] *Stromata* III, 13.92.

Hermetic philosophy, the hermaphrodite becomes the symbol of totality.

386   In Perpetua's case, however, it is not a union of opposites that takes place, but an inversion, which corresponds to a complete extinction of the previous ego-consciousness, in place of which, in the state of ecstasy, there appears another spiritual consciousness.

387   The extent to which St. Augustine intuitively grasped these psychological facts and expressed them in the language of his time is almost unbelievable. Referring to Ephesians 4:13 ("Till we all come in the unity of the faith, and of the knowledge of the Son of God, unto a perfect man ... and so on), Augustine says that because the devil "felt himself to be in the presence of a woman who behaved to him like a man" *(viriliter secum agentem feminam sensit),*[24] he determined to tempt her by means of a man, choosing for this purpose her father, who besieged her with his arguments. And in *de Anima* he even adds:

388   In a dream, Perpetua saw herself *changed into a man,* fighting with an Egyptian. Who, however, can doubt that it was her soul that appeared in this [masculine] bodily form, not her actual body, which latter, having remained completely feminine, lay unconscious, whereas *her soul* fought in the aforesaid form of a masculine body.[25]

389   In effect, she becomes identical with the animus. The Montanist prophetess Maximilla provides another striking parallel when, in her prophecies inspired by the Spirit, she speaks of herself in the masculine form.

390   Inasmuch as the Christian symbols rose to the light of day as a new and creative content coming from the depths of the collective unconscious, the people of that time were drawn into the unconscious by them. In Perpetua's case, too, the Christian symbols appear in the unconscious (the shepherd in the Beyond and the

---

[24] See C.J.M.J. van Beek, *Passio Sanctarum Perpetuae et Felicitatis,* p. 155.
[25] IV: 18, 26.

Hermaphrodite on the winged globe of chaos.
(Jamsthaler, *Viatorium spagyricum*, 1625)

fountain of life in the underworld). The conflict is not one between a consciousness newly converted to Christianity and the still-pagan unconscious; on the contrary, the Christian symbol itself also appears in the unconscious, and it is there that the opposites clash. The same phenomenon occurs in a reversed form in the case of the author of the *Shepherd of Hermas:* thanks to a woman, to his meeting with the anima, he is initiated into a new doctrine.

391   This whole period of evolution, when the Christian world was coming into being, is characterized by a powerful influx of the collective unconscious. Miracles were in the air; and in the catacomb pictures, the people of that time wear a peculiarly eager expression, their glance directed inward, as though they expected something tremendously fascinating to emerge from that direction.

392   The young men in the dream who anoint Perpetua with oil after her transformation are helpful figures like Pomponius, but they are split up into a plurality—a typical characteristic of an animus figure.

393   Oil, especially in the form of scented ointment *(unguentum)*, plays an important role in all primitive rites. It is a fluid charged with power and is a means of healing, of beautifying, of preserving the dead, and so on. The ancient images of the gods were also anointed with oil in order to bring them to life. The Roman Catholic Church likewise uses scented oil *(myron)*, which has been consecrated by the priest, especially in the case of extreme unction, to impart spiritual strength. Thus, Cyrillus, a Father of the Church, says:

394   The oil which has been consecrated by the priest is no longer mere oil, but in the same way as the bread becomes the body of Christ, the oil becomes the *charisma* of Christ and of the Holy Ghost in an energized form *[energetikon charisma].*[26]

395   In other words, it becomes the archetype of the Holy Ghost, who was frequently thought of as a nourishing, satisfying perfume. Therefore, oil also meant Gnosis. Honorius of Autun says: "Naked of all vices and anointed with the oil of the *charisma,* must we fight

---

[26] Migne, ed., *Patrologiae*, Greek series, vol. 30, col. 1089.

the devil."[27] So, here likewise, the laying aside of the garment is a laying aside of vices, of the *agnosia* or unconsciousness.

396   Moreover, this passage in the vision bears a close resemblance to a part of the Slavonic *Book of Enoch* (22:8); before entering into the highest Heaven, Enoch is divested of his earthly garments by the angel Michael, anointed with fine oil, and arrayed in the garment of God's majesty.[28] This ointment "resembled a great light . . . and shone like the rays of the sun." According to the rules of the Church established by Hippolytus, the catechumens were also anointed by the bishop with the laying on of hands as a transmission of the spirit.

397   So, this anointing with oil means a spiritual strengthening and enlightening by means of these animus figures. (In the Greek text, they appear as a youth who sends forth flashes of lightning, and other fair youths. To send forth lightning means to enlighten.) These unite to form the figure of the giant *lanista*. He is of such enormous size that he almost towers above the whole amphitheater. He carries a rod or staff in one hand and, in the other, a green bough bearing golden apples, which he promises to Perpetua as a reward of victory. Like Pomponius, he has a loose toga with a broad purple stripe across the middle of his chest between two others, and he wears "manifold shoes made of gold and silver." Since Pomponius promised to help Perpetua, we may assume that he has, as it were, been transformed into the *lanista*, or at least that he was an early form of this figure.

398   The staff is evidently a sign that this daimon is also a guide. The staff is generally associated with Hermes, messenger of the gods and leader of souls; it is a golden rod which is similar to the magic wand of the magician. The shepherd-deity likewise carries a staff and shares with the *lanista* the characteristic of supernatural size. At bottom, it is the same figure. The staff gives him the quality of a guiding and judging principle. Honorius of Autun, for instance, interpreted the bishop's staff as *auctoritas doctrinae* (the authority of the doctrine).[29] The staff characterizes the *lanista* as a personification

---

[27] *Ibid.*, Latin series, vol. 172, col. 857.
[28] See W.R. Morfill, ed., and R.H. Charles, trans., *The Book of the Secrets of Enoch.*
[29] Migne, ed., *Patrologiae*, Latin series, vol. 172, col. 610.

of the right faith, the *pistis*—that is, the personification of a guiding principle which will settle the conflict and be the absolute judge of the life and death of the soul.

399   Judging also plays a remarkable role with St. Paul. According to him, "He that is spiritual [the *pneumatikoi*] judgeth all things, yet he himself is judged of no man" (1 Cor. 2:15). This absolute infallibility of the *pneumatikoi* is based on the fact that he possesses, so to speak, the mind *(Nous)* of Christ, and the *Nous* of God judges absolutely. In the *Magic Papyri*, as we saw earlier, the Egyptian *Agathodaimon* is addressed as "thou who sittest on the head of the cosmos, and judgest everything, surrounded by the circle of truth and faith." On the last day Christ will also appear as such a judge of the world.

400   Thus, the *lanista* carries the symbol of unshakable faith, which definitely settles the conflict. In this sense, he is truly the "spirit of truth" which "shall be with you." In the presence of such an inviolable faith, every human criterion comes to an end: The individual is enabled to suffer even death willingly for its sake.

401   The gold and silver shoes of the *lanista* point to an analogous psychic factor. As an aspect of clothing that mirrors one's attitude to one's surroundings, one's standpoint, shoes stand for a component of our inner attitude which is especially concerned with the earth— that is, with reality. In this sense, shoes might be looked upon as representing how one relates to earthly things. The German saying "to lay aside children's shoes," for instance, means to outgrow an infantile attitude toward reality. In folklore, shoes often have an erotic meaning, particularly as the feminine, receptive principle. That they are also a symbol of power is perhaps most clearly expressed in the expression "to be completely under someone's heel."

402   The shoes of the *lanista* thus symbolize a psychic attitude which is receptive to reality, and at the same time, they express unshakable steadfastness. They show that he not only embodies a directing principle but also bestows a standpoint both incorruptible and secure.

403   In addition, the *lanista* wears a white garment with three purple stripes across the chest. According to Shewring, this means that a

purple undergarment was visible between the two end stripes of the toga.[30] White and red are the colors of the priests of the African Saturn and of the Egyptian mysteries in general, and in alchemy, they represent the two highest stages—the *albedo* and *rubedo*. (Here, the equivalent of the alchemical *nigredo* appears separately in the form of the Egyptian.) White indicates the first transfiguration in alchemy and also the dominance of the feminine principle; red implies the dominance of the masculine principle and is the color of the new Sun King. According to Mithraic texts also, the god Helios wears a white garment and a scarlet mantle.

404   Therefore, the garment of the *lanista* contains an allusion to the highest stages of initiation into the mysteries and also to the reconciliation of the opposites in the unconscious. The presence of the three red stripes might point to the fact that here an upper triad has detached itself from a lower fourth element. A higher triad has appeared in opposition to the dark power represented by the Egyptian, which in alchemy, for instance, was looked upon as the fourth factor and the foundation of a uniform development.[31] The dark *prima materia* was frequently described in alchemy as *caput draconis* (dragon's head), or as *draco,* whose head represented man as the *vita gloriosa* to which the angels minister. The *prima materia* was also occasionally portrayed as an Ethiopian.

405   The vision of one of the martyrs in the "Passio Mariani et Jacobi" provides a strikingly close parallel to the *lanista:*

406   I saw a youth of incredibly gigantic stature, whose loose garment shone with such a bright light, that our eyes could not dwell on it. His feet did not touch the ground and his countenance was above the clouds.

407   As he hastened past us, he threw us each—into thy lap, Marianus, and into mine—a purple girdle, and spake; "Follow me!"

---

[30] See *The Passion of SS. Perpetua and Felicity,* p. 109.
[31] See *Scriptum Alberti super arborem Aristotelis,* in *Theatrum Chemicum,* vol. 2, p. 525.

408   The martyrs interpret this apparition as Christ. According to the "Apocalypse of Peter," also, the bodies of the righteous "were whiter than snow and redder than any rose, and the red thereof was mingled with the white."[32]

409   Thus, the conflict in the middle of the magic circle which Perpetua has reached reveals itself as a clash between two suprapersonal, spiritual powers: the Egyptian as the spirit of paganism, of the *pneuma* projected into the cosmos, and a new spiritual power which confronts him, tending entirely in the opposite direction, toward the Beyond, and laying claim to the absolute truth. But this spirit is nevertheless also a *kosmokrator* and *pneuma* which reaches from heaven to earth. Like the lord of the Egyptian earth, it is also an *Agathodaimon* and a shepherd of men.

410   Indeed, perhaps the most singular feature in Perpetua's fourth vision is that, when one probes deeply into the conflicting, opposite principles, one is confronted with their peculiar similarity. This comes from the fact that they are both in the unconscious.

411   It is really astounding that the spiritual power which has the casting vote in this conflict should be personified by a figure belonging most unmistakably to the pagan world, the trainer of gladiators, and not by a Christian figure such as Saturus or Pomponius, for instance, or Christ himself. This can only be explained by the fact that the unconscious as a whole, in its still pagan aspect, was actually working to build up a Christian consciousness. Hence, to be a Christian in those days meant unconditional obedience to the inner voice.

412   We might also say that had Christ appeared as the *lanista*, he would have been taking sides in the fight, so to speak. But the decisive factor which desired Perpetua's victory was the Self in a form which showed itself to be beyond the opposites, *Christus et eius umbra*. The non-Christian nature of the *lanista* is again expressed in a significant detail—in his garment. His garment, with the peculiarly broad purple stripes on the toga and the scarlet

---

[32] A. Dieterich, *Nekyia*, pp. 3f.; see also "The Revelation of Peter," in M.R. James, ed., *Two Lectures on the Newly Discovered Fragments, etc.,* p. 46.

undergarment, is very similar to that worn by the African priests of Saturn, who was especially honored as a god of vegetation and of the underworld. Thus, it represented the very Deity against whom the Christians had to fight the hardest battle. Saturn was looked upon as the special tutelary god of animal fights[33]—so that he was also a *lanista* and umpire par excellence—the spirit of the amphitheater. One could almost fancy that it was this spirit which appeared to Perpetua as the *lanista*.

413   It is remarkable how similar the images and texts of budding Christianity were to those of the Gnostic and pagan mysteries which it fought against with such ardor. Indeed, the Fathers of the Church themselves who inveighed against paganism were not blind to this fact and could only explain it as a subtle *diabolica fraus*. The then widespread conception of a *Daimort Antimimos* (hostile and mimicking) who stands in the Redeemer's way was doubtlessly founded on such facts. For instance, Zosimos says:

414   [Christ] appeared to the very feeble as a man capable of suffering and like one scourged. And after he had privily stolen away the Men of Light that were his own, he made known that in truth he did not suffer, and that death was trampled down and cast out. ... Thus they [the men of light] kill their Adam. And these things are so until the coming of the daemon Antimimos, the jealous one, who seeks to lead them astray as before, declaring that he is the Son of God, although he is formless *[amorphos]* in both body and soul.[34]

415   Curiously enough, the Poimandres of the *Corpus Hermeticum* is opposed by a similar "fire-breathing" daimon of vengeance and punishment, a similar power of destiny.[35] We meet the same idea when St. Paul draws a comparison between the first "earthy"

---

[33] See Lactantius Firmianus, *Divinarum Institutionum Libri Septem*, vol. 6, p. 20. [For English see Roberts and Donaldson, eds., *Ante-Nicene Fathers*, vol. 7.—Ed.]

[34] Berthelot, ed., *Collection des Anciens Alchimistes Grecs*, vol. 3, p. 49; also quoted by Jung in *Psychology and Alchemy*, CW 12, par. 456. (In the Greek text of the "Passio Perpetua," the Egyptian is likewise called *amorphos.)*

[35] See Scott, ed., *Hermetica*, vol. 13.

(*choikos*) Adam and the second Adam, who is "a quickening spirit" (*pneuma zoopoion*). And lastly, this opposition appears also in the idea of the Antichrist.

416   Perpetua herself does not use the designation *Antimimos* but simply calls the Egyptian *diabolus;* yet, he possesses this peculiar quality of an antigod in matter, a nature-spirit which, while aping the Christian spirit, is nevertheless its opponent. If we ask ourselves what is actually taking place autonomously in the collective unconscious, we can perceive a splitting-up, as it were, of the archetype into a light and a dark aspect. This happened first of all to the image of God, inasmuch as the ambivalent, primordial father, Yahweh, approached the human sphere in the form of the two sons, Satan and Christ.[36] This tearing apart of the light and dark aspects of the image of God, as it is described by Jung, is true of all the other symbolic images. In Rhabanus Maurus's list of *flgurae,* for instance, nearly all the *typi* (allegorical images), such as fire, eyes and lion, have one aspect which alludes to Christ and another which alludes to the devil.[37]

417   The split into two aspects of the image of God, and at the same time of all other archetypal images, appears to be connected—as Jung states in his Eranos article on the mother archetype[38]—with the differentiation of feeling and, consequently, with moral judgment in Western culture. This subsequently made it impossible to endure the paradoxical character and moral ambivalence still retained by, for instance, the Indian gods.

418   However, this moral reaction was preceded and induced by the constellation of the new archetypal situation itself, first revealed in the form of a transcendent psychic presence, as Perpetua's visions show so clearly. Splitting the image of God into *Christus-Diabolus* constellated a problem of the opposites which was to lead to a schism

---

[36] For a fuller description of this inner divine drama, see various essays by Jung, including "The Spirit Mercurius" *Alchemical Studies,* CW 13; "A Psychological Approach to the Dogma of the Trinity," *Psychology and Religion,* CW 11; and "The Phenomenology of the Spirit in Fairy Tales," *The Archetypes and the Collective Unconscious,* CW 9i.

[37] See Migne, ed., *Patrologiae,* Latin series, vol. 112, cols. 907ff.

[38] "Psychological Aspects of the Mother Archetype," *The Archetypes and the Collective Unconscious,* CW 9i.

in times to come. The one-sided belief in the light side which characterized the exponents of early Christianity—such as Perpetua—was bound, in obedience to the law of enantiodromia,[39] to be followed by the problem of the Antichrist, "Lord of This World." This question, however, was only to arise in the second era of the astrological age of Pisces.

419   It is particularly interesting in the visions of St. Perpetua to be able to observe this splitting-up process in the unconscious psyche itself. An equally remarkable fact is that the *lanista* still incorporates a remnant of the pagan spirit in which the opposites are united, but whose aim is unmistakably to urge humanity to be partisan of the light side.

420   The daimon who guides Perpetua in the person of the *lanista* carries yet a third attribute, the green bough with the golden fruit. This is a bough from the Tree of Life, a general archetypal image which is to be found all over the world. It is the tree of the Hesperides, whose fruit signifies eternal life. It is also important in alchemy as *arbor solis et lunae.* It is no accident that Perpetua receives this bough at the hands of the leader of souls, for the tree grows in the west, the way of the night sea journey. In the *Aeneid,* before the hero can enter the land of the dead, he must break the "golden bough."[40] So the bough is at the same time the promise of eternal life and a means of passing over into the kingdom of the dead, of descending into the unconscious. This vision is particularly impressive when one considers that Perpetua had the dream on the eve of her actual death.

421   In the *Passio Mariam et Jacobi,* a boy who had been put to death three days before appeared to one of the martyrs, wearing a wreath of roses around his neck and carrying the greenest branch of a palm tree *(palma viridissima)* in his right hand. He tells them that he is feasting merrily and that they will soon eat with him. The bough of the Tree of Life with the golden apples corresponds to the milk in the first vision and to the water of life in the Dinocrates dream. Gold

---

[39] [Enantiodromia, literally "running counter to," refers to the emergence of the unconscious opposite in the course of time.—Ed.]
[40] *Aeneid,* Book 6, pp. 140ff.

is a symbol for the highest value (Dinocrates also drank out of a golden phial). The green bough points to the fact that this highest value is a living element which has grown naturally.

422   Accordingly, the new spirit which towers above humanity fills Perpetua with absolute and unshakable conviction, and at the same time, it transmits to her from the unconscious the highest living value, which one may surely look upon as the Deity. This spirit gives her the inner conviction of God's existence, which makes it easy for her to die. But again, for this very reason, her actual death becomes simply one more step in the inner development which is implied.

423   It is the Saint herself who now wins victory as "lifted up in the air," she tramples her foe, singing hymns as she does so. She is thrown into a state of enthusiasm, an ecstatic condition in which she sings hymns as a means of banishing her doubts—which are embodied in the Egyptian. Praising God meant at the same time making a mental sacrifice *(thysia logike)* for the purpose of receiving the divine help. It was really a means of fighting. In this connection, Clement of Alexandria says:

424   Out of Zion shall go forth the law, and the word of the Lord from Jerusalem, the heavenly word, a true fighter crowned in the theater of the whole cosmos.[41]

425   Ecstatic prophesying played a particularly important role among the Montanists. Montanus even once said of himself:

426   Behold, man is like a lyre and I myself play on it as the plectron [being himself the Paraclete], Man is asleep, but I am awake.[42]

427   It is interesting that the Montanist prophetess Maximilla should also have said of herself: "I am the word, *pneuma* and *dynamis*.[43]

---

[41] *Protreptikos,* 1.3.
[42] See Epiphanius, *Panarion,* 48. 4.
[43] Kirsopp Lake, *The Ecclesiastical History with an English Translation,* p. 26.

428   Thus, Perpetua also becomes the pure Logos (hence her masculinity). In this way, she overcomes the spirit of doubt and attains the living, unquestionable faith, symbolized in the bough which the *lanista* presents to her with a kiss. This is the kiss of peace, which was a custom in the early Church; the kiss of life, of which the 28th ode in *Odes of Solomon* says: "Immortal life has come forth and has kissed me, and from that life is the Spirit within me, and it cannot die, for it lives."[44]

429   As the outer destruction draws nearer, the comforting images in Perpetua's dreams increase. It is also doubtless owing to the general compensatory function of the unconscious that it was particularly the martyrs in prison and the monks who gave themselves up to a life of asceticism in the desert who enjoyed frequent dreams of wonderful banquets and beautiful heavenly gardens.

430   The terrible events actually connected with the martyrdom of Perpetua and her fellow-sufferers parallel the dream images. They are their outer fulfillment and, at the same, their denial. As Saturus takes the lead in the dream, so he is the first to be put to death; as Perpetua lays aside her garment in the dream, so the mad cow tears her dress to shreds, exposing her nakedness; and just as the Egyptian threatens to pierce her with his sword, so she is actually pierced by the sword of the gladiator (and this contrary to all expectation, thanks to the intercession of the crowd on her behalf).

431   Therefore, one might even say that in outer reality the Egyptian conquered. But his triumph was like the victory of Hell and death when Christ was crucified. Through suffering these, Christ remained victorious.[45] Thus, in a certain sense, Perpetua suffers the very fate of Christ; in the words of St. Paul, "Christ" is "formed in" her (Gal. 4:19). Because consciously she is entirely on the side of one of the pairs of opposites in the unconscious and becomes identical with it, the other appears as her outer fate. Yet the very fact of being torn by the conflict (whose truest symbol is the cross of Christ) also offers

---

[44] Bernard, *Odes of Solomon*, ode 28. Literally, "for it is life itself."
[45] "Death is swallowed up in victory. O death, where is thy sting? O grave, where is thy victory?" (1 Cor. 15:54-55)

the possibility of a new life (alluded to in the vision as the bough with the golden apples).

432   When the deepest layers of the collective unconscious are stirred, as they were at that time, with an emerging new symbol of God, outer events also seem to take part in the process—miracles come to pass. For instance, when the martyrs were put to death, incidents occurred whose unconscious logical sequence seems hardly credible to rational consciousness: Not only did the Egyptian apparently conquer with his sword, but also at first, it was even decided by the organizers of the games that the women martyrs should appear in white robes, as priestesses of Ceres, and the men, in scarlet, as priests of Saturn.

433   The martyrs protested on the grounds that they gave their lives precisely to avoid having to do anything of the kind. The suggestion was finally dropped. It was, in fact, a widespread custom at that time to make criminals who had been sentenced play such roles in the amphitheater, but the extraordinary thing is the choice of the gods whose priests the martyrs would have to impersonate. The women were to serve Ceres, the greatest Mother-Deity of antiquity, the Earth Mother and Mother of the Corn, the protectress of young women.

434   It was just this principle, however, that Perpetua and her fellow martyr Felicitas had repudiated. Perpetua forsook her infant son; Felicitas gave birth to a child in prison only shortly before her martyrdom. And what is still more amazing is that they were thrown to a mad cow.

435   The cow itself is a widespread ancient symbol of the feminine and maternal principle. The author of the "Passio Perpetuae" seems somehow to have sensed the singularity of this coincidence, for he says:

436   As to the young women, the devil had kept a mad cow in store for them—which had been provided quite exceptionally [praetor consuetudi-nem]—in order by means of the animal, to insult their sex still further by aping it [sexui earum etiam de bestia aemuiatus].

437 An equally astonishing coincidence of outer circumstances is to be found concerning the male martyrs. They were to appear as priests of Saturn, and two of them bore names which happen to be derivations of Saturn: one was Saturus, the other Satuminus.

438 In Africa, the Roman Saturn was identified with a native Punic-Phoenician deity and played a significant role in the cult of the country. In the old inscriptions, he is called *frugifer* (fruit-producing) or *deus frugum* (god of fruit) and is compared to Ceres. The cult of this god was exceptionally widespread in Africa, as the apologetic writings of Tertullian show.[46] In a list of bishops recorded by Cyprian (Epist. 557), no fewer than four bear the name Satuminus. According to Tertullian, the priests of Saturn had particularly broad purple stripes on their togas, also a loose garment in Galatian red.[47] So they wore exactly the same clothing as the gigantic *lanista* in Perpetua's vision—evidence yet again of the bewildering similarity of the opposites.

439 Saturday was the day consecrated to Saturn, and it also coincided with the Sabbath of the Jews, so it was believed at the time that Saturn was the highest god of the Jews. Since no distinction was generally made between Christians and Jews, he was also thought of as the God of the Christians. So, the idea which occurred to the organizers of the games—to dress up the martyrs specifically as priests of Saturn—undoubtedly had its origin in these connections.

440 Thus, the law of the enantiodromia of all archetypal opposites fulfilled itself in the martyrs up to the bitter end, and the tension of the wrenching apart of those opposites produced a new life-energy with which the Christian culture of the following centuries was to build afresh. But the unconscious itself sustained the martyrs with images which held the promise of new life, thereby giving them the inner strength to stand unwaveringly by their decision.

441 These visions of the "Passio Perpetuae" therefore reveal in a singularly complete form the whole unconscious situation of humanity at that time, pagan as well as Christian. They also show

---

[46] See Franz Joseph Dölger, *Ichthys,* vol. 2, pp. 277ff.
[47] *De Pallio. 4.* [For English, see Roberts and Donaldson, eds., *Ante-Nicene Fathers,* vol. 3.—Ed.]

Chapel dedicated to St. Perpetua.
(National Shrine of the Little Flower Catholic Church,
Royal Oak, Michigan)

the conflict the Christians experienced in endeavoring to tear themselves free from the spirit which was bound up in nature and in matter. Martyrdom itself had indeed no other meaning than to demonstrate to the pagan world this complete separation and the absolute belief in a world beyond. But the visions also show what hard battles the believers had to fight within themselves, how deep the inner struggle, which in reality had broken out between two divine, suprapersonal unconscious powers.

442   In truth, viewed psychologically, the martyrs can be seen as tragic, unconscious victims of the transformation which was then being fulfilled deep down in the collective stratum of the human soul. This was the transformation of the image of God, whose new form was to rule over the aeons to come.

Appendix
Saturus's Vision

443   We had died and had put off the flesh, and we began to be carried towards the east by four angels who did not touch us with their hand. But we moved along not on our backs facing upwards but as though we were climbing up a gentle hill. And when we were free of the world, we first saw an interior light. And I said to Perpetua (for she was at my side): "This is what the Lord promised us. We have received his promise."

444   While we were being carried by these four angels, a great open space appeared, which seemed to be a garden, with rose bushes and all manner of flowers. The trees were as tall as cypresses, and their leaves were constantly falling. In the garden there were four other angels more splendid than the others. When they saw us, they paid us homage and said to the other angels in admiration: "Why, they are here! They are here!"

445   Then the four angels that were carrying us grew fearful and set us down. Then we walked across to an open area by way of a broad road, and there we met Jucundus, Satuminus, and Artaxius, who were burnt alive in the same persecution, together with Quintus, who had actually died as a martyr in prison. We asked them where they had been. And the other angels said to us: "First come and enter and greet the Lord."

446   Then we came to a place whose walls seemed to be constructed of light. And in front of the gate stood four angels, who entered in and put on white robes. We also entered and we heard the sound of voices in unison chanting endlessly: "Holy, Holy, Holy!" In the same place we seemed to see an aged man with white hair and a youthful face, though we did not see his feet. On his right and left were four

elders, and behind them stood other aged men. Surprised, we entered and stood before a throne: Four angels lifted us up, and we kissed the aged man, and he touched our faces with his hand. And the elders said to us: "Let us rise." And we rose and gave the kiss of peace. Then the elder said to us: "Go and play." To Perpetua I said: "Your wish is granted." She said to me: "Thanks be to God that I am happier here now than I was in the flesh."

447   Then we went out, and before the gates we saw the bishop Optatus on the right and Aspesius the presbyter and teacher on the left, each of them far apart and in sorrow. They threw themselves at our feet and said: "Make peace between us. For you have gone away and left us thus." And we said to them: "Are you not our bishop, and are you not our presbyter? How can you fall at our feet?" We were very moved and embraced them.

448   Perpetua then began to speak with them in Greek, and we drew them apart into the garden under a rose arbor. While we were talking with them, the angel said to them: "Allow them to rest. Settle whatever quarrels you have among yourselves." And they were put to confusion. Then they said to Optatus: "You must scold your flock. They approach you as though they had come from the games, quarrelling about the different teams."

449   And it seemed as though they wanted to close the gates. And there we began to recognize many of our brethren, martyrs among them.

450   All of us were sustained by a most delicious odor that seemed to satisfy us. And then I woke up happy.[1]

---

[1] Musurillo, trans., "Perpetua," in *Acts of the Christian Martyrs,* pp. 119ff.

◆

Bibliography

Adlington, W., trans. *The Golden Ass of Apuleius* (1566). New York: Modern Library, 1932.

Allendy, Rene, *Le symbolisme des nombres,* Paris: Chacornac Freres, 1948.

Bächtold-Stäubli, H., (ed.), *Handwörterbuch des deutschen Aberglaubens*, Berlin, 1927–1942.

Basel, *Rosarium Philosophorum*, Vol. 1, 1610.

Bernard, J.H., ed. *The Odes of Solomon.* In J.A. Robinson, *Texts and Studies: Contributions to Biblical and Patristic Literature.* Cambridge; Cambridge University Press, 1891.

Berthelot, M. *Collection des Anciens Alchimistes Grecs.* Paris: Ministry of Public Information, 1887.

Betz, Hans Dieter, ed. *The Greek Magical Papyri in Translation: Including the Demotic Spells.* Chicago: University of Chicago Press, 1992.

Blanke, F., *Bruder Klaus von Flüe*, Zürich: Zwingli, 1948.

Bolte, J., and Polivka, G., (eds), *Anmerkungen zu den Kinder- und Hausmärchen der Brüder Grimm,* Vol. 3, Leipzig: de Gruyter, 1918.

Brandstetter, R., *Die Wuotansage im alten Luzern. Der Geschichtsfreund,* Vol. 62, Stans, 1907.

Buehlmann, J., *Christuslehre und Christusmystik des Heinrich Seuse,* Lucerne, 1942.

Cabrol, Fernand, ed. *Dictionnaire d'Archeologie Chretienne et de Liturgie.* Paris: Letouzey et An6, 1907.

Cassells, Ian, *The Raven Banner: A guide to Viking Caithness,* Thurso, 1995.

Cavalieri, P. Franchi de. *La Passio SS. Perpetuae et Felicitatis.* Rome, 1896.

Colson, F.H., and Whitaker, G.H., eds. *Philo with an English Translation.* New York: G.P. Putnam's Sons, 1929.

Cumont, F. *Textes et monuments figures relatifs aux mysteres de Mithra,* Brussels: H. Lamertin, 1896-99.

Davids, R., "Zur Geschichte des Rad-symbols," *Eranos-Jahrbuch,* Zurich: Rhein Verlag, 1934.

Dieterich, A. *Nekyia.* Leipzig, 1893.

Dieterich, A., *Eine Mithrasliturgie,* Leipzig: Leipzig, 1903.

Dölger, Franz Joseph *Antike Parallelen zum Leidenden Dinocrates in der Passio Perpetuae, Antike und Christentum.* Münster, 1930.

_____. *Ichthys,* vol. 2. Münster, n.d.

Dronke, Peter. *Women Writers of the Middle Ages: A Critical Study of Texts from Perpetua to Marguerite Porete.* Cambridge: Cambridge University Press, 1984.

Duerrer, R., *Bruder Klaus. Die ältesten Quellen über den seligen Niklaus von Flüe, sein Leben und seinen Einfluss,* Sarnen: Ehrli, 1917–1921.

Duerrer, Werner, *Augenzeugen berichten über Bruder Klaus,* Lucerne: Rex Verlag, 1941.

Dyrenkova, N.P., "Bear-worship among Turkish tribes in Siberia," *Proceedings of the 23rd International Congress of Americanists,* New York, September 1928.

Edinger, Edward F. *The Aion Lectures: Exploring the Self in C.G. Jung's* Aion. Toronto: Inner City Books, 1996.

_____. *The Psyche in Antiquity, Book 2: Gnosticism and Early Christianity.* Toronto: Inner City Books, 1999.

Eliade, M., *Shamanism: Archaic Techniques of Ecstasy,* Princeton, NJ: Princeton University Press, 1964.

Ephraem Syrus, *Hymni et Sermones,* Lamy (ed.), Mechliniae, Vol. 1 and 2, 1902.

Federer, B. H., *Niklaus von Flüe,* Frauenfeld, 1928.

Federer, H., *Wander- und Wundergeschichten aus dem Süden,* Berlin: G. Grote'sche Verlagsbuchhandlung, 1924.

Findeisen, H., "Zur Geschichte der Bärenzeremonie," *Archiv für Religionswissenschaften,* Vol. 37, Berlin, 1941.

Forde, Cyril Daryll, *Ethnography of Yuma Indians: American Archaeology and Ethnology,* Oakland, CA: University of California Press, 1931.

Frischknecht, M., "Das schreckliche Gesicht des Klaus von Flüe," *Theologische Zeitschrift,* Vol. 1, Universitat Basel, 1946.

Goethe, J.W., "Die Sonne tönt nach alter Weise," *Faust,* Taylor, B., (trans.), Boston: Houghton, Mifflin and Co., 1870.

Goldschmidt, Günther, and Reitzenstein, Richard, eds., *Heliodori Carmina quattuor ad fidem codicis Casselani. – Alchemistische Lehrschriften und Märchen bei den Arabern,* Giessen: Töpelmann, 1913.

Hallowell, A.F., "Bear-ceremonialism in the Northern Hemisphere," *American Anthropologist,* Vol. 28, 1926.

Hauer, I.W., '*Symbole und Erfahrung des Selbstes*', *Eranos-Jahrbuch 1934,* Zürich: Rhein Verlag, 1935.

Heidel, A., *The Gilgamesh Epic and Old Testament Parallels,* Chicago: Chicago University Press, 1949.

Hemleben, J., *Niklaus von Flüe,* Frauenfeld: Huber, 1977.

Hentze, C., *Le culte de l'ours ou du tigre et le t'aotie,* Zalmoxis I, 1938.

Herrmann, P., *Das altgermanische Priesterwesen,* Jena: Eugen Diederichs Verlag, 1929.

Jacobsohn, H., *Das Gespräch eines Lebensmüden mit seinem Ba. Zeitlose Dokumente der Seele,* Zürich: Rascher Verlag, 1952.

James, M.R., ed. *Two Lectures on the Newly Discovered Fragments, etc.* 2nd ed. London: 1892.

Journet, Charles, *Saint Nicolas de Flüe,* Neuchâtel/Paris: Cahiers du Rhône, 1947.

Jung, C.G., *The Collected Works* (Bollingen Series XX). 20 vols. Trans. R.F.C. Hull. Ed. H. Read, M. Fordham, G. Adler, Wm. McGuire. Princeton: Princeton University Press, 1953-1979.

_____., *Letters,* Vol. 1, London: Routledge and Kegan Paul, Ltd., 1973.

_____., *Symbols of Transformation,* CW 5, London: Routledge & Kegan Paul Ltd, 1956.

_____., *Psychological Types,* CW 6, London: Routledge & Kegan Paul Ltd, 1971.

_____., *Two Essays on Analytical Psychology,* CW 7, London: Routledge & Kegan Paul Ltd, 1953.

_____., *The Structure and Dynamics of the Psyche,* CW 8, London: Routledge & Kegan Paul Ltd, 1960.

_____., *The Archetypes and the Collective Unconscious,* CW 9/i, London: Routledge & Kegan Paul Ltd, 1959.

_____., *Aion,* CW 9/ii, London: Routledge & Kegan Paul Ltd, 1959.

_____., *Civilisation in Transition,* CW 10, London: Routledge & Kegan Paul Ltd, 1964.

_____., *Psychology and Religion: West and East,* CW 11, London: Routledge & Kegan Paul Ltd, 1958.

_____., *Psychology and Alchemy,* CW12, London: Routledge & Kegan Paul Ltd, 1953.

_____., *Alchemical Studies,* CW 13, London: Routledge & Kegan Paul Ltd, 1967.

_____., CW 14, *Mysterium Coniunctionis,* London: Routledge & Kegan Paul Ltd, 1963.

_____., *The Practice of Psychotherapy,* CW 16, London: Routledge & Kegan Paul, Ltd, 1954.

_____., *The Symbolic Life,* CW 18, London: Routledge & Kegan Paul Ltd, 1977.

Jung, E., "Die Anima als Naturwesen," in Studien zur analytischen Psychologie C.G. Jungs, Zürich: Rascher Verlag, 1955.

Jung, Emma. *Animus and Anima.* Zürich: Spring Publications, 1978.

Kerényi, K., and Jung, C.G. *Essays on a Science of Mythology.* Princeton: Princeton University Press, 1969.

King, Charles William *The Gnostics and Their Remains: Ancient and Medieval.* London, 1864.

Kirfel, W., *Die dreiköpfige Gottheit,* Bonn: Dümmler, 1948.

Labriolle, Pierre de. *La Crise Montaniste.* Paris: Ernest Leroux, 1913.

Lake, Kirsopp. *The Ecclesiastical History with an English Translation.* New York G.P. Putnam's Sons, 1926-32.

Landesdörfer, P.S., ed. *Ausgewahlte Schriften der syrischen Dichter.* *Kempten, 1913.*

Lavaud, M.-B., *Vie profonde de Saint Nicolas de Flüe*, Switzerland: Library of the University of Friborg, 1942.

Lütolf, Alois, *Sagen, Bräuche, Legenden aus den fünf Orten*, Lucerne, 1862.

Méautis, G., *Nicolas de Flüe,* Neuchatel: Secrétariat de l'Université, 1940.

Menzel, W., *Odin*, Stuttgart, 1855.

Migne, Jacques Paul, ed. *Patrologiae cursus completus.* Latin series: 221 vols., Paris, 1844-64. Greek series; 166 vols., Paris, 1857-66.

Moret, A., *Mystères égyptiens,* Paris: Librairie Armand Colin, 1927.

Morfill, W.R., ed., and Charles, R.H., trans. *The Book of the Secrets of Enoch* (1896). Escondido, CA: Book Tree, 1999.

Muncey, R. Waterville. *The Passion of Perpetua: An English Translation with Introduction and Notes.* London: J.M. Dent, 1927.

Musurillo, Herbert, trans. *The Acts of the Christian Martyrs.* Oxford: Oxford University Press, 1972.

Mylius, J.D., *Philosophia reformata,* Jennis: Frankfurt am Main, 1622.

Nielsen, D., *Der dreieinige* Gott, Copenhagen: Gyldendalske Boghandel, 1922.

Nietzsche, Friedrich, *Also sprach Zarathustra,* Leipzig: Alfred Kroner, 1923.

Ninck, M., *Wodan und germanischer Schicksalsglaube,* Jena: Eugen Diedrichs Verlag, 1953.

Oehl, W., "Bruder Klaus und diedeutsche Mystik," *Zeitschrift für Schweizer Kirchengeschichte,* Vol. 11, Stans, 1917.

Onians, R.B., *The Origins of European Thought about the Body, the Mind, the Soul, the World, Time and Fate,* Cambridge: Cambridge University Press, 1951.

Owen, E.C.E. *Some Authentic Acts of Early Martyrs.* Oxford: Oxford University Press, 1927.

Pfeiffer, F., *Marienlegenden,* Stuttgart, 1846.

Platonici, Apulei, *De deo Socratis*, Madaurensis de Philosophia libri rec., Leipzig: Leipzig, Teubner, 1908.

Preisendanz, Karl L., ed. *Papyri Magicae Graecae*. Leipzig: E.G. Teubner, 1928.

Rahner, H., "Flumina de ventre Christi," *Biblica*, Vol. 22, Rome, 1941.

Rahner, Hugo. "Antenna Crucis II." In *Zeitschrift fur Katholische Theologie*, 1942.

Reitzenstein, Richard. *Hellenistische Mysterienreligionen*. Leipzig: B.G. Teubner, 1908. [English: *Hellenistic Mystery Religions: Their Basic Ideas and Significance*. Trans. J.E. Steely. Pittsburgh: Pickwick Press, 1978.]

_____. *Das Iranische Erlösungsmysterium*, Bonn: A. Marcus & E. Weber, 1921.

_____. *Hellenistische Wunderzahlungen*. Leipzig: B.G. Teubner, 1906.

_____. *Poimandres*. Leipzig: B.G. Teubner, 1904.

Renner, Eduard, *Goldener Ring über Uri: ein Buch vom Erleben und Denken unserer Bergler, von Magie und Geistern und von den ersten und letzten Dingen*, Zürich: Helvetische Bücherei, 1941.

Robert-Tornow, W., *De apium mellisque apud veteres significatione et symbolica et mythologica*, Berlin: Weidmann, 1893.

Roberts, A., and Donaldson, J., eds. *The Ante-Nicene Fathers: Translations of the Writings of the Fathers Down to A.D. 325*. Grand Rapids, MI: Wm. B. Eerdmans Publishing Co., 1986.

Robinson, J.A. *Texts and Studies: Contributions to Biblical and Patristic Literature*. Cambridge: Cambridge University Press, 1891.

Ruska, J., ed., *Tabula Smaragdina*, Heidelberg: Winter, 1926.

_____. *Turba Philosophorum*, Berlin: Julius Springer, 1931.

Salisbury, Joyce E. *Perpetua's Passion: The Death and Memory of a Young Roman Woman*. New York: Routledge, 1997.

Sarasin, P., *Helios und Keraunos*, Innsbruck: Verlag der Wagner'schen Universitaĭˆts-Buchhandlung, 1924.

Scott, W., ed. *Hermetica*. Oxford University Press, Oxford, 1924.

Shewring, W.H. *The Passion of SS. Perpetua and Felicity.* London: Sheed and Ward, 1931.

Stoeckli, A., *Die Visionen des seligen Bruder Klaus*, New York: Benziger, 1933.

Stucken, E., *Astralmythen*, Leipzig: Pfeiffer, 1907.

Suzuki, T., *An Introduction to Zen Buddhism*, Kyoto: Eastern Buddhist Society, 1934.

Tacitus, *Germania*, Munich: Verlag der Bremer Presse, 1922.

Theatrum Chemicum. 6 vols. Ursell and Strasbourg, 1602-61.

Thiriot, P. G., des Frères Prêcheurs, *Oeuvres mystiques du bienheureux Henri Suso*, Vol. 2, Paris: Librairie Victor Lecoffre, 1899.

Trevisanus, Bernhardus, "Parabel von der Fontina" in: Jean-Jacques Manget, *Biblioteca Chemica Curiosa*, Vol. 2, Geneva: Chouet, 1702.

van Beek, C.J.M.J. *Passio Sanctarum Perpetuae et Felicitatis.* Vol. 1 of *Textum Graecum et Latinum ad Fidem Codicum MSS.* Nijmegen, 1956.

Vandryes, J., and Tonnelat, E., *Les religions des Celtes, des Germains et des anciens* Slaves, Mana: Presses Universitaires de France, 1948.

Vetter, F., (ed.), *Die Predigten Taulers*, Vol. II, Berlin: Weidmann, 1910.

Vokinger, K., *Bruder-Klausen-Buch*, Stans: von Matt, 1936.

von der Leyen, F., and Zaunert, P., (eds), *Indianer Märchen aus Südamerika*, "Die Märchen der Weltliteratur," and *Indianer Märchen aus Nordamerika*, Jena: Eugen Diedrichs Verlag, 1921.

von Franz, Marie-Louise, *Archetypal Symbols in Fairy Tales*, CW 1. Asheville, NC: Chiron Publications, 2020.

_____. *Aurora Consurgens*, Toronto: Inner City Books, 2000.

von Matt, Leonard, *Der heilige Bruder Klaus. Offizielles Gedenkbuch der Heiligsprechung*, Zürich: NZN Verlag, 1947.

Wilhelm, Richard, trans. *The I Ching or Book of Changes.* London: Routledge and Kegan Paul, 1968.

Winckelmann, E., *Geschichte der Angelsachsen*, Stuttgart: Hoffmannsche Verlagsbuchhandlung, 1847.

Wunderlich, Eva, "Die Bedeutung der roten Farbe im Kultus der Griechen und Römer" in *Religionsgeschichtliche Versuche uned Vorarbeiten,* Giessen, 1925.

Wyss, K., *Die Milch im Kultus der Griechen und Römer,* Giessen, 1914.

Zimmermann, Joh. J. *Disquisitiones Historicae et Theologicae, de Visionibus.* Tiguri, 1738.

Index